TOUR BOOK

For Antique Car Buffs

3rd Edition

by Richard E. Osborne

Riebel-Roque Publishing
Indianapolis, Indiana

Library of Congress Catalog Card Number 98-092101

ISBN 0-9628324-4-8

First Edition, Date of Publication, December 1990
Second Edition, Date of Publication, September 1994
Third Edition, Date of Publication, November 1998

Published and printed in the U. S. A.
Book design and production by Steve Miller

RIEBEL-ROQUE PUBLISHING COMPANY

6027 CASTLEBAR CIR.
INDIANAPOLIS, IN 46220
Distributed by:
SEVEN HILL BOOK DISTRIBUTORS, INC.
CINCINNATI, OHIO

INTRODUCTION

The purpose of this book is to provide the antique car buffs in The United States and Canada with a directory that they can use to identify and find the many antique car museums, displays, dealers, salvage yards, historic sites, libraries, restaurants and other business and public organizations specializing in displaying antique vehicles and preserving their history.

I have sought to locate and list only those organizations that welcome visitors, have permanent facilities, staff and regular hours. I am well aware that some organizations might have been overlooked and I welcome information from readers and interested parties regarding those organizations for future listing. There is no charge for being listed in this book. My intention is to provide the motoring car buff with a tour upon which book he can rely on with confidence.

Listings in this book are in alphabetical order by states, provinces and cities within the states and provinces.

—*Richard E. Osborne*

SPECIAL THANKS

I would like to express my gratitude to David L. Lewis, Professor of Business History at The University of Michigan, author of the book "Ford Country" and many magazine articles for his aid in helping me locate some of the historic Ford sites around the US, and to Ray Featherstone, my Research Associate, who discovered places I didn't know existed. Thanks also to Sara Streeter for her technical guidance and assistance.

Tour Book for Antique Car Buffs

IMPORTANT NOTE—Please Respect Businesses

While "tourists" are welcome at museums, restaurants and historic sites, this is not always the case at salvage yards, antique car dealerships and restoration shops. The latter are businesses and exist to make a profit, not to entertain the public. The motoring public must keep in mind that while businesses welcome potential customers they may not welcome "lookers" and the "curious". Please use good judgement when visiting such places.

FINDING PLACES

Whenever possible the street address and/or highway number has been given for the listings in this book to make it as easy as possible for the readers to find the places they seek.

In large cities that is not easy. Please be reminded, however, that detailed city maps are usually available at most convenience stores that sell gasoline. These maps cost about $3 to $4and give an alphabetical listing and map grid location of every street covered.

ORDERING ADDITIONAL COPIES OF THIS BOOK

Additional copies of this book may be ordered from:

Riebel-Roque Publishing Co.
6027 Castlebar Cir.
Indianapolis, IN 46220
317-849-3680

Price per book $15.95
Postage & handling (1 book only) 2.00
Postage & handling (Ea. addl. book) 1.00
Indiana residents please add $.80 sales tax.

CONTENTS BY STATE AND PROVINCE

THE UNITED STATES

CANADA

CELEBRITY CARS

AUTOMOBILES AND OTHER VEHICLES
ASSOCIATED WITH FAMOUS PEOPLE

Tour Book for Antique Car Buffs

ALABAMA

Barber Vintage Motorsports Museum has on display the largest collection of motorcycles in the United States.

BARBER VINTAGE MOTORSPORTS MUSEUM
512 28th Street South
BIRMINGHAM, AL 35233
Phone: 205-252-8377
Hours: W-F 9-11 and 1-3, closed holidays.
Admission charged.

There are more than 325 motorcycles on display at this relatively new museum making it the largest motorcycle mu-

seum in America. The oldest motorcycle is a 1904 Shaw. The others represent motorcycle manufacturers around the world. You'll see street bikes, race bikes, military motorcycles, side cars and specialty bikes, all in restored condition and most in running conditon. Barber's has its own restoration shop. There is also a racing shop and Barber's sponsor an antique motocycle racing team. Museum founded in 1995.

Alabama

The International Motorsport Hall of Fame and Museum.

INTERNATIONAL MOTORSPORTS HALL OF FAME AND MUSEUM

4000 Speedway Blvd (Off I-20)
TALLADEGA, AL 35160 (40 miles east of Birmingham)
Phone: 205-362-5002
Hours: Daily 9-5, closed holidays. Admission charged.

This is a three-building museum on the grounds of the Alabama International Motor Speedway complex. The museum displays famous race cars such as Sir Malcolm Campbell's "Blue Bird", which achieved a record speed of 276 mph in 1935. Also displayed are cars driven by Richard Petty, Bobby Allison, Buddy Baker, Bobby Isaac, Marty Robbins and Ron Bouchard. Other displays include pace cars, go-karts, drag racers, antique automobiles stock cars, trucks, motorcycles and memorabilia of famous drivers, inventors and racing events. Tickets to speedway events are sold in the visitors orientation center. There is a gift shop, a game room, a camp ground and a concessions area. Guided tours of the Alabama Motor Speedway are available.

MERCEDES-BENZ VISITORS CENTER (Factory visitors center and museum)

I-20/59 at Exit 89 (East of Tuscaloosa)
TUSCALOOSA, AL 35403 (50 miles southwest of Birmingham on I-20/59)
Phone: 205-507-3300 or 888-2-TOUR-MB
Hours: M-F 9-5, Sat 10-5. Plant tour available. Admission charged to the Visitors Center.

The Mercedes-Benz Visitors Center, Tuscaloosa, AL.

There is 24,000 square feet of space in this new visitors center and museum attached to the huge Daimler-Benz manufacturing complex outside Tuscaloosa. This is the only such Mercedes-Benz facility in North America. Visitors follow a self-guided tour through the center that traces the history and current operations of the Daimler-Benz Corporation. One display stresses Daimler-Benz's commitment to safety and tells of its auto testing program. A 30-seat theater shows the company's worldwide advertisements and other films pertaining to the company. A second theater shows a film on Mercedes-Benz's history in racing from the early 1920s to the present.

Of interest to antique car buffs is the display of old Mercedes-Benz automobiles which includes a 1905 American Mercedes, a 1936 Nurburg 500 Cabriolet F, a 1957 gull-wing coupe, a 1995 DTM race car, a camouflaged M-Class from the movie "The Lost World" and the company's first M-Class SUV. There is also a replica of the world's first motorcycle.

A tour of the factory can be arranged at the museum. Reservations are required for the factory tour and no sandals, open-toe shows or shorts are allowed. The factory tour is free.

ALASKA

MUSEUM OF ALASKA TRANSPORTATION AND INDUSTRY

Milepost 46.7 Parks Highway (near the Wasilla Airport)
WASILLA, AK 99687 (28 miles north of Anchorage)
Phone: 907-376-1211
Hours: Memorial Day through Labor Day, M-Sat 10-6. Rest of year Tues-Sat 8-4. Admission charged.

Alaska's transportation and industrial history is amply preserved in this museum for the educational and scientific benefit of current and future generations. On the museum's grounds and inside the spacious museum building are displays of trains, aircraft, mining equipment, firetrucks, farm equipment, construction equipment, boats, dog sleds and about 25 antique cars. Antique automobiles of interest include a 1923 Dodge Touring Car used by President Harding during his trip to Alaska, a 1926 Mack truck, a 1931 Hupmobile, a 1921 American LaFrance firetruck, a 1947 Studebaker, a 1939 Plymouth, a 1950 Nash Ambassador and a 1964 Cadillac hearse. The museum has a gift shop and a picnic area.

The "Chitina Auto Railer" was a 1935 Chevrolet bus fitted to run on railroad tracks and operated in the Matanuska Valley.

ARIZONA

▼ U.S. 66:

Arizona has been in the forefront of preserving sections of old highway U.S. 66 and many of the sites along its way. Some of those sites include (from east to west):

HOLBROOK: "The Wigwam Village" is a restored and operating motel in which each cottage is a wigwam. These particular wigwams were patented in 1936 and were erected in many parts of the country. This is the only location in the U.S. where these particular wigwams have been restored and put back into service.

WILLIAMS: Stretches of U.S. 66 on both sides of Williams are on the National Register of Historic Places and various sites along the road have been preserved.

ASH FORK to **SELIGMAN**: This stretch of U.S. 66 was one of the first stretches of U.S. 66 to be preserved thanks to the efforts of the citizens of Seligman.

CROZIER: U.S. 66 through Crozier Canyon was the last stretch of the highway to be paved in the late 1930s.

OATMAN: The Oatman Hotel on old U.S. 66 is listed on the National Register of Historic Places and was the honeymoon hideaway of Hollywood legends Clark Gable and Carol Lombard.

WISEMAN'S AUTO SALVAGE
900 W Cottonwood Ln
CASA GRANDE, AZ 85222 (45 miles southeast of Phoenix on I-10)
Phone: 520-836-7960
Hours: M-F 8-5:30, Sat 9-1:30.

This is a large salvage yard containing 3000 rust-free cars and trucks from the 1920s to the 1970s. Browsers welcome. Customers may remove some parts themselves. Inquiries accompanied by SASE will be answered. Master Card and Visa accepted on phone orders.

DREAM MACHINE
(Dealer and restorer)
119 Andy Divine Av
KINGMAN, AZ 86401
Phone: 520-753-1314
Hours: M-F 8-5

On the strip in downtown Kingman you'll find this combination antique car dealership and restorer. The restoration shop is behind the showroom. Some of the cars on display have been restored by Dream Machines. All makes and models are offered. The company offers a repair service and towing. There is a small museum inside the showroom.

HOCTOR'S HIDDEN VALLEY
AUTO PARTS (Salvage)
21046 North Rio Bravo Rd
(Off SR 238)
MARICOPA, AZ 85239 (27 miles south of downtown Phoenix)
Phone: 602-568-2945 and
602-252-2122
Hours: M-F 8-5, Sat 9-3.

An 80-acre salvage yard with about 8000 American and some imported cars and trucks, many 20 years and older. Vehicles are available for parts or sold whole for restoration. Most vehicles are rust-free. The Hoctor family runs several yards in central Arizona and almost all vintage tin is sent to this yard. A record is kept on every car in this yard so customers can be told immediately what parts are available. Since most vehicles are Arizona cars that were originally equipped with air conditioning, making this yard a good source for early air conditioning parts. Customers may browse the yard. Every vehicle is marked as to year, make and yard number. Location: Exit I-10 on Maricopa Rd. and proceed west to SR 238 (approximately 6 miles). Turn right onto SR 238 and proceed approximately 2 miles to Rio Bravo Rd. (a dirt road) and turn left down that road several hundred yards to the yard.

▼ THE PHOENIX AREA

BONEYARD STAN (Salvage)
218 North 69th Av
PHOENIX, AZ 85043
Phone: 602-936-8045
Hours: Daily, Please phone first.

A salvage yard of over 300 vehicles specializing in PONTIACS from the 1950s to the late 1970s. Other makes of cars also available. Boneyard Stan will locate cars and parts and will ship anywhere in the world. Guaranteed replies to all mail inquiries with SASE.

Owners are Stanley and Kathy Jones.

ART COFFER AUTO
DISMANTLERS, INC. (Salvage)
3127 W Broadway Rd
PHOENIX, AZ 85041
Phone: 602-276-7377 and
800-960-7377
Hours: M-F 8-5, Sat 8-noon.

A salvage yard of 500 to 600 vehicles specializing in CHRYSLER and MOPAR parts from 1960 to the present. Dodge and Plymouth pickup truck are included. No General Motors or Fords. Coffer will search other salvage yards for parts and sells used cars, used trucks and used tires. Customers may browse the yard. Car clubs welcome. In business since 1967.

CNV CORVETTE SALES (Dealer)
2166 E University Dr
TEMPE, AZ 85282 (Eastern suburb of Phoenix)
Phone: 602-994-8388 and
800-875-8390
Hours: M-F 8:30-7, Sat 9-6.

This is Arizona's only full-service CORVETTE dealership with between 70 and 80 Corvettes and other collectible cars in inventory at all times. Cars are kept in an indoor showroom and on an adjacent lot. An inventory list is available. CNV will help arrange financing, takes trades, searches for a specific vehicle and arranges transportation. They can provide full service, parts, upholstery and detailing. Car clubs welcome.

DESERT VALLEY AUTO PARTS (Salvage)
22500 N 21st Av
PHOENIX, AZ 85027
Phone: 800-905-8024,
602-780-8024
Hours: M-F 8-5, Sat 8-2.

This is a relatively new salvage yard with about 2500 vehicles on 45 acres of land. The yard is exceptionally clean with many of the cars resting on concrete slabs. The vehicles, which range in age from the 1940s to the 1990s, are of mixed makes although there is a large number of Chevrolets. Desert Valley Auto Parts has a towing service and can provide repair services. Customers may browse the yard. In business since 1991.

LEO GEPHART, INC. (Dealer)
7360 E Acoma Dr, Suite 14
SCOTTSDALE, AZ 85260
Phone: 602-948-2286
Hours: M-F 9-5, Sat 9-noon

You will find beautiful machines here in Gephart's spacious showroom. They specialize in fine quality American-made classics and often have in inventory such cars as Duesenbergs, Pierce-Arrows, Packards, Cadillacs and the like. They carry about 45 cars in inventory and can provide an inventory list. Gephart's take trades, arranges financing and transportation, will search for specific vehicles and sells on consignment. The company is one of the few places in the world where you can find Duesenberg parts. Leo Gephart, the owner, says car clubs are welcome to visit.

HALL OF FLAME MUSEUM OF FIREFIGHTING
6101 E Van Buren St
PHOENIX, AZ 85008
Phone: 602-ASK-FIRE
(602-275-3473)
Hours: M-Sat 9-5; closed Thanksgiving, December 25 and January 1. Admission charged.

This interesting museum, located across Van Buren Street from the Phoe-

Arizona

nix Zoo, has 30,000 square feet of floor space and is the largest museum of its type in the world. Over 100 fire engines, dating from 1725 to 1961, are on view along with one engine once owned, and later donated to the museum, by movie star Gene Autry. There are helmets, badges, firemarks, lithographs, photographs, paintings and other firefighting memorabilia on display. Displays rotate so frequent visits are recommended. Car clubs welcome.

One of the many fire trucks at the Hall of Flame Firefighting Museum in Phoenix, AZ.

SPEEDWAY AUTOMOTIVE (Salvage)
  2300 W Broadway
  PHOENIX, AZ 86041
  Phone: 602-276-0090
  Hours: M-F 8:30-5:30, Sat 9-3.

This is a 400 vehicle salvage yard specializing in BUICKS and FORDS from 1961 to 1987. NOS and reproduction parts also available. Customers may browse the yard. In business since 1978.

TRI-STATE PETE (Salvage)
  1988-$^{1}/_{2}$ E First St
  TEMPE, AZ 85281
  (Eastern suburb of Phoenix)
  Phone: 602-829-7826

There are over 550 MERCEDES BENZ automobiles in this salvage yard. MBZs are their specialty and range in age from 1951 to 1991. New and used parts available and Tri-State Pete will locate parts on their satellite locator system. Model 300 SEL parts also available. Tri-State Pete buys "tired" MBZs.

End of Phoenix Area △

▼ THE TUCSON AREA

CLASSIC AUTO PARTS (Salvage)
  4865 E Cindrich
  TUCSON, AZ 85706
  Phone: 602-574-0308
  Hours: M-F 8-5

They're stacked two high at this small but densely-packed salvage yard. Some 1500-plus cars of all makes, mostly postwar, are available. Many of the cars are from the mid-1950s and many have

One of the beautifully restored Franklins in display at the H. H. Franklin Foundation Museum in Tucson, AZ.

early model air conditioners—a hard-to-find item. Yard personnel have good knowledge of parts available. Classic Auto Parts has been in business since 1976.

H. H. FRANKLIN FOUNDATION MUSEUM

3420 N Vine St
TUCSON, AZ 85719
Phone: 520-326-8038
Hours: Open Sept 15th to Memorial Day. Phone for hours at other times. Donations accepted.

One of the largest collections of Franklin automobiles in the country is on display at this museum. The museum currently has 19 Franklins ranging from 1926 to 1934 and is constantly looking for additional models. The Franklins were unique in that they had air-cooled engines and were constructed for light weight. Aluminum was used extensively in their manufacture. About a dozen antique cars of other marques can also be seen as well as historic items and literature relating to the Franklin automobile. The museum has its own library. This is a non-profit corporation founded by the late Tom Hubbard, a well-known collector and restorer of automobiles, and run primarily by volunteers.

REVOLVSTORE (Salvage)

5275 E Drexel Rd
TUCSON, AZ 85706
Phone: 800-28-VOLVO,
602-574-1717
Hours: M-F 8-5, Sat 8-noon.

As the name implies, this salvage yard specializes in Volvos. The yard is small, only two acres, but about 300 Volvos pass through the yard each year. Revolvstore tracks Volvos in other salvage yards and has a computerized

The Willys Works in Tucson, AZ.

hookup with some 2000 other salvage yards. Many parts are removed and stored inside. New parts also available. Established in 1983.

T-BIRD SPECIALISTS (Salvage)
3156 E President
TUCSON, AZ 85714
Phone: 520-889-8634
Hours: M-Sat 1:30-5:30

This salvage yard has about 100 THUNDERBIRD parts cars from 1958 thru 1976. They can provide parts, re-pairs and service for Thunderbirds from 1955 thru 1976. Dick Hoaglund, owner.

WILLYS WORKS, INC (Dealer & restorer)
1933 W Gardner Ln
TUCSON, AZ 85705
Phone: 520-888-5082
Hours: Tues-F 10-6, Sat 9-4

Specializes in the sales, restoration, and modernization of post-World War II JEEPS. Can provide parts and service.

End of Tucson Area △

ARKANSAS

The Last Precinct Police Museum, Eureka Springs, AR.

BIG BEN'S USED CARS AND SALVAGE

924 North Highway 79
FORDYCE, AR 71742
(South-central part of the state)
Phone: 870-352-7423
Hours: M-Thurs 8-5, F 8-6.

A 40 acre salvage yard with approximately 1500 cars of all makes from the '60s and '70s. Customers remove their own parts thus keeping the cost of parts to a minimum. Bring your own tools. There is a good selection of CHRYSLER products and some antique pickup trucks. Big Ben's will search other salvage yards for parts and offers antique Arkansas license plates. Customer may browse the yard. Car clubs welcome. In business since 1984.

THE LAST PRECINCT (Museum)

Highway US 62 West (5.3 Mi. west of Jct. US 62 and SR 23)
EUREKA SPRINGS, AR 72632
(Northwest corner of the state)
Phone: 501-253-4948
Hours: Tues-Sat 10-6.
Admission charged.

Over 150 years of law enforcement history is on display at this museum including the largest collection of police cars in the country. One of the cars is a 1979 Carmaro Z-28, one of only twelve, built especially for the California Highway Patrol. Also to be seen are motorcycles, uniforms, weapons, badges, police toys and more. Displays are arranged in chronological order with the first display being that of a sheriff's office of the 1880s. Confiscated weapons are shown and there is information on such famous law enforcement agencies as the Royal Canadian Mounted Police, Texas Rangers, New York City Police Department and others. A large display of "Hollywood Cops" is on view as well as the "Bluesmobile" and "Dick Tracy" movie cars. The museum has a gift shop with a wide array of police and fire department collectibles.

▼ FORT SMITH AREA
(West-central part of the state on the Texas state line)

RANDY BLYTHE'S (Dealer)
4210 Towson Av
FORT SMITH, AR 72901
Phone: 501-646-6351 or
800-297-4298
Hours: M-F 8:30-6:30, Sat 9-5.

Randy and his friends specialize in MUSCLE CARS and will have between 50 and 60 of them in their showroom to offer at any one time. They also work in a few classics, special interest cars and other collectibles from time-to-time. An inventory list is available. The company takes trades, does appraisals and helps arrange financing and shipping. Randy Blythe's has been in business since 1977.

CARDINAL MOTORS
(Dealer and restorer)
5610 Powson Av
FORT SMITH, AR 72901
Phone: 501-646-2302 or
501-646-6526
Hours: Summer M-Sat 8-5, Winter M-Sat 8-6:30.

This dealer has a showroom and lot with additional storage facilities and offers, on average, 15 cars for sale at all times. Cardinal does restoration work, repairs, arranges financing, sells on consignment and takes trades. Car clubs welcome.

End of Fort Smith Area △

▼ HOT SPRINGS AREA

DUCK RIDES
(Amphibious vehicle tours)
There are three companies in the Hot Springs area offering land/water rides in World War II-era amphibious vehicles known as DUWKs (ducks). Passengers board the ducks at the companies' offices or pickup locations, proceed down city streets and into Lake Hamilton. They then take a trip around the lake and return to their starting points. Tours are colorfully narrated by the driver. The ducks are a very safe mode of transportation and are inspected regularly by the Coast Guard.

The duck ride companies operate

Two White & Yellow Ducks that take passengers on land and water tours in the Hot Springs area.

every day during the season. Check locally for departure times, costs and pickup locations.

DUWKs were used extensively during World War II to transport men and supplies from ships to shore.

The duck ride companies in Hot Springs are:

DUCKS IN THE PARK
Phone: 501-624-DUCK (3825)

NATIONAL PARK DUCK TOURS
Phone: 501-321-2911 or
800-682-7044

WHITE AND YELLOW DUCKS
Phone: 501-623-1111 or
800-934-0374

End of Hot Springs Area △

THE MUSEUM OF AUTOMOBILES
State Rd 154 at Petit Jean Mountain State Park (Southwest of Morrilton)
MORRILTON, AR 72110
(Northwest of Little Rock)
Phone: 501-727-5427
Hours: daily 10-5. Closed Christmas. Admission charged.

An outstanding museum founded by the late Arkansas Governor Winthrop Rockefeller containing some 50 antique cars including several from the Rockefeller collection. The cars on display change regularly because most are on loan from private collectors. Included in the collection is a 1923 Arkansas-built Climer, a 1913 Metz and a 1929 Ford Towncar. Also on display are motorcycles, guns, antique gas pumps, engines and signs. A gift shop and an old-

Arkansas

The Museum of Automobiles at Petit Jean Mountain State Park, Morrilton, AR.

fashioned drug store are part of the museum.

The museum is the national headquarters for The Mid-State Old-Time Automobile Assn. An annual swap meet is held here in June.

CALIFORNIA

A stretch of old U.S. 66, now known as the "Old National Trail Highway", is maintained in southeastern California.

The economy of California, as we know it today, could not exist without the automobile. This dependence on the automobile has carried over in a very unique way in that cars which are considered to be antiques by most other Americans are still on the streets of California and being driven every day. It is not uncommon to see cars 20 years and older whizzing along the state's freeways keeping pace with their present-day counterparts. A thriving business exists within the state of rebuilding old cars, not for the collector, but for ordinary citizens to use on the road. Therefore, a trip to California is an interesting experience for an antique car buff because he or she can still see the old cars in action.

California has also made efforts to preserve sections of historic roads. A section of old U.S. 66 has been preserved in the desert country of southeastern California from Ludlow to an interchange 21 miles west of Needles. It is known as the "Old National Trail Highway" and still serves the local communities along its route. The road is well maintained and many old buildings and businesses can be see along its length. In the Los Angeles area there is a museum devoted to U.S. 66.

California

In the southeastern corner of the state along I-8, 15 miles west of Yuma, AZ, sections of an old plank road can still be seen from the interstate highway. The plank road was built in 1914-15 across the shifting sands of Algodones Dunes. It was 6 miles long, single lane and built of wooden sections laid end-to-end and then covered over with asphalt. There were turnouts along the road where one vehicle could pass another. Travellers often travelled this route in caravans carrying extra tires, water, tools and food. In 1926 the road was replaced by a conventional asphalt highway.

▼ THE FRESNO AREA

ROMO AUTO WRECKING (Salvage)

4625 N Golden State Blvd
FRESNO, CA 93722
Phone: 209-275-4823
Hours: Tues-Sat 8-5, Sun 9-4

Romo's is one of the oldest auto salvagers in California. Located on a 10-acre site outside Fresno, the lot has more than 1500 vehicles, including trucks, from the 1930s to the 1980s. Muscle cars are also to be found here. Employees remove all parts to ensure that quality is maintained. The company was founded in the 1920s and manager Ron Romo is the third generation of the family to run the place.

TURNER'S AUTO WRECKING

(Salvage)
4248 S Willow Av
(Old Highway 99)
FRESNO, CA 93725
Phone: 209-237-0918
Hours: M-Sat 8-5

This is a large salvage yard of about 100 acres covered with cars dating back to the 1940s. This is one of the oldest salvage yards in California and has some 10,000 vehicles including trucks, commercial vehicles and a few hearses and ambulances. Row after row of orphan cars, such as Packards, Nashes, Hudsons, Kaisers, etc. can be found here at Turner's. Turner buys about 1500 cars a year and scraps out about half that many. Yard personnel remove all parts. In business since the 1950s. Jerry Turner is the manager and has a large personal collection of antique cars.

End of Fresno Area △

▼ THE LOS ANGELES/LONG BEACH AREA

Autobooks/ Aero Books, Etc. in Burbank, CA offers a wide selection of automobile- and aviation-related literature.

AASE BROTHERS, INC. (Salvage)
701 E Cypress St (Cypress is two blocks north of Lincoln Ave.)
ANAHEIM, CA 92805 (South-eastern suburb of Los Angeles in Orange County)
Phone: 800-444-7444 or 714-956-2419
Hours: M-F 8:30-5:30

This yard specializes in PORSCHE and MERCEDES and has about 200 cars in their lot. Many parts are stored in-side. Customers may browse the lot su-pervised. Mail orders welcome. Several Porsches are on display in an inside showroom. In business since 1971.

ALL CADILLACS OF THE FORTIES
(Parts dealer and auto display)
12811 Foothill Blvd
SYLMAR, CA 91342 (Northern end of San Fernando Valley)

Phone: 818-361-1147
Hours: M-F 8-4:30

As the name implies, this company sells parts for 1940s-era CADILLACS. Engines, transmissions and major body parts are available as well as smaller parts and chrome. Inside All Cadillacs' spacious building is one of the finest collection of 1940s Cadillacs in the country. It is the private collection of the Ed Cholakian family and is available for viewing by customers and interested parties.

AUTOBOOKS/AERO BOOKS, ETC.
(Bookstore)
3524 W Magnolia St
BURBANK, CA 91505
(Northern suburb of Los Angeles)
Phone: 818-845-0707
Hours: M-Sat 9:30-6

27

California

This is a retail book store specializing in automotive, motorcycle and aviation subjects. Their selection of auto-related books is very extensive. They also sell used books, magazines and repair manuals. Mail inquiries and orders welcome.

AUTOMOTIVE BOOK STOP (Bookstore)
1508 W Magnolia Blvd
BURBANK, CA 91506
(Northern suburb of Los Angeles)
Phone: 818-845-1202
Hours: Tues-F noon-6, Sat 10-4.

This book shop specializes in out-of-print automotive publications, automotive magazines, shop manuals, owners manuals, sales literature, racing books, etc. They also offer automobilia items such as badges, pins and posters.

BEST DEAL, INC. (Salvage)
8171 Monroe St
STANTON, CA 90680 (10 miles west of Long Beach, CA)
Phone: 800-354-9202 or 714-995-0081
Hours: M-F 8:30-5, Sat 9-3.

This salvage yard specializes in PORSCHE and BMW automobiles. The company inventories from 50 to 100 cars at all times. Many of the best cars, and parts from about 1000 dismantled cars, are stored inside for maximum preservation. All dismantling is done indoors. There is a showroom and counter at the front of the building but more than half of Best Deal's business is done by phone and mail order. Customers may browse the yard. In business since 1975.

BOYD'S HOT RODS & COLLECTIBLE CARS (Dealer)
10971 Dale St
STANTON, CA 90680
(East of Long Beach)
Phone: 714-220-9870
Hours: M-F 9-6, Sat 9-4

If you like hot rods, you'll like Boyd's. There are between 30 and 40 hot rods and affordable collectible cars on sale inside the showroom of this dealer at all times. Boyd's also leases cars, takes trades, publishes an inventory list, helps find financing, sells on consignment, does appraisals and will search for specific vehicles. Hot rod accessories, T-shirts and other items of interest are also on sale at Boyd's. Owned by Stecher Enterprises, Jim Stecher, President.

CARS WITH CLASS (Dealer)
1115 Wilshire Blvd
SANTA MONICA, CA 90401
Phone: 310-656-3444
Hours: M-F 9-6, Sat 10:30-4:30

You'll find between 40 to 45 affordable collector cars at this dealership. Cars With Class offers a general line of vehicles in their attractive indoor showroom which was once a Cadillac agency. They can arrange financing, do appraisals, sell on consignment, take trades, lease cars, publish an inventory list and will, in a limited manner, search other dealers for specific vehicles. Car clubs are welcome. Cars With Class is owned and operated by Grant Wood, native of New Zealand.

CHECQUERED FLAG INTERNATIONAL, INC. (Dealer)
4128 Lincoln Blvd
MARINA DEL RAY, CA 90292
Phone: 310-827-8665
Hours: M-F 9-5, Sat-Sun 10-3

You'll see a lot of British cars here was well as other European makes and some American cars—some 120 in all. Checquered Flag has an active export business and sells cars worldwide. Visitors usally arrive at the Los Angeles Interantional Airport which is only three miles away. The company will help arrange nearby hotel accomodations. Checquered Flag will search for specific vehicles and can help arrange financing. They provide an inventory list, lease cars, sell on consignment, take trades and do appraisals. Owner is Britisher Neil Jaffe. Car clubs welcome.

COAST GM SALVAGE
1400 W Anaheim
LONG BEACH, CA 90813
Phone: 213-437-1247
Hours: M-F 8-5, Sat 9-2.

This salvage company specializes in CHEVROLET PICKUPS from 1960, CAMAROS from 1967, CORVETTES from 1968 and GM cars, vans and trucks from 1978. They have approximately 1500 vehicles in the yard and have been in business since 1979.

CORVETTE MIKE
(Dealer and restorer)
1133 N Tustin Av
ANAHEIM, CA 92807

Phone: 800-327-VETT
Hours, Sales: M-F 9-6, Sat 11-4, Sun 11-2 (Phone first)
Service: M-F 8-5

CORVETTES, CORVETTES, CORVETTES, that's what they do at Corvette Mike. This company buys, sells, trades, leases, repairs and offers complete or partial restorations of Corvettes. They also arrange financing, do appraisals, sell on consignment, publish a newsletter and will search for a specific vehicle. Corvette Mike deals in automotive art and there is a boutique offering Corvette accessories such as custom wheels and Corvette apparel. The owner, Mike Vietro, has one example of every major Corvette body style on exhibit inside the ballroom of his headquarters hotel, and has some 50 Corvettes for sale in his indoor showroom at all times. Car clubs are welcome. There is a second "Corvette Mike" location in Plymouth, Massachusetts.

CROSSROADS CLASSIC MUSTANG (Salvage)
12421 Riverside Av
MIRA LOMA, CA 91752 (40 miles east of downtown Los Angeles and just west of Riverside, CA)
Phone: 714-986-6789 or
800-GIDDY-UP
Hours: M-F 8-5, Sat 8:30-2.

This salvage yard specializes in MUSTANGS from 1964-$^{1}/_{2}$ and up. They have about 250 vehicles in the yard and offer used, new and reproduction parts. Catalog and inventory list available. Customers may browse the yard supervised. In business since 1967.

California

Henry Ford Avenue in Long Beach, CA was named after the famous Detroit automaker.

HENRY FORD AVENUE: One of the main streets in Long Beach is Henry Ford Avenue. It is named after the famous Detroit automaker and there once was a Ford Motor Co. plant near its southern end.

GIANT AUTO WRECKERS (Salvage)
  23944 Pine St
  NEWHALL, CA 91321 (Northwest of Los Angeles near junction I-5 and SR 14)
  Phone: 805-259-4678 and 818-704-4205
  Hours: M-F 8-5

This salvage yard, which has up to 150 vehicles, specializes in dismantling FIATS of all years. They also have a general line of vehicles including some trucks. They carry a large selection of new and used hub caps and wheel covers. Giant will search other yards for hard-to-find parts. Customers may browse the yard escorted. The owner is Derrick Frerichs.

MEMORY LANE COLLECTOR CAR DISMANTLERS (Salvage)
  11311 Pendleton
  SUN VALLEY, CA 91352 (At the east end of the San Fernando Valley off I-5)
  Phone: 800-281-9273 or 818-504-3341
  Hours: M-Sat 8-5, Sun 8-4

This yard has about 700 vintage cars of all makes from the 1940s thru the 1970s, the bulk being CHEVROLETS and FORDS. Some of the vehicles have been used in movies. Many cars are offered as complete units. Yard personnel do all parts removal and the company has a nationwide computerized parts locator service. Customers may browse the yard and Memory Lane offers towing and mail order services. The owner-operator is Tony Martinez.

30

This Twenty Grand Duesenberg is typical of the quality of the vehicles in the Merle Norman collection.

MERLE NORMAN CLASSIC BEAUTY COLLECTION (Museum)

15180 Bledsoe St
SYLMAR, CA 91324 (Northern end of the San Fernando Valley near the junction of I-5 and I-210)
Phone: 818-367-2251
Hours: Visitors are escorted thru the museum on regularly scheduled 2-hour tours. Please phone for tour reservations. Free. Children under 12 not admitted.

Here is one of the premier collections of classic cars in all the world. This museum was founded by J.B. Nethercutt, president and co-founder of Merle Norman Cosmetics, and his wife, Dorothy. The museum building itself is a thing of beauty and lavishly decorated on the inside with marble columns, mirrors, chandeliers and works of art. The automotive section is divided into two salons, the Grand Salon, which houses about 30 ultra-expensive and meticulously restored classics and sports cars, and the Rolls-Royce Salon which houses nothing but Rolls-Royces. The total collection consists of over 200 vehicles which are rotated regularly in and out of the museum. Outstanding cars include a 1933/34 "Twenty Grand" Duesenberg, a 1934 Packard V-12 Dietrich sedan, a 1913 Rolls-Royce Town Carriage, a 1912 Premier roadster and Rudolph Valentino's 1923 Voisin. On the top floor of the museum is one of the world's largest and finest collections of music boxes and orchestrions. Tours include both the auto and music collection.

This is a "must see" museum for any antique car buff visiting the Los Angeles area. There is a souvenir and gift shop, a restoration shop and The Nethercutt Automotive Research Library.

METROPOLITAN HISTORICAL COLLECTION (Museum and parts dealer)

5330 Laurel Canyon Rd
NORTH HOLLYWOOD, CA 91607 (Eastern end of San Fernando Valley)
Phone: 818-769-1515
Hours: M-F 9:30-6

This is a collection of 8 NASH Metropolitans. Included in the collection is

The NHRA Motorsports Museum, Pomona, Ca. The very roots of hot-rodding come alive with the cars and memories inside this museum.

the world's only Metropolitan station wagon, the "Astra-Gnome", a dream car built on a Metropolitan for the 1956 International Auto Show in New York to preview what Metropolitans would be like in the next millennium. There is a Metropolitan fire truck, a right-hand drive Met, one of the very first Mets with all original equipment and one of the last Mets made: a show car named "The Westerner" exhibited at all of the West Coast auto shows in 1961-62. This company is also a supplier of all Nash Metropolitan parts.

DENNIS MITOSINKA'S CLASSIC CARS (Dealer)
619 E 4th St
SANTA ANA, CA 92701
(15 miles east of Long Beach)
Phone: 714-953-5303
Hours: M-F 9-5. Admission charged to "lookers".

This is a dealer of antique and special interest cars with about 20 cars in an indoor showroom. Mitosinka offers appraisals and does some of his own restoration on the premises. They offer a large collection of automotive literature, photos and books for sale including literature on motorcycles, race cars, test cars and aircraft.

NATIONAL HOT ROD ASSOCIATION MOTORSPORTS MUSEUM

Pomona Fairplex
(County Fair Grounds)
1101 W McKinley Av
POMONA, CA 91768 (Eastern edge of metropolitan Los Angeles)
Phone: 909-622-2133
Hours: W-Sun 10-5.
Admission charged.

There's about 50 vintage vehicles at this museum and as the name implies, they're hot rods, street rods, drag racers, dry-lake racers and vehicles run on the Bonneville Salt Flats. There are also Indy cars and midget racers. On display, too, are fire suits, helmets, trophies, photos, art and other memorabilia. The museum has an interesting gift shop, a research library, art gallery and multimedia classroom. This is a new museum opened in April 1998 and expansions are planned. The museum's facilities are available for private parties, weddings and meetings. Group tours are provided upon request.

RICHARD NIXON PRESIDENTIAL LIBRARY AND BIRTHPLACE

18001 Yorba Linda Blvd
YORBA LINDA, CA (40 miles southeast of downtown Los Angeles)
Phone: 714-993-3393
Hours: M-Sat 10-5, Sun 11-5.
Admission charged.

This is a memorial complex dedicated to the life and career of President Richard Nixon. There is a museum, gardens, the house in which Nixon was born as well as the gravesite of Former President Nixon and his wife, Pat. Many items relating to the Nixon family and presidency are on display including two automobiles of interest. One of the vehicles is Nixon's bullet-proof 1967 Lincoln limousine. This vehicle was made for presidential use and has many built-in and sophisticated safety and communication devices as well as fold down bumpers and hand rails for Secret Service agents. Presidents Ford, Carter and Reagan also used the car and many world leaders were passengers.

The second vehicle on display is a 1949 Mercury woody station wagon which is a replica of the vehicle Nixon used during his 1950 senatorial campaign. Throughout the museum are many photographs showing Nixon and the automobiles he used.

PETERSEN AUTOMOTIVE MUSEUM (A member of the Los Angeles County Museum of Natural History Family)

6060 Wilshire Blvd (In the "Miracle Mile" District of Los Angeles)
LOS ANGELES, CA 90036
Phone: 213-930-2277 recording, 213-964-6315 information, 213-964-6324 book store and gift shop.
Hours: Tues-Sun 10-6, closed holidays. Admission and parking charged.

This fine museum, in one of Los Angeles' most colorful areas, has a size-

Inside the Petersen Museum.

able collection of antique automobiles, many of them quite unique. Included in the collection is a 1932 Model J Duesenberg, 1915 Stutz racer with overhead cams, 1927 Miller race car with front wheel drive, 1907 air-cooled Aerocar, 1911 American Underslung, 1906 Black Motor Buggy, 1912 Little, 1910 Welch, 1917 Woods dual Power, 1963 Chrysler Turbine Car and a 1957 BMW designed by Raymond Loewy that served as the prototype for the Studebaker Avanti. There are also celebrity cars such as Greta Garbo's 1925 Lincoln Limousine, Rita Hayworth's 1953 Cadillac, Clark Gable's 1956 Mercedes 300 SC Coupe and Dick Van Dyke's 1963 Studebaker Avanti. The museum has a large book store and gift shop offering items related to the hobby of antique car collecting.

PRESTIGE THUNDERBIRD
(Restorer and dealer)
10215 Greenleaf Av
SANTA FE SPRINGS, CA 90670
(12 miles southeast of downtown Los Angeles)
Phone: 562-944-6237 or
800-423-4751
Hours: M-F 8-5:30, Sat 8:30-4.

Prestige Thunderbird is the world's largest restorer of 1955-56-57 Thunderbirds and can offer restored Thunderbirds ready to drive.

This is the world's largest restorer of 1955-56-57 THUNDERBIRDS. Prestige will restore your Thunderbird or you may buy one restored from the showroom floor. There are between 40 and 50 cars in inventory at all times in various stages of restoration. Many of their cars have been show winners. The company can arrange financing and transportation. They also do appraisals, have a service department and sell NOS, new and used parts. Parts catalog available. Contact Rick, Rod or Frank.

VINTAGE COACH (Salvage)
16593 Arrow Blvd
FONTANA, CA 92335 (46 miles east of Los Angeles, 5 miles west of San Bernardino)
Phone: 909-823-9168
Hours: M-Sat 9-5

This is a small salvage yard specializing in HUDSONS, especially the "Step-down" models of the late 1930s and 1950s. Twin-H has between 70 and 80 cars including some pre-war Hudsons, Hudson pickup trucks and some "Nash" Hudsons. They also do some restoration and service work and the yard is decorated with Hudson dealership and service signs. The owner has a personal collection of about 30 restored Hudsons, most of which are usually on display. Founded in 1971.

Z & Z AUTO SALVAGE (Salvage & restorer)
233 N Lemon
ORANGE, CA 92666
(18 miles east of Long Beach)
714-997-2200
Hours: M-F 8-5

This salvage yard specializes in CAMAROS and FIREBIRDS and also does restorations. In business since 1974.

End of Los Angeles/Long Beach Area △

California

3 BOYS AUTO WRECKING
(Salvage)
19480 Highway 99 south
MADERA, CA 93637 (20 miles
northwest of Fresno on SR 99)
Phone: 209-674-7374
Hours: M-F 8-5, Sat 8-noon

This is a large salvage yard divided into two sections, one with antique cars known as 3 Boys Auto Wrecking and the other with later model cars known as Pick-A-Part. In the antique section will be found cars dating from the 1930s thru the 1960s. Most cars are American-made, but there are some imports. 3 Boys will search for parts from other yards in the area. 3 Boys Auto Wrecking and Pick-A-Part can be seen from SR 99.

PEARSON'S AUTO DISMANTLING
AND USED CARS (Salvage)
2343 Highway 49 (About 8 miles
south of town)
MARIPOSA, CA 95338
(30 miles east of Merced and
near the entrance to
Yosemite National Park)
Phone: 209-742-7442
Hours: W-F 9-6, Sat 9-5

This is an old salvage yard nestled in the foothills of the Sierra Nevada Mountains on 80 acres of land. It has about 1500 vehicles, mostly from the 1940s thru the 1960s, but there are no classics. Customers may browse the yard. Pearson's sells complete cars as well as parts. Chrome pieces will not be sold off of doors, fenders, windows or trim panels. Customers must take entire assembly. In business since 1968.

MARKS OF OROVILLE
(Dealer and restorer)
1108 Oro Dam Blvd West
(SR 162 west)
OROVILLE, CA 95965
(64 miles north of Sacramento)
Phone: 530-534-1144
Hours: M-F 8-5

Pearson's Auto Dismantling and Used Cars in nestled in the foothills of the Sierra Nevada Mountains 8 miles south of Mariposa, CA.

Marks of Oroville sells antique cars as is or restored to your specific-ations.

This is a body and paint shop that sells antique cars as is or restored to your specifications. About 50 cars are kept in inventory on a lot adjacent to the shop. Marks will also locate cars and does appraisals. In business since 1972.

PEARSON'S (Salvage)
236 Pearson Rd
PEARSONVILLE, CA 93527
(In the Mojave Desert 74 miles east northeast of Bakersfield on US 395)
Phone: 619-377-4585
Hours: M-Sat 8:30-5

"Hubcap Lucy" they call her. That's Lucille Pearson. She got the name because she handles the yard's vast collection of wheel covers and knows just about everything there is to know about hubcaps. Husband Andy and their two boys handle the rest of the 30-acre lot and some 3000 vehicles. Most of the vehicles are post-war sedans, wagons and pickups of all makes. The family owns two other lots, one in Lancaster and the other in Ridge Crest, but the older stuff is here. They also own the Pearsonville Raceway, a dirt track, site of the locally famous "Turkey Classic" race, which is run each Thanksgiving, and an adjacent service station. The Pearsons are a busy bunch. If you can catch one of them, they'll escort you around the lot.

PLACERVILLE, CA (35 miles east of Sacramento on U.S. 50):
One of the heros of this town is John M. "Wheelbarrow Johnny" Studebaker, one of the famous brothers of the Studebaker Corp. of South Bend, IN. As a young man John Studebaker came west to this gold mining area to seek his fortune and found it, not in gold, but in wheelbarrows. Studebaker was a blacksmith and wheelwright and soon discovered that there was a tremendous need for wheelbarrows in the gold fields. He established a shop at 534 Main St. in Placerville and produced wheelbarrows from 1853 to 1858. Studebaker

The Placerville Town Hall now rests on the site of "Wheelbarrow Johnny" Studebaker's wheelbarrow shop in downtown Placerville. A bronze plaque on the wall (behind the fire plug) commemorates Studebaker and his Wheelbarrow shop.

eventually sold out and returned to Indiana where he went into business with his brothers making wagons and eventually automobiles. The money he made in Placerville helped finance that business.

The Placerville Town Hall now rests on the site of Studebaker's wheelbarrow shop and a bronze plaque commemorates Studebaker and his enterprise. Every year at the county fair Studebaker is further remembered in a unique way when they hold the "Johnny Studebaker Wheelbarrow Races". The El Dorado County Museum, 100 Placerville, Dr. has displays and exhibits on Studebaker.

GILLY'S AUTO WRECKERS
(Salvage)
2561 Blacks Ln (visitors please phone for directions)

PLACERVILLE, CA 95667
Phone: 916-622-4052 and
888-622-4052
Hours: M-Sat 8-5

Gilley's is a 12-acre salvage lot in the hill country outside Placerville on an old country road. It's an old lot, started in the 1940s, and still has some 1940s vehicles among its 600+ car inventory. There are lots of pickup trucks from the 1940s and 1950s and some of Gilley's vehicles are whole and restorable. There is a nice selection of Chevys, other GM makes, some Studebaker Larks and some early 1960s T-birds. In addition to cars this lot has an interesting collection of car emblems, insignias, nameplates and tailights. Customers may browse the yard and, with permission, remove their own parts.

**TOWE AUTO MUSEUM OF
AUTOMOTIVE HISTORY**
2200 Front St
SACRAMENTO, CA 95818
Phone: 916-442-6802
Hours: Daily 10-6. Closed Dec 25,
Thanksgiving and Jan 1. Admission
charged. Free parking.

This area of Sacramento is called
"museum row" and right in the middle
of it is this fine auto museum. Displays
in the museum are based on "dream
themes" with many of the museum's 140
vehicles worked into the displays. The
themes are "Dream of Mobility",
"Dream of Luxury", "Dream of Independence", "Dream of a Rich Harvest",

"Dream of Speed" and "Dream of Cool".
Other museum themes include displays
entitled "Down Memory Lane" and
"Hall of Technology". A highlight of
the museum's auto collection is some
30 antique Fords.

Other displays include period costumes, tools, equipment, license plates
and miscellaneous artifacts. The
museum has a fine gift shop and a growing automotive library.

This museum hosts numerous
events such as swap meets, antique toy
sales, organ concerts, dances, musical
shows, etc. Phone for information on
these events. Ask for Kristin Hartley,
Business Manager.

▼ SAN DIEGO AREA

BONANZA CORVETTES (Dealer)
1600 Broadway
(Down town San Diego)
SAN DIEGO, CA 92101
Phone: 619-239-1646
Hours: M-F 9-5, Sat 10-4

They've got only six CORVETTES in
this former Chevrolet dealership showroom, but nearly a hundred more in the
rear and elswhere. That's a lot of Corvettes. On occasion, other makes of cars
are offered. Bonanza sells cars on con-

*Three of
the many
vehicles on
display at the
Towe Auto
Museum of
Automotive
History in
Sacramento,
CA.*

The Deer Park Auto Museum is part of the Deer Park Market Place in Escondido, CA.

signment, takes trades, arranges financing and shipping, leases cars, does appraisals and has a repair shop and sells parts. They will also search for specific vehicles for customers. Car clubs are welcome. Bonanza is owned and operated by a father and son team, Jim and Glenn Haight.

DEER PARK AUTO MUSEUM

29013 Champagne Blvd
(Parallels I-15 north of Escondido)
ESCONDIDO, CA 92026
(Northern suburb of San Diego)
Phone: 760-749-1666
Hours: Daily 10-4. Closed Jan 1,
Thanksgiving and Dec 25. Admission charged.

This museum is part of a large winery which has a tasting room, a wine shop, a market/deli and a gift shop. The auto collection of some 150 cars consists primarily of convertibles, retractables and early open cars. Most of the cars are American-made. Cars of interest include a 1908 Buick Model 10, a 1931 Chrysler roadster, a 1949 Crosley Hot Shot, a 1915 Ford Model T Speedster, a 1928 Franklin Runabout, a 1954 Kaiser Darrin, a 1950 Hudson Pacemaker, a 1955 Muntz Jet, a 1950 Nash Rambler, a 1935 Packard Model 120 and a 1952 Studebaker Champion 100th Anniversary car. There are many activities at this establishment such as weddings, car shows, wine-tasting dinners and parties.

FIREHOUSE MUSEUM

1572 Columbia St
SAN DIEGO, CA 92101
Phone: 619-232-3473
Hours: Thurs-F 10-2, Sat-Sun 10-4.
Donations requested.

This fire museum displays antique fire trucks, hand pumpers, steamers, helmets and uniforms, bells, alarms, speaking trumpets, fire extinguishers and other firefighting equipment and devices. It is located in the city's old Fire Station #6.

**THE GRAND GARAGE
(Dealer)**
1212 Knoxville St
(location #1)
1400 Garnet Av
(location #2)
SAN DIEGO, CA 92110
Phone: 619-276-0323
Hours: M-Sat 10-5

One of several antique fire trucks on display at San Diego's Firehouse Museum.

The Grand Garage has two locations, both in the beach and bay sections of town and near Sea World. They offer between 60 to 70 vehicles for sale, mostly hot rods, muscle cars, antiques, Corvettes and other vehicles of quality. The Grand Garage takes trades, sells on consignment, helps arrange financing and shipping, does appraisals and some repair work and will search for specific vehicles. They also arrange and promote local hot rod cruises and tours. Car clubs are welcome. Here to serve you is General Manager, Bruce Brown.

**HORSELESS CARRIAGE
FOUNDATION LIBRARY AND
RESEARCH CENTER**
8186 Center St, Suite F
LA MESA, CA 91942 (10 miles east of San Diego off I-8)
Phone: 619-464-0301,
Fax 619-464-0361
Hours: Tues-Sat 10-4

The Horseless Carriage Foundation Library, founded in 1995, is a must for hobbyists seeking information on restoration projets. Here is one of the finest public-accessible collections of original factory literature in the U.S. The Library features a pleasant reading room, research service center, climate controlled archival storage and warehouse. A librarian will assist on-site patrons in self-directed research at no charge. Phone, Fax or mail requests for research by Library staff are accommodated for a modest charge.

The Horseless Carriage Foundation Library has a working relationship with other automotive libraries around the country including the Smithsonian Institute. They also work with legal firms, the media and the IRS. On occasion they sell surplus automotive literature. For information contact Roberta Watkins, manager.

California

President Ronald Reagan's assassination attempt car, a bulletproof 1968 Lincoln Limousine, is on display at the San Diego Automotive Museum.

SAN DIEGO AEROSPACE MUSEUM
Pan American Plaza in Balboa Park
SAN DIEGO, CA 92112
Phone: 619-234-8291
Hours: Daily 10-4:30, closed Jan. 1, Thanksgiving and Dec. 25. Admission charged. Free to all on the 4th Tuesday of each month.

This is a large museum devoted primarily to aerospace displays, but scattered among the exhibits are about a dozen antique cars. The building housing the museum is unique in that it is built in the form of Ford Motor Company's "V-8" trademark. It was built for Ford's exhibit during the 1935 California-Pacific International Exposition. The museum has a sizeable gift shop.

SAN DIEGO AUTOMOTIVE MUSEUM
Pan American Plaza in Balboa Park
SAN DIEGO, CA 92112
Phone: 619-231-2886
Hours: Daily in the summer 10-5:30, rest of year 10-4:30. Closed Jan. 1, Thanksgiving, Dec. 25. Admission charged. Free to all on the 4th Tuesday of each month.

A publicly owned museum with a large collection of rare and historic cars and motorcycles. The cars are rotated every 3 to 4 months. Examples of the cars in the collection are an 1889 Benz, a 1948 Tucker, a 1906 Thomas Flyer, a 1931 Duesenberg Model J and President Ronald Reagan's 1968 assassination attempt limousine. There is also an automotive library and art gallery. The museum solicits memberships and produces a quarterly publication called "Auto Museum News". There is a fine gift shop offering automotive literature, souvenirs and automobilia.

End of San Diego Area △

▼ SAN FRANCISCO BAY AREA

**BLACKHAWK AUTOMOTIVE
MUSEUM**
3700 Blackhawk Circle
DANVILLE, CA 94506
Phone: 925-736-2280
Hours: W-Sun 10-5. Open major
holidays except Christmas and
New Years Day. Admission charged.

The Blackhawk Automotive
Museum presents and displays histori-
cally-significant and artistically inspired
automobiles, automotive art and related
artifacts from the very earliest to the
contemporary for public enjoyment
and educational enrichment.

The 100,000 square foot multi-level
glass and gran-
ite architec-
tural master-
piece show-
cases an ever-
changing exhi-
bition of over
120 of the
world greatest
autos dating
from the 1890s.

Included are cars formerly owned by
Roscoe "Fatty" Arbuckle, Lucille Ball,
Clark Gable, Al Jolson and Andre
Dubonnet.

The Automotive Art wing features
"Moving Inspiration: Artistic Interpre-
tations of the Motor Age", a rotating
exhibition of nearly 1000 artifacts in an
amazing variety of media from the
automobile's first 110 years.

The Museum's Shop and Bookstore
is open during Museum hours and has
a large selection of automotive books,
posters, die-cast models and kits in plastic and metal of varied skill levels.

The Museum and its facilities are
totally wheelchair-accessible. Docent-

*The Blackhawk Automotive
Museum is one of the finest
automotive museums in the
world and has an oustanding
collection of meticulously
restored vehicles.*

led tours of the automobile exhibition are conducted at 2 pm every weekend, and docent-led tours of the Automotive art exhibition are conducted *the first Sunday* of each month at 2 pm. Visitors will not be disappointed. This is one of the finest automotive museums in the world.

CARS DAWYDIAK (Dealer)
1450 Franklin St.
SAN FRANCISCO, CA 94109
Phone: 415-928-CARS (2277)
Hours: M-F 10-7, Sat 10-5 & Sun 10-4.

This is a dealer of classic, sports and antique luxury vehicles in downtown San Francisco. Cars Dawydiak carries anywhere from 35 to 55 restored or fine original cars in inventory at all times and specialize in PORSCHE. An inventory list is available. All of their cars are rust-free California cars. They have their own restoration facility and also do service and repair work. Company personnel will help arrange financing and world-wide transportation, search for specific vehicles and make appraisals. Cars are sold on consignment, leased and the company takes trades. Cars Dawydiak is the exclusive San Francisco-area dealer for the PANOZ Roadster. They have a gift store and car clubs are welcome. The owner is Walter Dawydiak.

FANTASY JUNCTION (Dealer)
1145 Park Av
EMERYVILLE, CA 94608 (A northern suburb of Oakland)
Phone: 510-653-7555
Hours: M-Sat 9:30-5:30

This dealer specializes in post-war European sports cars and carries about 50 cars in inventory at all times in the indoor showroom. Race cars are also available from time to time. Fantasy Junction sells cars on consignment, will search for specific vehicles, does appraisals and can provide an inventory list. Car clubs are welcome. The manager is Bruce Trenery.

Fantasy Junction of Emeryville, CA specializes in the sale of post-war European sports cars.

O'Connor Classic Autos of Santa Clara specializes in MGs.

**THE MARITIME MUSEUM at the
SAN FRANCISCO MARITIME
NATIONAL HISTORICAL PARK**
Hyde Street Pier
SAN FRANCISCO, CA 94100
Phone: 415-556-3002
Hours: Daily 10-5. Closed Jan. 1,
Thanksgiving, Dec. 25. Free.

This museum is devoted primarily to
the naval and maritime history of the
west coast from 1800 to the present, but
it has a collection of about a dozen antique cars from the 1920s and 1930s.

**O'CONNOR CLASSIC AUTOS
(dealer)**
2569 Scott Blvd.
SANTA CLARA, CA 95050
(a suburb of San Jose)
Phone: 408-727-0430
Hours: Tues.-F 9-5,
Sat. by appointment.

This dealer specializes in all years of
MGs and normally carry 7 to 8 affordable cars in stock at all times. O'Connor
sells on consignment, offers appraisals
and takes MGs only in trade. They also
sell MG parts and accessories. Car clubs
are welcome at O'Connor's.

**SHOWROOM AUTO SALES
(Dealer & restorer)**
960 S Bascomb Av
SAN JOSE, CA 95128 (At the
southern end of San Francisco Bay)
Phone: 408-279-0944
Hours: M-F noon-7, Sat. noon-5.

This company specializes in the restoration and sales of MERCEDES-
BENZ automobiles and other fine automobiles. At any time they will have 60
or more vehicles in their showroom.
The company sells cars on consignment,
takes trades, offers leases, does appraisals, will search for specific vehicles and
arranges financing and transportation.
Car clubs are welcome. Ron Perry is the
owner of the company.

California

SPECIALTY SALES
(Dealer and bookstore)
4321 First St.
PLEASANTON, CA 94566 (18 miles southeast of Oakland near the junction of I-580 and I-680)
Phone: 925-484-2262 or 800-600-2262
Hours: M-F 9-6, Sat-Sun 10-6.

This is a large dealer of antique, classic, muscle and special interest cars, most of which are sold on consignment. Specialty Sales has a 14,000 Sq. ft. showroom and carries an average inventory of 70 vehicles. About 80% of the vehicles are in the "affordable" range and an inventory list is available. The company will help arrange financing and transportation, does appraisals, takes trades, offers leases and will search for specific vehicles. Specialty Sales is the exclusive locator for American Express Co. Inside the showroom is a very large gift and book shop offering a wide selection of automotive reading materials and automotive-oriented souvenirs and gifts. Car clubs are welcome at Specialty Sales. Steve Barlow is the manager.

VALLEJO (On the east shore of San Pablo Bay which is the northern extension of San Francisco Bay):

When this town was laid out in the early 1900s the city planners named the town's alleys after popular automobiles of the day. They were named in alphabetical order from "A" thru "T", with "T" being the last of the original alleys. Over the years Alleys "A" thru "C" have disappeared due to urban renewal but the others remain. From south to north they are; Dodge, Everett, Ford, Garford, Hudson, Indian (the motorcycle), Jeffry, Kissel, Lozier, Maxwell, National, Overland, Packard, Quincy, REO, Stutz and Templar.

Packard Alley, Vallejo, CA.

End of San Francisco Bay Area △

The Pontiac Grill in Santa Cruz, CA.

PONTIAC GRILL
(Theme restaurant)
  429 Front St.
  SANTA CRUZ, CA 95060
  (30 miles southeast of San Jose at
  the north end of Monterey Bay)
  Phone: 408-427-2290

  This is a 1950s-style restaurant designed around a PONTIAC theme and
located in a former Pontiac-Cadillac
dealership building. Old Pontiac advertisements and memorabilia add to the
decor as do items on the menu such as
"Pontiac Splits" (omelets) and
"Bonneville Burgers".

ALMEIDA'S CLASSIC CARS
(Dealer)
  551 N. Tully Rd.
  TURLOCK, CA 95380 (Midway
  between Merced and Modesto on
  SR 99)

Phone: 209-667-7828
Hours: Tues-Sat 10-5.

  This dealer carries an average inventory of between 30 and 35 antique and
classic vehicles for sale in an indoor
showroom. They buy vehicles and sell
on consignment. Almeida's also offers
appraisals, detailing and can arrange
domestic and export shipping. Car clubs
are welcome.

CALIFORNIA ROUTE 66 MUSEUM
  Old U.S. 66 in downtown
  Victorville
  VICTORVILLE, CA 92392
  (28 miles north of San Bernardino
  on I-15)
  Phone: 760-951-0346 or
  760-261-US66
  Hours: Thurs-M 10-4. Free.

  There are Route 66 museums spring-
ing up in various places all along the old

California

Almeida's Classic Cars of Turlock, CA.

historic Route 66 and this is one of the best. The California Route 66 Museum is located in the heart of Victorville in an old (1918) bank building and has numerous displays on the road. There's an art gallery, exhibits on the Route itself as well as on other great roads and Indian trails. Other exhibits provide information on books and movies which involved Route 66 including John Steinbeck's "Grapes of Wrath" and, of course, the famous TV series. A gift shop offers items of interest including the newest maps showing where the old road might still be found. A library contains old literature about Route 66 and has a copy of every book published on the road.

HAYS ANTIQUE TRUCK MUSEUM

1962 Hays Ln.
Heidrick Ag History Center (On I-5 & Road 102 five miles west of Sacramento Airport)

WOODLAND, CA 95776 (18 miles northwest of Sacramento)
Phone: 530-666-1044
Hours: Easter Week to Labor Day M-F 10-5, Labor Day to Easter Week W-F 10-5 and Sat-Sun 10-6. Admission charged (one admission price for two museums).

You can see two museums at this location: the Hays Antique Truck Museum and the Fred C. Heidrich Antique Ag Collection. The Hays Antique Truck Museum was founded in 1982 by A. Wayne "Pop" Hays and is dedicated to the procurement, care and display of antique trucks and truck-related artifacts. There is also an archive and library specializing in literature related to trucks. On display are 123 trucks, representing 94 manufacturers and dating from 1903 to the mid-1950s. The museum owns the only remaining Breeding Steam Truck as well as several electric trucks. One display features a Museum truck on a large section of the old plank road which crossed the sand dunes of Yuma, AZ to El Centro, CA in the early 1900s.

The Museum provides evidence of the industry's effort to meet the needs of the drivers and the demands of the builders, providers and the consumers to deliver bigger loads more efficiently. Changes in the design and engineering of the cabs, bodies, wheels and tires can be seen. Interactive and reactive displays are being planned and developed.

A restored 1929 Chevrolet truck, similar to the one used by "Pop" Hays when he started in the trucking business in 1929.

The History Center operates a gift shop, has a 300-seat conference center, is wheelchair accessible and provides guided tours.

ALLCHEVY AUTO PARTS (Salvage)
4999 Vanden Rd.
VACAVILLE, CA 95687
(Midway between Oakland and Sacramento on I-80)
Phone: 707-437-5466
Hours: M-F 8:30-5:30.

This salvage yard specializes in CHEVROLET auto and truck parts from 1955 to the present. There are about 200 cars and trucks in the yard and most of their inventory is computerized. Vacaville Auto Parts will search sources throughout the nation for hard-to-find parts. Customers may browse the yard. In business since 1984.

COLORADO

L & M USED AUTO PARTS (Salvage)

8151 Rd 8 South
ALAMOSA, CO 81101
(South-central part of the state)
Phone: 719-589-6191 or
719-589-9205
Hours: M-F 8-5, Sat 8-noon

You are not far from New Mexico when you visit L & M. It is high and dry here and that means very little rust in old cars. L & M has some 1400 vehicles on the lot of mixed makes and many years. There are also trucks. If L & M does not have it they will try to find it. Car clubs are welcome. L & M started in 1963 and is owned by Leroy Martinez.

PIKES PEAK AUTO HILL CLIMB MUSEUM

135 Manitou Av (At intersection of US 24 and Manitou Av.)
COLORADO SPRINGS, CO 80829
Phone: 719-685-4400 or
800-307-8168
Hours: M-Sat 9-5, Sun 12-5.
Admission charged.

This museum is dedicated to the world-famous Pikes Peak Hill Climb Race held each year in July on Pikes Peak Mountain. On display in the museum are 24 cars and four motor bikes, all associated with the race since it first started in 1916, as well as lots of photographs and memorabilia. Included in

The Pikes Peak Auto Hill Climb Museum in Colorado Springs, CO.

the collection: Bobby Unser's 1968 winner #92, the Lexington that won the 1920 race, the Ford racer that won in 1922, a 1957 Frenzel Lincoln special, and a dramatic open wheel car that set the 1992 record. Visitors may also watch videos that include "Riding Along" to the summit. The museum's gift shop offers items of interest to racing and antique auto fans. Mary Elizabeth Ruwell is the museum's archivist and curator.

▼ DENVER AREA

COLORADO CAR BOOKS
(Book store)
　5138 S Broadway at Bellview
　ENGLEWOOD, CO 80110 (Southwestern suburb of Denver)
　Phone: 303-762-8595
　Hours: M-F 10-7, Sat 9-4

This book store specializes in literature for automobile hobbyists and has numerous books on antique cars, trucks, motorcycles, hot rods, racing, auto history, restorations, repairs and modifications. They carry current and back-issue magazines and out-of-print books. Also available are posters, prints, original works of automotive art and models. Colorado Car Books buys auto-related books and magazines.

FORNEY HISTORIC
TRANSPORTATION MUSEUM
　1416 Platte St
　DENVER, CO 80202

Phone: 303-433-3643
Hours: May thru Sept M-Sat 9-5, Sun 11-5. Rest of year M-Sat 10-5, Sun 11-5. Closed Jan 1, Thanksgiving, Dec 25, New Years Day and Easter. Admission charged.

This museum is housed in the former power station of the Denver trolley system and displays a wide range of transportation equipment including trains, airplanes, carriages, sleighs, motorcycles and about 150 classic and antique autos. In the auto collection is Amelia Earhart's 1923 Kissel, Ali Kahn's Rolls-Royce and movie producer D. W. Griffith's 1923 six-wheel Hispano-Suiza which was used in some of his movies. The museum has a gift shop.
　Location: From I-25 northbound, exit 211 onto 23rd St. turn east on 23rd St. which will take you to Platte St. and the museum. Steve Meyer is the museum's curator.

End of Denver Area △

THE STANLEY HOTEL AND
CONFERENCE CENTER
　333 Wonderview Av
　ESTES PARK, CO 80517 (55 miles northwest of Denver)

Phone: 800-976-1377 or 970-586 3371

This famous hotel was build in 1909 by F. O. Stanley, inventor of the Stanley

Colorado

The famous Stanley Hotel and Conference Center in Estes Park, CO. It was build by F. O. Stanley, inventor of the Stanley Steamer automobile.

Steamer Automobiles. Stanley's idea was to provide a fine hotel to house summertime tourists to the fabulous Rocky Mountain region and to carry those tourists into the mountains and to and from the rail heads in Stanley Steamer motor coaches.

The hotel was completely renovated in 1997 featuring 133 guest rooms with refurbished antiques, down comforters, new bedding, and much more! Additionally, the Stanley Hotel is the site of the Stanley Museum, built in conjunction with the Stanley Museum in Kingfield, Maine, and displays items of interest regarding Stanley automobiles. Other hotel features include award-winning dining with their famous Holiday and Sunday brunches, a fine gift shop, outdoor heated pool, poolside dining, weekend jazz programs, and a popular Sunday concert series. The hotel is often used for meetings, weddings, reunions, etc.,

and of course, antique car meets.

The Estes Park Area Historical Museum, 200 4th St., has further information on the Stanley family, their automobile business and has on display a 1909 Stanley Steamer automobile.

AMERICAN AUTO SALVAGE
2773 D Rd
GRAND JUNCTION, CO 81501
(West-central part of state on I-70)
Phone: 970-243-0373
Hours: M-F 9-5, Sat 9-noon

Bill "Butch" Jarvis, the yard's manager, knows every vehicle and part in the yard without the aid of a computer. That's quite a feat considering there are 550 vehicles. Some 250 of them, though, are whole and restorable and will only be sold as a complete unit. Most of American Auto Salvage's cars and parts are in very good condition because of the dry and sunny climate. The company does not offer mail order services, but does have a towing service capable of handling rigs up to 80,000 pounds. Customers may browse the yard.

▼ GREELEY AREA (50 miles north of Denver on US 85)

CLASSICAL GAS
(Dealer and museum)

245 E Collins
EATON, CO 80615 (8 miles north of Greeley on US 85)
Phone: 800-453-7955 or
907-454-1365
Hours: M-F 9-5, Sat 9-2

This is a large antique vehicle dealer with a 12,000 sq ft showroom and museum. They carry dozens of antique vehicles of all makes in inventory ranging in age from the mid-1920s to the mid-1960s. Classical Gas sells on consignment, takes trades, provides an inventory list and does minor repairs and service work. They will search for a specific vehicle and financing is available. The company also sells antique auto-related signs and pedal cars.

DEALS ON WHEELS (Dealer)

1320 8th Av
GREELEY, CO 80631
Phone: 970-356-9232
Hours: Spring thru Fall M-Sat 8-8, Winter M-Sat 9-6

This is northern Colorado's largest muscle car and antique car dealer. They carry between 25 to 30 fine cars in inventory at all times. Deals on Wheels takes trades, sells on consignment, does appraisals, helps arrange financing and transportation and will search for specific vehicles for customers. An inventory list is available and car clubs are welcome. The company's owner is Dean Jule.

End of Greeley area △

PIONEER MUSEUM

South Adams St/Hwy 50 (at the east edge of town)
GUNNISON, CO 81230 (120 miles west of Pueblo on US 50)
Phone: 940-641-4530
Hours: Memorial Day thru Labor Day M-Sat 9-5. Admission charged.

This is a large museum complex of 8 buildings displaying historic items from Gunnison County Colorado and else-where. There is a restored schoolhouse, a collection of mineral and Indian artifacts, a narrow-gage D & RG steam train, displays of antique farm equipment, horse-drawn vehicles and about a dozen antique cars. Most of the cars are on loan from local collectors. Permanent cars on display include a 1908 Oldsmobile, a 1916 Cadillac convertible, and 1939 hearse and a 1931 custom-made Buick roadster. There is also a Simplex motorcycle and an antique

53

Colorado

The Dougherty antique car collection is open to the public on weekends only and is south of Longmont, CO. on US 287.

1923 Model T firetruck. Most of the cars are driveable and are used in local parades and other events. The museum has a small gift shop which offers locally-made craft items and other things of interest. August Grosland is the museum's manager and curator.

WOLLER AUTO PARTS, INC. (Salvage)

8227 Road SS
LAMAR, CO 81052 (Southeastern part of the state)
Phone: 719-336-2108
Hours: M-F 8-5:30, Sat 8-noon

A large salvage yard with about 4000 vehicles of all makes & models, mostly domestic, from 1955 to the mid-1980s. Many pickups available. Woller provides several services including body work, painting, glass work and mechanical repairs. In business since 1973.

DOUGHERTY MUSEUM COLLECTION

One mile south of Longmont on US 287
LONGMONT, CO 80501 (30 miles north of downtown Denver)
Phone: 303-776-2520
Hours: Weekends 11-4. Admission charged.

A privately owned museum displaying some 35 vehicles ranging in age from 1902-1937. They include a 1902 Mobile Steamer, a 1908 Packard 30 Runabout, a 1910 Lozier Type I Briarcliff, a 1913 Lozier Type 72 Riverside, a 1915 Stanley Mountain Wagon and a 1920 Pierce-Arrow Type 48 five-passenger touring car. There are also displays of carriages, steam engines, musical instruments and a collection of Springfield guns from 1812 to World War I.

**ANTIQUE AUTO HOUSE—
ANTIQUE FIRE HOUSE (Dealer)**
1825 E 18th St
LOVELAND, CO 80538 (48 miles
north of downtown Denver)
Phone: 970-667-7040
Hours: M-Sat 9-5:30. Admission
free.

This is an antique car dealer that buys and sells antique, special interest automobiles and fire trucks, all pre-1970s. They carry about 20 cars and trucks in inventory at all times in their showroom. Some vehicles are on consignment. Visitors will also see fire trucks and fire equipment and memorabilia. The facility is accessible to the physically impaired. John R. and Nancy J. Bergquist are the owners.

▼ PUEBLO AREA

MORGAN AUTO PARTS (Salvage)
722 Kennie Rd
PUEBLO, CO 81001
Phone: 303-545-1702
Hours: M-F 8-5, Sat 8-1

This salvage yard has some 450 vehicles of all makes and models. Mail orders are welcome and customers many browse the yard. In business since 1963.

WEST 29th AUTO, INC. (Salvage)
3200 W 29th St
PUEBLO, CO 81003
Phone: 719-543-4247 or
719-543-4249 or 800-550-4247
Hours: Tues-Sat 8-5

This is an 80-acre salvage yard with approximately 4000 vehicles of all makes and models of cars accumulated over 30 years. Employees remove all parts and the company welcomes mail orders. Some new parts are available. In business since 1957.

End of Pueblo Area △

EDDIE PAUL (Salvage)
9150 Boone Rd
YODER, CO 80864 (30 miles east
of Colorado Springs)
Phone: 719-478-2723
Hours: M-F 8 am to 9 pm, Sat 8 am
to 9 pm by appointment only.

A small salvage yard of approximately 35 vehicles including 1933-1951 Chevrolet cars, 1936-1941 Chevrolet trucks, 1936 Oldsmobiles, 1951 Cadillacs, 1940, 1950 and 1953 Buicks, 1946, 1947 and 1955 Dodges, 1940 Hudsons, 1942, 1948 and 1950 Plymouths, 1939, 1951 and 1959 Chryslers, 1953 Fords and 1936 International pickups. In business since 1977.

CONNECTICUT

DRAGONE CLASSIC MOTORCARS, INC. (Dealer & restorer)
1797 Main St
BRIDGEPORT, CT 06604
Phone: 203-335-4643 and
203-375-8624
Hours: M-Sat 8-6

Here you will find a large dealer and restorer of vintage automobiles specializing in exotic vehicles and convertibles from the 1950s and older. Between 35 and 50 cars are in their showroom, a 15,000 sq. ft. restored 1880s stable. Dragone does full restorations, repairs and service work on antique cars. They can arrange financing, offer leases, do appraisals, take trades and provide an inventory list. They also actively search other dealers for specific vehicles for customers. Once a month, on the last Saturday, Dragone's holds an open house for friends and customers. Visitors and car clubs, though, are welcome at other times.

There is an automobilia gallery on the second floor offering for sale such items as period oil paintings, toys, books and a wide variety of collectibles. The owners are George and Manny Dragone.

CONNECTICUT FIRE MUSEUM
58 North Rd (Behind the Connecticut Trolley Museum)
EAST WINDSOR, CT 06088
(Northern suburb of Windsor Locks)
Phone: 860-623-4732
Hours: June-Aug M-F 10-4, Sat 10-5, Sun noon-5; Apr thru May and Sept thru Oct Sat-Sun noon-5. Admission charged.

This is a large fire museum displaying some 20 firefighting vehicles including a 1913 Seagrave ladder truck, a 1927 Bulldog Mack pumper and a 1929 Ahern-Fox pumper. Also on display is a 1939 Yellow Coach transit bus, model fire engines, antique alarm systems and various other items of the firefighting profession. The museum has its own repair shop and a gift shop.

GHOST PARKING LOT (Curiosity)
Hamden Shopping Plaza
Dixwell Av
HAMDEN, CT 06517 (Northern suburb of New Haven)

In the parking lot of this shopping plaza are 20 automobiles permanently

Cars in the Ghost Parking Lot of Hamden Plaza, Hamden, CT.

molded into the surface of the lot and covered with asphalt so as to blend in with the lot itself. It is a one-of-a-kind attention-grabber.

LEO WINAKOR & SONS, INC
(Salvage)
470 Forsyth Rd
SALEM, CT 06415
(11 miles east of Norwich)
Phone: 203-859-0471
Hours: Sat 10-3, Sun 10-2, other times by appointment.

This is a 30-acre salvage yard with about 1500 vehicles of all makes and models ranging in age from 1930 to 1981. Many cars are from the 1950s. Some vehicles are complete and suitable for restoring. In additon there is a respectable number of trucks. Customers may browse the yard. Towing service

available. In business since 1949. The owners are Art Winakor and Rick Holmwood.

ALPLEX AUTOMOTIVE RESTORATIONS
(Dealer and restorer)
79 Commercial St
WATERTOWN, CT 06795 (North-western suburb of Waterbury)
Phone: 203-274-2547
Hours: M-F 8-5, Sat 8-noon

Alplex is both a dealer of antique vehicles and a restorer. They have a 10,000 square foot facility and do partial or complete restorations of classics, special interest vehicles and sports cars. All body work, painting and mechanical work done in-house. Autos for sale are on display in their showroom. Visitors welcome.

57

DELAWARE

NEMOURS MANSION AND GARDENS (Historic home)

Rockland Rd (3.5 miles NW on Rockland Rd between US 202 & SR 141)

WILMINGTON, DE 19899

Phone: 320-651-6912

Hours: May thru Nov two-hour tours offered Tues thru Sat at 9, 11, 1 and 3; Sun 11, 1 and 3. Children under 16 not admitted. Admission charged.

This is the 300-acre estate, home and gardens of Alfred I. du Pont. The 102-room mansion is lavishly furnished in fine examples of antique furniture, tapestries, rare rugs and works of art. Included in the tour of the estate is a display of several antique automobiles including a 1912 Cadillac, a 1924 Cadillac, a 1951 Rolls-Royce Silver Wraith and a 1960 Rolls-Royce Phantom V, of which only 10 were built.

DISTRICT OF COLUMBIA

NATIONAL MUSEUM OF AMERICAN HISTORY

On Constitution Av Between
12th & 14 Sts N W
WASHINGTON, DC 20560
Phone: 202-357-2700
Hours: Daily 10-5:30 with
extended hours in the summer.
Closed Dec 25. Admission free.

This museum is one of several in the large and magnificent Smithsonian museum complex along the Mall in our nation's capital. The museum depicts the cultural, technological, scientific and political development of the United States. Venerated objects such as The Star-Spangled Banner are on display as well as such unusual objects as the ruby slippers from the movie "The Wizard of Oz" and one of the first "Teddy" Bears.

Also on display are large collections of coins, First Ladies' dresses, musical instruments, graphic arts and printing; and for the antique car buff, there is a display of several automobiles, motorcycles, truck tractors, race cars and busses. The automotive display includes an 1866 Dudgeon steam carriage, an 1893 Duryea, an 1894 Haynes, a 1903 Winton touring car, a 1913 Ford Model T touring car, a 1929 Miller Indianapolis race car, Bruce Larson's championship funny car dragster and Don Garlits' Swamp Rat XXX dragster. The museum has well-stocked shops, a cafeteria, a restaurant and three gift shops.

FLORIDA

B & B USED AUTO PARTS (Salvage)
Industrial Rd
BIG PINE KEY, FL 33043
(In the Florida Keys)
Phone: 305-872-9761 and
305-745-3517
Hours: M-F 9-5:30, Sat 9-?.

A salvage yard in the beautiful Florida Keys with some 1200 vehicles from 1950 forward. The yard specializes in CADILLACS, CHEVROLETS, CHRYSLERS, BUICKS, INTERNATIONALS and FORDS. There is a selection of Volvos and Citroens from 1968 and later. Customers may browse the yard. In business since 1982.

PAST GAS (Automobilia)
308 Willard St (SR 520)
COCOA, FL 32922 (18 miles south of Titusville on US 1)
Phone: 407-636-0449 (Days),
407-631-1227 (Evenings)
Hours: M-F 9-5

Past Gas restores old gas pumps and other antique service station-related items and offers them for sale in their showroom. They also have automobilia items such as traffic lights, bumper cars, gas globes, signs and decals. Other antique items for sale include juke boxes, coin-operated machines, neon clocks, coke machines, and barber poles. Catalog available for $1.00.

▼ DAYTONA BEACH AREA

DAYTONA USA (Museum)
Daytona International Speedway
1801 W International Speedway
Blvd (U.S. 92 just east of I-95)
DAYTONA BEACH, FL 32114-1243
Phone: 904-947-6800
Hours: Daily 9-6 with extended hours during peak seasons. Closed Dec 25.

They call it "The Ultimate Motorsport Attraction". This fine mu-
seum is on the grounds of the Daytona International Speedway. Visitors enter the museum through twin tunnels which are replicas of the famous twin tunnels at the Speedway through which millions of fans have passed as they entered the infield. Once through the tunnels the world of racing opens up in a fascinating array of displays, race cars, racecar drivers, racing events, great moments in racing and much more. Six rear-projected video screens, complete

The Twin-tunnel entrance to the Daytona USA museum at the Daytona International Speedway.

with surround-sound, show visitors actual stock car, sports car and motorcycle races—the things that made Daytona famous. The museum's Great Moments Theater also shows films of historic moments in racing.

Sir Malcolm Campbell's Bluebird V is on display. This famous machine attained the incredible speed of 276.820 mph in 1935 at Daytona and was the fastest man had yet travelled in a race car at the time. Also on display is the Chrysler-powered "Mad Dog" racer, with stubby wings, which set a world closed-course speed record in 1961. Lee Petty's 1959 Daytona 500-winner Olds is on display as is "Fireball" Robert's 1962 Pontiac, Richard Petty's 1964 Plymouth, Cale Yarborough's 1968 Mercury, Dale Earnhardt's 1990 Chevrolet and other well-known cars. The museum's gift shop, the Daytona USA Pit Stop, offers Nascar-related merchandise, clothing, postcards, books and a

61

The Klassix Auto Museum focuses on the Corvette automobile, but also has antique cars, race cars and motorcycles.

wide variety of collectibles. Tours of the Speedway's track are available through the museum.

KLASSIX AUTO MUSEUM

2909 W International Speedway Blvd (1 miles west of Daytona Speedway)
DAYTONA BEACH, FL 32124
Phone: 904-252-3800
Hours: Daily 9-9, closed major holidays. Admission charged.

There's a magnificent mix of vintage machines in this museum including muscle cars, classics, sports cars, motorcycles and celebrity cars. Among the celebrity cars is Burt Reynolds's 1957 Thunderbird, "Hulk" Hogan's 1956 Cadillac Eldorado convertible and Humphrey Bogart's 1956 Thunderbird. This was the last car "Bogey" bought. He died in January 1957. There are about 120 cars and 40 motorcycles. Twenty of the motorcycles are Indians.

Displays of individual cars are highlighted by elaborate period-accented backdrops and manikins. The museum has a movie tracing the history of stock car racing and, on the second floor, there's a mockup of a drive-in theater with modern corvette tailcones used as seats where visitors can watch a movie on the development of the Corvette. The museum's large gift shop is filled with interesting souvenirs for the car enthusiast. Klassix Auto Museum was founded by Bill Carlson and his son, Dean.

End of Daytona Beach area g

▼ FORT MYERS AREA

Henry Ford's winter home, "Mangoes", in Ft. Myers, FL. To the right is a bust of Henry Ford.

HENRY FORD AND THOMAS EDISON WINTER ESTATES
(Historic homes)

2350 McGregor Blvd (SR 867)
FORT MYERS, FL 33901
(in the southwest part of the Florida peninsula near the coast and on I-75)
Phone: 941-334-7419 or 941-334-3614
Hours: Admission by guided tour only, M-Sat 9-3:30, Sun noon-3:30, closed Thanksgiving and Dec. 25. Admission covers both estates.

These are the winter homes of two famous Americans, Henry Ford and Thomas Edison who, as close friends, built their homes side-by-side in this winter resort town. Ford's home is known as "Mangoes" and Edison's as "Seminole Lodge". Both homes are open to the public. Edison's extensive botanical garden and laboratory are preserved much as they were at the time of his death in 1931. On display in an adjoining museum are many artifacts and personal belongings of both men as well as several antique automobiles. One of the vehicles is a Model T Ford given to Edison by Ford.

SHOW CARS (Dealer)
US 41 South near Sam's Plaza
(mail address 1435 Larkspur)
FORT MYERS, FL 33901
Phone: 941-277-9911
Hours: M-F 10-4, Sat 10-1

This is the closest thing you'll find in America to an EDSEL dealership. Show Cars specializes in that marque and has upwards of a dozen EDSELs on the floor at any one time. They also are strong in LINCOLNs. Yet other makes, Corvettes, Cadillacs, Fords, etc. might be offered too. Most of the non-Edsels are cars from the 1940s through the 1960s. Show Cars sells on consignment, takes trades and will arrange financing and transportation. Robert Mayer, Show Cars' owner, participates in several local shows and cruises each year. Car clubs are welcome.

End of Fort Myers Area △

SUNRISE AUTO SALES (Salvage)
Aero Av
LAKE CITY, FL 32055
Phone: 904-755-1810 or
904-755-0441
Hours: M-F 8-5:30, Sat 8-1

This yard has over 1000 cars and trucks ranging from the 1930s and up. They specialize in vehicles from the 1940s thru early 1970s with the highest concentration of cars being from the 1950s and 1960s. Customers may browse the lot. Sunrise has a brisk mail order business. In business since 1989.

▼ MIAMI/FORT LAUDERDALE AREA

AUTO WAREHOUSE (Dealer)
5810 N Federal Hwy
FORT LAUDERDALE, FL 33308
Phone: 954-492-4242
Hours: M-F 9-6, Sat 10-2

Auto Warehouse carries a wide variety of affordable makes and models of antique and collectible vehicles. They have over 100 vehicles in stock, many of them convertibles. Pickup trucks also available. Auto Warehouse takes trades, sells on consignment and can arrange financing and transportation. Stop by and take a look. You may find your next car here.

BERLINER CLASSIC MOTOR CARS, INC. (Dealer)
1920 Stirling Rd
DANIA, FL 33004 (Southern suburb of Ft. Lauderdale)
Phone: 954-923-7271 and
954-920-0753
Hours: M-F 9-5, Sat 10-1

This is an antique auto dealer offering a wide variety of fine quality automobiles and motorcycles. Berliner takes trades, sells on consignment, assists in financing and shipping, and searches for specific vehicles. They also offer jukeboxes, old cash registers, gas pumps,

Berliner Classic Motor Cars of Dania, FL.

radios, phonographs, slot machines, bicycles, barber chairs, Coke machines, carousel horses, auto couches, scales and more. Their facilities are available for corporate or private parties. Berliners is a fun place to visit.

DEZERLAND SURFSIDE BEACH HOTEL
8701 Collins Av
MIAMI BEACH, FL 33154
Phone: 800-331-9346

Hours: Hotel open 24 hours.
Restaurant daily 7 am to 10 pm.

This is a unique beach-front hotel decorated throughout in an antique car motif. There are antique cars around the entrance, in the lobby, restaurant and at the bottom of the swimming pool. All of the hotel's rooms are named after cars. One of the vehicles in the lobby, a 1956 Ford truck, is a lobster tank. Most of the cars are kept in running order and are used from time-to-time in events

One of the booths in the restaurant of the Dezerland Surfside Beach Hotel.

throughout the country. In the restaurant are booths made from old car bodies. Car clubs are welcome and are offered discounts. There is a large gift shop filled with items of interest to antique car buffs.

MOTORCAR GALLERY (Dealer)
715 N Federal Hwy (US 1)
FT. LAUDERDALE, FL 33304
Phone: 954-522-9900
Hours: M-F 9:30-8:30, Sat 9:30-5

Here is a dealer that specializes in top-of-the line vintage cars, sports cars and European exotics. Prices range from $40,000 to $200,000. Visitors will see LAMBORGHINIs, FERRARIs, MASERATIs and coach-builder limited-production ROLLS-ROYCEs and BENTLEYs. Other fine quality cars will

also be seen here. Motorcar Gallery carries up to 40 cars in inventory at all times, will take trades and arrange transportation. Ed Waterman is the owner. He knows quality cars.

TED VERNON (Dealer)
471 NE 79th St
MIAMI, FL 33138
Phone: 305-754-2323
Hours: M-F 9-5

Ted Vernon has a garage-type indoor showroom and an adjacent lot with some 100 to 125 antique, classic and collectible cars available for sale. Vehicles range from $1000 fixer-uppers to $100,000 ready-to-go Rolls-Royces. Limousines are something of a specialty here and up to 40 might be on hand at any one time. The owner is Ted Vernon.

End of Miami/Fort Lauderdale Area △

▼ OCALA AREA (35 miles south of Gainesville on I-75)

E-ONE FACTORY TOURS
(Manufacturer)
1601 SW 37th Av
OCALA, FL 32676
Phone: 904-854-3524
Tour hours, M-F 8-3, closed
holidays and Dec 26-31.
Admission charged.
Reservations strongly suggested.

This is a company that make fire trucks and offers walking tours thru their factory to see how fire trucks are made. Tours are two miles long and can be noisy. Children under 6 not admit-

ted. A special tour demonstrating lights and sirens is available. Groups welcome.

FLORIDA'S SILVER SPRINGS
(Theme park)
SR 40 East
SILVER SPRINGS, FL 32688-0370
(An eastern suburb of Ocala)
Phone: 800-234-7458 and
904-236-2121
Hours: Daily 9-5:30.
Admission charged.

This is a large theme and wildlife

park built around the world's largest fresh water springs area. Among the many activities and displays in the park is a collection of some two dozen antique and classic cars. Autos of particular interest include a 1958 Chrysler Imperial, 1934 Ford, 1938 Cadillac, 1955 Chevrolet and a 1932 fire truck. Many movies and TV shows have been filmed at Silver Springs and the area was used for jungle warfare training during World War II.

DON GARLITS' ATTRACTIONS (Museum)
　　I-75 Exit 67
　　OCALA, FL 34473
　　Phone: 352-245-8661
　　Hours: Daily 9-5:30. Closed Dec 25.
　　Admission charged.

A large and impressive museum complex featuring racing machines, especially drag racers, dating back to the '40s, plus antique vehicles. Twenty-four of the drag racers are Don Garlits' own cars, including several of his "Swamp Rats". Others cars on display include those driven by Don Prudhomme, Tom McEwen, Dean Moon, Shirley Muldowney and Chris Karamesines.

There are a number of vintage Fords and Dodges in a separate museum and several rare Metz automobiles. Altogether, there are over 160 cars in the collection. Two attractive gift shops offer a large selection of racing and antique car memorabilia and souvenirs. You'll have fun here.

Don Garlits' Attractions display both racing vehicles and antique cars.

End of Ocala Area △

Florida

OLD GOLD CARS AND PARTS (Salvage)

Hwy 349 north, HC4 Box 630
OLD TOWN, FL 32680
(38 miles west of Gainesville)
Phone: 352-542-8085
Hours: M-Thurs 8-5, F 8-noon

This is a large salvage yard with approximately 5000 vehicles, all of which are American-made. The yard specializes in vehicles from 1948 thru 1978 and does a brisk mail order business. In business since 1987. Ask for Shannon, the Manager.

▼ ORLANDO AREA

CLASSIC CHEVY INTERNATIONAL (Dealer, parts)

8235 N Orange Blossom Trail
ORLANDO, FL 32810
Phone: 800-456-1957 and
407-299-1957
Hours: M-F 8-5, Sat 9-3

This is an organization devoted to the restoration and preservation of CHEVROLET cars and trucks from 1955 to 1972. In their large indoor showroom are restored Chevrolets of these years offered for sale. Most of the facility consists of a restoration department and a warehouse operation stocking Chevrolet parts. Tours of the warehouse and restoration facilities are available. Classic Chevy also operates a club devoted to 1955-1972 Chevrolet cars and trucks. Car clubs welcome.

J AND B AUTO PARTS (Salvage)

17105 E Highway 50
ORLANDO, FL 32820
Phone: 305-568-2131
Hours: M-F 8-5:30, Sat-Sun 8-4

This is a large salvage lot with some 1500 American-made and imported cars and trucks. J and B has a radiator shop, and a service department. They install glass and offers towing. Customers may browse the yard. In business since 1954.

Classic Chevy International of Orlando, FL.

RADER'S RELICS (Dealer)
2601 W Fairbanks Av (Off I-4)
WINTER PARK, FL 32789 (Northeastern suburb of Orlando)
Phone: 407-647-1940
Hours: M-F 9-5

This is a well-established dealer of antique autos with approximately 40 autos offered for sale at all times. Cars are sold on consignment and Rader's buys cars, takes trades and arranges shipping. Walt Disney World is only 25 minutes away.

End of Orlando Area △

ST. PETERSBURG (See Tampa/St. Petersburg, Area)

▼ SARASOTA AREA

CARS & MUSIC OF YESTERDAY MUSEUM
5500 N Tamiami Trail (Just south of the airport)
SARASOTA, FL 34234
Phone: 813-355-6228
Hours: M-Sat 8:30-6, Sun 9:30-6.
Admission charged. Tours available.

A large and interesting museum with approximately 2000 mechanical music machines such as nickelodeons, calliopes, music boxes, penny-arcades, Hurdie Gurdies—and some 170 antique cars. Among the cars on display is a 1917 Simplex, a 1932 Auburn Boattail Speedster, a 1959 Scimitar, 1978 Bricklin, two Rolls-Royces and two Pierce-Arrows owned by the late John Ringling of circus fame. There is a large gift shop offering a wide variety of European music boxes, clocks, dolls, etc., some of which cannot be purchased anywhere else in the United States.

THOROUGHBRED MOTORS (Dealer & Parts)
3935 N Washington Blvd
SARASOTA, FL 39324
Phone: 941-955-5960 or 941-359-2277
Hours: M-Sat 9-7

A dealer specializing in vintage European cars; Jaguars, Rolls-Royces, Aston Martins, Austin Healeys, MGs, Triumphs, etc. Some cars are in their original state and are offered as rebuildable automobiles. Normally there are some 30 cars on display. Thoroughbred Motors does appraisals, takes trades, makes repairs and publishes an inventory list. They also carry a large inventory of Jaguar parts. Car clubs are welcome. The owner is Rodney Dessberg.

69

Florida

VINTAGE WHOLESALE OF SARASOTA, INC. (Dealer)
2836 N Tamiami Trail
SARASOTA, FL 34234
Phone: 941-355-6500
Hours: M-F 9-6, Sat 10-4

This is a large dealership with a wide variety of cars ranging from week-end run-abouts to chairman-of-the-board Rolls-Royces. They carry between 70 and 100 cars in inventory. An inventory list is available. Vintage also does appraisals, helps arrange financing, exports, sells on consignment, takes trades and will search for that very special vehicle you've always wanted. Martin Godbey is the owner and welcomes car clubs to come visit.

End of Sarasota Area △

ELLIOTT MUSEUM
825 NE Ocean Blvd (SR A1A)
STUART, FL 34996 (30 miles north of West Palm Beach)
Phone: 407-225-1961
Hours: Daily 11-4. Admission charged.

A large and diversified museum showing displays of Americana from 1835 to 1930. One wing includes some 30 vintage autos, plus motorcycles and bicycles. Among the auto collection is a 1914 Packard touring car, a 1953 Briggs-Cunnigham Cabriolet and a 1930 Lincoln. There is also a display of the many industrial inventions of Sterling Elliott, the father of Harmon Parker Elliott, museum founder.

The Elliott Museum of Stuart, FL.

▼ TAMPA/ST. PETERSBURG AREA

Golden Classics, Clearwater, FL where you'll find "Toys for Big Boys".

GOLDEN CLASSICS (Dealer)
1928 Gulf-To-Bay Blvd
CLEARWATER, FL 33765
Phone: 813-449-1962 or
813-726-1957
Hours: M-F 9-5, Sat-Sun vary

This dealer has four showrooms and carries about 120 vehicles in stock at all times. They offer antique cars, muscle cars, street rods and Fifties cars. There is a 300 ft model train layout in the main showroom. In showroom #4 you will find a life-size drive-in scene where visitors can sit in a collector car with drive-in speakers and watch a classic movie. Golden Classics sells cars on consignment, offers appraisals and can arrange financing and shipping. There is a large memorabilia store selling jukeboxes, antique Coke machines, slot machines, gas pumps and many other items. Free popcorn and small Cokes are available. On the second floor is a 3000 sq. ft. lounge available for parties, wedding receptions, meetings etc. Dan Newcombe is the company president.

THE OLD CAR COMPANY (Dealer)
1022 S 50th St
TAMPA, FL 33619
Phone: 813-247-6700
Hours: M-F 8-5, Sat 8-noon

This is a dealer that specializes in FORD MODEL As. They carry about 40 to 50 affordable vehicles in stock at all times in their indoor showroom. The Old Car Company also handles other cars, especially from the Model A time period. They offer repair services, sell cars on consignment, take trades, and can provide an inventory list. Car clubs are welcome at The Old Car Company. Marvin Goldenberg is the owner. (Photo next page).

71

The Old Car Company of Tampa, FL offers a generous selection of Ford Model A vehicles as well as other collectible cars. (See listing on prior page.)

End of Tampa/St. Petersburg, Area △

UMATILLA AUTO SALVAGE
19714 Saltsdale Rd (2 miles east of town)
UMATILLA, FL 32784 (30 miles northwest of Orlando)
Phone: 904-669-6363
Hours: M-F 9-5, Sat 8-noon

This salvage yard, near the small town of Umatilla, has about 1000 ve-hicles. They are mostly American-made and mostly from the mid-1960s to 1970s. There are some older vehicles, however, including some pre-war cars. A number of vehicles are whole and re-storable. Customers may browse the yard. This is a 32-year-old salvage yard under current management since 1986.

▼ WEST PALM BEACH AREA
(65 miles north of Miami)

CLASSIC DREAMCARS, LTD.
(Dealer)
161 US Hwy 1 North
TEQUESTA, FL 33469 (A northern
suburb of West Palm Beach)
Phone: 561-743-0008
Hours: M-F 9-5

This is the multi-story facility of Ragtops Motorcars of West Palm Beach. FL.

...and Dreamcars they are! Classics, muscle cars, sports cars, antiques... everything for which the car buff could hope. Classic Dreamcars carries several dozen fine automobiles in stock for the customers' inspection. They take trades, export, do appraisals, help arrange financing, buy and sell. Stop on by!

RAGTOPS MOTORCARS (Dealer)
2119 S Dixie Hwy (US 1)
WEST PALM BEACH, FL 33401-7701
Phone: 561-655-2826 or 800-655-2119
Hours: M-Sat 9-6, Sun (during the season) 9-5

This is the country's largest dealer of vintage convertibles. There are facilities on both sides of the street. The main office and showroom is located in an ornate old building that was originally designed for a Hudson dealer. Ragtops offers approximately 70 classic, luxury and sports convertibles at all times. The cars are displayed in a very unique way in this three-floor facility. Customers may find the vehicle of their dreams parked in a simulated drive-in theater, a gas station, a barn, an old-fashioned main street, a car-as-art gallery, a working soda bar or at the beach in real sand.

Ragtops helps arrange financing, offers leasing, storage and sells cars on consignment. There is a gift shop offering automotive memorabilia and Ragtops has an interesting display of memorabilia from the 1950s.

Ragtops' owner, Ty Houck, has restored and put back into service a 1954 "Silver Diner". Why not pop in for a soda and some 1950s Rock and Roll? Inquire at Ragtops about location and details.

end of West Palm Beach △

Florida

HOLDER'S AUTO SALVAGE
12404 Highway 231
YOUNGSTOWN, FL 32466 (In the Florida Panhandle 20 miles northeast of Panama City)
Phone: 850-722-4993
Hours: Tues-Sat 8-5

This salvage lot specializes in pre-1975 cars and trucks with some cars back to the 1920s. Most of the vehicles are American-made. The owner's brother operates a wheel cover/hub cap business on the same site with thousands of wheel covers from 1934 up. In business since 1984.

GEORGIA

▼ ATLANTA AREA

ANTIQUE AUTO & MUSIC MUSEUM

Georgia's Stone Mountain Park
STONE MOUNTAIN, GA 30086
(An eastern suburb of Atlanta)
Phone: 404-981-0194
Hours: Summer, daily 10-8:30, rest of year 10-5:30. Closed Dec 25. Admission charged.

This is a very nice museum, located inside beautiful Stone Mountain Park, displaying some 40 antique vehicles. There are also collections of antique musical instruments, toys, clocks and other items. Among the antique vehicles is an 1895 Fugier, a 1904 Oldsmobile truck, a 1905 Stanley Steamer, a 1920 Wurlitzer, a 1928 Martin aeroplane car inspired by the famous aviator, General Billy Mitchell and a "Buck Rogers" car. The museum has an interesting and well-stockerd gift shop.

The Antique Auto & Music Museum has many interesting vehicles on display and is located in Georgia's famous Stone Mountain Park.

AUTO MOTIF, INC. (Automobilia)

2941 Atlanta Rd
SMYRNA, GA 30080
(A northern suburb of Atlanta)
Phone: 770-435-5025
or 800-367-1161
Hours: M-Sat 10-6

This is an automotive theme gift shop offering over 10,000 auto-related items such as books, models, kits, glassware, apparel, posters, puzzles, magazines, key rings, reproduction signs and more. Drop in and browse around. Milton S. Hill is the owner.

Georgia

EMBEE PARTS, INC. (Salvage)
4000 Lee Rd
SMYRNA, GA 30080
(A northwestern suburb of Atlanta)
Phone: 770-434-5686 or
800-234-5239
Hours: M-F 9-6, Sat 9-noon

This rare 1951 Mercedes 220 4 dr sedan is stored inside at Embee Parts, Inc. as are other valuable parts cars. Standing beside the car is George Wolfes, Embee's owner.

Embee stands for MERCEDES BENZ. This 500-car salvage yard specializes in the dismantling of that marque. The oldest Mercedes goes back to 1934. In recent years other makes of hard-to-find parts cars have been added such as MG's, Jaguars and some of the rare models of Cadillacs. Many parts are stored inside. Customer may browse the yard supervised. John Wolf is the man to see.

RED BARON'S (Dealer)
6450 Roswell Rd
ATLANTA, GA 30328

Phone: 404-252-3770
Hours: M-F 10-6, Sat 10-4

This is an antique dealer with a large showroom offering architectural antiques, furniture, chandeliers, cut glass, statuary, merry-go-rounds and antique cars. They carry about 25 antique vehicles in stock at all times and will sell cars on consignment. Two or three times a year Red Baron's conduct their own antique vehicle auction.

End of Atlanta Area △

PARK'S USED AUTO PARTS (Salvage)
Friendship Rd
EATONTON, GA 31024 (65 miles southeast of Atlanta)
Phone: 706-485-9905
Hours: M-F 2-6, all day Sat

This salvage yard specializes in muscle cars, antique cars and street rods. They also have a selection of trucks and mobile home axles. Mail-order business welcome.

CLARKE'S AUTO PARTS (Salvage)
Hwy 341 North
HELENA, GA 31037 (Suburb of
McRae, a county seat, 75 miles
southeast of Macon)
Phone: 912-868-6071
Hours: M-Sat 8:30-5:30

There is about 4000 vehicles in this
rural salvage yard. It covers about 200
acres and 60 to 70 of those acres contain the "old stuff". Some vehicles date
back to the 1930s. There is a generous
mix of makes, models and some light
trucks. Customers may browse the yard.
Clarke's is off the beaten path and may
be hard to find. Phone for directions if
necessary. Car clubs are welcome. In
business since 1947. Rodney Byrd is the
man to contact.

RICHMOND HILL (13 miles
southwest of Savannah on I-95):
They call this town "The Town That
Henry Ford Built". That's not exactly
true, but it is the town that Henry Ford
greatly improved and made more liveable for its citizens. In the mid-1930s
Ford bought a plantation nearby and
built a winter home in which he and his
wife, Clara, stayed for one month each
year. Ford named his Georgia home the
Richmond Plantation. At that time
Richmond Hill was known as Ways Station and was an impoverished community whose citizens suffered a high rate
of illiteracy, chronic unemployment and
chronic maladies such as malaria and
venereal diseases. Ford's chauffeur
caught malaria soon after his arrival
here. Ford saw the great needs of the
community and went to work to improve the local conditions. He had an
extensive drainage system built to drain
off standing water and by 1940 these
efforts had eradicated the malaria problem. He also built a medical clinic and
staffed it with nurses. Ford then built
chapels for whites and blacks, a school
for blacks, a sawmill, an industrial arts
and trade school, a large community
center and an agricultural research center that experimented on producing
starch from locally-grown sweet potatoes and water chestnuts, and on making alcohol from sweet potatoes and rice
for mixing with gasoline. In his schools,
Ford created one of the nation's first
school lunch programs. In 1941 the citizens of Ways Station renamed their
community Richmond Hill in honor of
Henry Ford and his nearby plantation.
Henry Ford's memory is still very strong
and cherished in this community.

PEBBLE HILL PLANTATION
(Historic home)
US Hwy 319 South
THOMASVILLE, GA 31779
(Southwestern part of the state near
the Florida state line)
Phone: 912-226-2344
Hours: Tues-Sat 10-5, Sun 1-5. Last
tour at 4. Closed the day after Labor
Day until Oct 1, Thanksgiving and
Dec 24 and 25. Children under 12
not admitted. Admission charged.

This is an old southern plantation
established in 1820. Through the years
it has had a succession of wealthy Yankee owners who converted the main
house into a lavish "winter cottage". The
main house is open to the public as are

Georgia

President Roosevelt's 1938 Ford convertible equipped with hand controls so that he could drive without the use of his legs. Behind is the entrance to his Warm Springs home.

the gardens and the other buildings on the plantation. In the garage is a collection of 8 antique cars, some of them used on the plantation.

LITTLE WHITE HOUSE STATE HISTORIC SITE (Historic home)
SR 85W South
WARM SPRINGS, GA 31830 (30 miles northeast of Columbus)
Phone: 706-655-5870
Hours: Daily 9-5. Admission charged.

This was the vacation home of President Franklin D. Roosevelt which he built for himself in 1932, and is the place where he died on April 12, 1945. Roosevelt chose this location so that he could be near the local waters and spa facilities of Warm Springs which he believed helped his lower-body paralysis —the result of polio. On display at the historic site are many items pertaining to his life and presidency including two of his personal pre-war automobiles. One is a Ford convertible and the other a Willys convertible. Both vehicles are specially equipped with hand controls that allowed him to drive without the use of his legs. Also on the site is a gift shop, snack bar and picnic area.

OKEFENOKEE HERITAGE CENTER (MUSEUM)
Augusta Av (2 miles NW via US 1/23, then 4 blocks west on Augusta St)
WAYCROSS, GA 31501 (Southeastern part of the state about midway between Brunswick and Valdosta)
Phone: 912-285-4260
Hours: M-Sat 9-5, Sun 1-5, closed major holidays. Admission charged.

The exhibits in this museum pertain mainly to the local history of Waycross, an important transportation center and

This is the unique entrance to Old Car City, USA.

lumber and tobacco growing area. To highlight Waycross' importance as a transportation center, there is on display a 1912 steam locomotive with rail cars, a railroad depot, and an assortment of horse-drawn vehicles and several early automobiles.

OLD CAR CITY, USA (Salvage yard with auto display)
3098 Hwy 411 N E
WHITE, GA 30184 (40 miles northwest of Atlanta off I-75)
Phone: 404-382-6141 and
404-974-6144
Hours: M-F 8-5, Sat 8-noon

There are over 4000 vehicles in this yard, mostly American makes, and most earlier than 1969. Some of the cars are driveable and hundreds more are restorable. A large showroom displays some of the best cars and some cars that are not for sale including a Lincoln Mark VII which was Elvis Presley's last car. There is a large display of antique toys and a store offering antique furniture and miscellaneous items. Old Car City sells vintage cars on consignment, provides inside and outside storage, does towing and offers appraisals. Customers may browse the salvage yard.

IDAHO

MUSEUM OF TRANSPORTATION, OLD IDAHO PENITENTIARY

2.5 Miles east on Main St at 2445
Penitentiary Rd
BOISE, ID 83712
Phone: 208-334-2844
Hours: Memorial Day to Labor Day
daily 10-5. Rest of year daily
noon-4. Closed holidays.
Admission charged.

This museum is one of several attractions at Idaho's old state penitentiary complex. There is also the Museum of Electricity in Idaho, the Bishop's House, a garden, and the penitentiary itself. The Museum of Transportation contains an Indian travois, a stagecoach, a 1903 steam-powered fire engine, various horse-drawn vehicles and a number of antique automobiles. One of the autos on display is a 1974 Leata, the only car to be assembled in Idaho. There is a unique custom-built trailer home, made in 1932 for a traveling evangelist. It was pulled by a 1929 Packard and later a Chevrolet Suburban.

A custom-built trailer-home built in 1932 for a traveling evangelist.

▼ COUER D'ALENE AREA

AUTO CLASSICS (Dealer)
1515 Northwest St
COUER D'ALENE, ID 83814
Phone: 208-765-2886
Hours: M-Sat 9-5

This is one of three antique car dealers in this community of 25,000 people. Auto Classics carries an inventory of about 50 vehicles of mixed makes and models. An inventory list is available. They sell on consignment, take trades, will search for specific vehicles and arrange financing and transportation. Car clubs are welcome. Contact Terry Godbout, the owner.

CLASSIC AUTO PARTS (Salvage)
18090 Hwy 95 North
HAYDEN, ID 83835 (A northern suburb of Couer D'Alene)
Phone: 208-667-3428
Hours: M-F 9-3, Sat by appointment.

This four-acre salvage yard has some 500 vehicles, mostly from the 1950s and 1960s. Most are American-made. Front ends and dog houses are neatly arranged in racks for easy inspection. This area of Idaho is relatively dry so many of the cars in the yard have little or no rust.

CORONADO CLASSICS (Dealer)
404 E. Indiana
COUER D'ALENE, ID 83814
Phone: 208-667-3445
Hours: M-Sat 9-5

This dealer carries an inventory of some 50 vehicles of various makes and types. Coronado Classics specializes in 1930s and 1940s FORDs but other makes and models are available. Motorcycles are offered, too. They do appraisals, will search for specific vehicles and arrange transportation. The company is a major sponsor of the annual "Car D'Alene" car show. Rick Cooper is the owner.

IDAHO AUTOMOBILE CO. (Dealer)
400 North 4th St
COUER D'ALENE, ID 83814
Phone: 208-765-1095
Hours: Appointment only

This dealer offers a variety of vehicles ranging from sporty European models to the gas-guzzlers of the 1960s. They also have post-1932 Fords and hot rods. The company takes trades and sells some cars on consignment. The owner, Dennis LeKander, will work with customers seeking specific cars.

PEGASUS AUTO WRECKING (Salvage)
18100 Hwy 95
HAYDEN LAKE, ID 83835 (A northern suburb of Couer D'Alene)
Phone: 208-772-3791
Hours: M-F 9-6, Sat 9-noon

Pegasus Auto Wrecking has about 600+ vehicles— and growing—on their lot with many of them dating back to

Idaho

the 1950s and 1960s. Some are restorable. There is a generous mix of makes and models. The man to see is owner "El Tee" Jones...when he not out stock car racing.

VICTORINO'S AUTO (dealer)
2420 Government Way
COUER D'ALENE, ID 83814
Phone: 208-665-2117 or 877-286-2886 (toll-free)

Victorino's offered a general line of antique vehicles from their showroom and adjacent lot. Normally about 15 cars are on hand. They can provide some repair and restoration work, take trades, arrange financing, provide appraisals, sell on consignment and will search for that special car you've always wanted. Paul Victorino is the owner and welcomes car clubs and interested visitors.

End of Couer D'Alene Area △

VINTAGE AUTOMOTIVE (Salvage)
2290 N 18th East
MOUNTAIN HOME, ID 83647 (42 miles southeast of Boise on I-80N)
Phone: 208-587-3743
Hours: M-F 9-6, Sat 10-5

This is a 1000-vehicle salvage yard with mixed makes and body styles from the 1930s thru the 1960s. There are a few late 1920s vehicles in the lot. Vintage Auto Parts has an unusually large number of NASH METROPOLITANS in the yard and the owner has several restored "Mets" in his personal collection. This is a relatively dry part of the state, and as a result many of the cars are rust-free, or nearly so. Vintage will search for parts in other yards. Customers may browse the yard supervised. Inventory list available. In business since 1980.

L & L CLASSIC AUTO (Salvage)
2742 S Hwy 46
WENDELL, ID 83355
(20 miles northwest of Twin Falls)
Phone: 208-536-6606 or
208-536-6607
Hours: M-F 8-6. Please phone ahead to make sure someone is in attendance.

This is one of the largest salvage yards in the west with some 5000 to 6000 vehicles on 100 acres of dry sagebrush-covered land. Vehicles run from the late 1920s to the 1980s with the highest concentration being in the 1950s and 1960s. The lot has an unusually large number of LINCOLNS and MERCURYS. Most of the other vehicles are American-made. Ron Ewing is the Manager.

ILLINOIS

ROUTE 66

It was in Illinois that the famous Route 66 began. Specifically, it started at the intersection of Jackson Blvd. and Lake Shore Dr. in downtown Chicago. From there it travelled some 300 miles southwest through Illinois before exiting the state at East St. Louis.

The State of Illinois has preserved much of the highway and marked it with signs noting "Historic Route 66". Many stretches of the old road still exist as local roads or frontage roads for I-55 which parallels the route. Most of the old route is two-lane and in some rare spots the original brick surface is still is use. Many historic buildings have been preserved along the way by communities and individuals. When the route leaves the state it crosses the Mississippi River at the Chain of Rocks Bridge, the longest bridge on all of Route 66.

Route 66 began in Chicago, travelled for over 300 miles through Illinois and exited the state at East St. Louis. Much of the famous route has been preserved and marked by the state.

▼ CHICAGO AREA

CHICAGO CAR EXCHANGE, INC
(Dealer and museum)

14084 W Rockland Rd
LIBERTYVILLE, IL 60048 (North-western suburb of Chicago)
Phone: 847-680-1950
Hours: M-F 10-6, Sat 10-5. Small admission charged.

They're on display in a museum setting here, but they're all for sale. There's some 150 vintage vehicles of all makes and models from pre-war to the latest exotics. An inventory list is available. The company has long been known as a dealer in vintage MERCEDES-BENZ cars and has highlighted that fact by putting all their M-Bs into one room called the "M-B Room". Chicago Car Exchange offers a repair service, takes trades, sells on consignment, arranges financing and transportation, provides appraisals, rents storage space and sells a few auto-related gift and collectible items. The company is very active in searching for specific vehicles and has a considerable waiting list for vehicles. Keep this in mind when you go to sell your car. Car clubs are always welcome and visit frequently. A father and son team, Philip Kuhn Sr. and Jr. run Chicago Car Exchange.

HARTUNG'S AUTOMOTIVE
MUSEUM

3623 W Lake St
GLENVIEW, IL 60025 (A north-western suburb of Chicago)
Phone: 847-724-4354

Hours: Open daily at various hours. Please phone. Donations accepted.

This is a large museum with over 150 vehicles, including motorcycles. There is a large collection of model cars, bicycles, scooters, hubcaps, radiator emblems and other automobilia. Some of the interesting cars on display include a 1926 Hertz touring car, a 1927 Henney limousine, a 1950 Veritas convertible, a 1950 Edwards convertible and 35 Ford Model As with different body styles. In addition to cars Hartung's visitors will see displays of hood ornaments, brass lights, old tools, spark plugs and the world's most complete collection of license plates. Hartung's is owned by Lee Hartung.

McDONALD'S DES PLAINES
MUSEUM

400 N Lee St
DES PLAINES, IL 60016 (A northwestern suburb of Chicago)
Phone: 847-297-5022
Hours: June, July and Aug W-Sat 10-4, Sun 1-4. Apr 15-May 31 and Sept 1-Oct 15 W, F and Sat 10-4. Closed rest of year. Free.

This was the first McDonald's restaurant opened in the Chicago area in 1955 by Ray Kroc, the founder of the McDonald's restaurant chain. The restaurant is preserved and looks as it did when it opened. There is a short movie explaining the history of the McDonald's chain of restaurants. In the lot are several antique autos of the 1950s. Food is not served in this McDonald's, but across the street is a modern-day McDonald's Restaurant.

MUSEUM OF SCIENCE AND INDUSTRY

In Jackson Park at S Lake Shore Dr and 57th St
CHICAGO, IL 60637
Phone: 773-684-1414
Hours: Memorial Day thru Labor Day: M-F 9:30-5:30. Labor Day thru Memorial Day: 9:30-4 on weekdays; 9:30-5:30 on weekends and holidays. Closed Dec 25. Admission charged. Parking is available.

Hands-on science fun awaits you at Chicago's favorite museum for all ages. More than 800 interactive exhibits. Touch, create and explore. Among the many and varied exhibits is an auto collection of some 30 vintage cars and race cars including a 1911 Simplex, 1924 Marmon, 1929 Duesenberg roadster, 1930 Alfa-Romeo, the 1949 Blue Crown Spark Plug Special race car, a 1972 Lola and Craig Breedlove's Spirit of America that set a 500 mph speed record. The museum has several gift shops and restaurants.

VOLO ANTIQUE MALL AND AUTO MUSEUM

Volo Village Rd (one block north of Rt. 12 & SR 120)
VOLO, IL 60073 (A northwestern suburb of Chicago)

Phone: 815-385-3644
Hours: Daily 10-5, closed Jan 1, Easter, Thanksgiving and Dec 25. Admission charged to the museum.

This is a complex of several buildings with antique cars as the main theme. There are about 250 vintage vehicles on display in four showrooms and many of the cars are for sale. Autos from the 1950s-1970s and muscle cars are their specialty, but there is also a generouse supply of pre-war cars. Throughout the year the museum has several antique car functions such as auctions, car shows and car club events. Antique vehicle services offered include appraisals, consignment sales and trades. In addition to cars there are some 150 antique dealers in the mall.

HARRY WOODNORTH AUTOMOBILES (Dealer)

1650 N Bosworth Ave
CHICAGO, IL 60622
Phone: 773-227-1340
Hours: M-F 9-5, Sat 10-5

This is a dealer of antique, luxury and exotic automobiles including Rolls-Royces, Mercedes-Benz, Aston Martins and Lamborghinis. There are usually about 40 vehicles in Woodnorth's showroom and the company takes trades and publishes an inventory list. They will sell on consignment, provide appraisals, search for specific vehicles, do service and restoration work and provide storage. Harry Woodnorth, the owner, welcomes car clubs and groups.

End of Chicago Area △

Illinois

MY GARAGE (Museum)

1 Mid America Place (Just off US
45 North)
PO Box 1368
EFFINGHAM, IL 62401 (South-
central part of the state at junction
of I-57 and I-70)
Phone: 217-347-4233
Hours: M-F 8-5, Sat 9-3

Here is a very unique collection of
CORVETTES. My Garage is a 13,000 sq.
ft. museum attached to the main building of Mid America Designs, Inc., the
world's largest supplier of Corvette parts
and accessories. The 39 Corvettes on
display are mostly low mileage originals
and the personal collection of Mid
America's president, Mike Yager. They
are often used by the company's engi-
neers in the design and manufacture of
their replacement parts and accessories.
The museum's 1954 Corvette is of interest because it has only 3000 miles on
the odometer. There is a 1972 Lemans
Corvette race car on display as well as a
CERV I test vehicle, several Challenge
Series race cars and several General
Motors experimental cars.

Also to be seen at My Garage is a
1910 Standard Oil of Indiana gas station, Corvette toys, model cars, pins,
posters, apparel, photos and memorabilia. An expansion of the museum is
planned. Dennis M. Gunning, the
museum's curator, welcomes car clubs
and tour groups.

Location: Exit I-70 at U.S. 45 and
proceed north on U.S. 45 to Mid
America Place.

GRANT HILLS ANTIQUE AUTO MUSEUM

US Highway 20
(1 mile east of Galena)
GALENA, IL 61036 (Northwest
corner of state 13 miles southeast
of Dubuque, IA)
Phone: 815-777-2115
Hours: Mid-May thru Oct 31, Daily
10-4. Closed Easter, Thanksgiving
and Dec. 25. Admission charged.

An interesting museum with some
40 antique cars, mostly American-made,
from the early 1900s to the 1960s. Several of the cars are national award winners. Included in the collection is a rare
1911 Case made by the J.I. Case Threshing Machine Co. There are many automotive artifacts in the museum including a large collection of Illinois license
plates. There are also displays of cast
iron banks and pottery made in Galena.
The museum has a gift shop.

WHEELS THROUGH TIME MUSEUM (Museum and dealer)

12th & Waltonville Rd
(South side of town)
MOUNT VERNON, IL 62864
(South-central part of state at the
junction of I-64 and I-57)
Phone: 618-244-4116
Hours: M-Tues, Thurs-F 9-5, Sat 9-
4. Closed holidays. Free.

A large indoor facility displaying
dozens of rare and antique motorcycles.
The museum has a three-wheeled util-
ity vehicle built by Harley-Davidson just

before World War II which was one of the competetors in the U.S. Army's search for a vehicle that eventually became known as the "Jeep". There is also a display of rare American-made motorcycles including one of Evil Knievel's jump bikes and a very rare 1910 Harley-Davidson. Wheels Through Time offers a large inventory of new and vintage Harley-Davidson parts for sale, does service work, restorations and has a gift shop. Tours and groups welcome. The museum is owned by Dale Walksler.

CASNER MOTOR CO. (Salvage)
US 36
OAKLEY, IL 62552
(9 miles east of Decatur)
Phone: 217-864-2162
Hours: M-F 9-5, Sat by appointment.

This salvage yard has a variety of cars and trucks, mostly of American manufacture. They also offer new and NOS parts, sell used cars and do repairs. Customers may browse the lot. In business since 1923.

HEARTLAND ANTIQUE CAR MUSEUM
1208 Main St.
PARIS, IL 61944 (East-central part of state near the Indiana border)
Phone: 217-463-1834
Hours: M-Sat 10-5. Admission free.

It ain't big but it's interesting - the Heartland Antique Car Museum. There is 13 or so cars here on display plus some memorabilia from World Wars I and II. The owner, Charles Glick, collects military memorabilia. Some of the cars are for sale and, in the back, there is a large restoration shop. Car clubs are welcome.

▼ PEORIA AREA

This is the oldest surviving three-wheeled 1899 Duryea trap and is on display at the Peoria Public Library in downtown Peoria.

Peoria was the home of the famous Duryea Brothers whom many believe built the first gasoline-powered horseless carriages in America. The Peoria Public Library, in downtown Peoria, has on permanent display the oldest surviving 1899 three-wheeled Duryea trap.

HUBCAP HOUSE
At the corner of SW Adams St (US 24 south) and S Stanley St is a house completely covered with hubcaps. (See photo, next page.)

The Hubcap House is at the corner of SW Adams St and S Stanley St in Peoria, IL.

WHEELS O' TIME MUSEUM
   11923 N Knoxville Av (SR 40)
   DUNLAP, IL 61525
   (13 miles north-northwest of
   downtown Peoria)
   Phone: 309-243-9020
   Hours: May thru Oct, W-Sun
   noon-5. Admission charged.

This is a private museum with about 30 antique automobiles on display along with many other antique items of the first half of the Twentieth Century. There are toy trains, clocks, cameras, musical instruments, a full-scale replica of the Red Baron's WW I tri-winged airplane, Caterpillar tractors, a country kitchen and many other items. Among the autos on display is a 1917 Glide built in Peoria.

The Wheels O' Time Museum at Dunlap, IL, just north of Peoria.

End of Peoria Area △

▼ QUAD-CITIES AREA (MOLINE, IL, ROCK ISLAND, IL, DAVENPORT, IA AND BETTENDORF, IA)

E & J USED AUTO & TRUCK PARTS (Salvage)
315 31st Av
ROCK ISLAND, IL 61204
Phone: 800-728-7686 or
309-788-7686
Hours: M-F 8-4:40, Sat 8-1

This is a 50-acre salvage yard with approximately 3500 vehicles ranging in age from 1937 to the present. There is a mix of American-made vehicles, imports and trucks. Parts are sold on a 6-month's warranty. Customers may browse the yard. In business since 1951.

VELIE MANSION (Historic home)
3551 7th St
MOLINE, IL 61265

This was the home of the Velie family, founders of the Velie Motor Vehicle Co. of Moline which manufactured the Velie automobile and a light airplane called the Monocoupe. The mansion was built in 1914 and has 46 rooms including 14 bedrooms and 12 baths. When the Velie family lived here it had terraced gardens, a greenhouse, high walls surrounding the grounds and was known locally as "Villa Velie". The Velie

The home of the Velie family, founders of the Velie Motor Vehicle Co., in Moline, IL.

Motor Vehicle Co. was sold in the late 1920s after the founder and his son died just a few months apart. The heirs vacated the mansion soon afterwards and it stood idle until 1945 when it was purchased by a new owner and converted into a fine dining restaurant. The restaurant closed in the mid-1970s and the mansion became a night club and an antique mall. These businesses closed in 1993 and still other ventures followed. Irrespective of its current use the mansion is of historic interest to car buffs.

End of Quad Cities Area △

▼ ROCKFORD/SOUTH BELOIT AREA

(North central part of state just south of the Wisconsin state line)

A & B AUTO AND TRUCK PARTS (Salvage)
1664 Guetschow
(West side of town)
SOUTH BELOIT, IL 61080
Phone: 815-389-2326
Hours: M-Sat 9-5

This salvage yard has some 1200 vehicles ranging in age from the 1940s through the 1970s. Most vehicles are American-made. There are many pickup trucks. Customers may browse the yard and remove small items themselves. In business since 1954. The owner is Art Chamblin.

COLLECTOR CARS U-CAN-AFFORD, LTD. (Dealer)
4046 11th St
ROCKFORD, IL 61109
Phone: 815-229-1258
Hours: M-F 9-5, Sat 9-2. Please phone first.

This is a large antique car dealer with a wide selection of domestic and imported vehicles for sale. Most cars are priced in the affordable range as the name of the company implies. Collector Cars takes trades, arranges delivery and has a gift shop. Ask for Mr. Lazarus.

End of Rockford/South Beloit Area △

ACE AUTO SALVAGE
Highway 51
TONICA, IL 61370
(North central part of state 7 miles south of LaSalle)
Phone: 815-442-8224 or 815-442-8225
Hours: M-F 8-5, Sat 8-noon

A large salvage yard with approximately 4000 vehicles. The best antique cars, collectibles, convertibles and muscle cars are stored in 3 buildings. Some cars are whole and restorable. Customers may browse the yard.

▼ WAUKEGAN AREA

AUTO PARTS CITY (Salvage)
3570 Washington
WAUKEGAN, IL 60085
Phone: 312-244-7171
Hours: M-F 8-5, Sat 8-3

This salvage yard has some 1500 vehicles of mixed makes and body styles. Customers may browse the yard. Mail orders welcome. In business since 1968.

B.C. AUTOMOTIVE (Salvage)
2809 Damascus
ZION, IL 60099 (A northern suburb of Waukegan)
Phone: 312-746-8056
Hours: M-Sat 8:30-5

This 600-vehicle yard specializes in domestic autos from 1960 to 1982 and imports from 1970 to 1984. They offer a towing service and customers may browse the yard. In business since 1983.

End of Waukegan Area △

BRYANT'S AUTO PARTS (Salvage)
RR 1
WESTVILLE, IL 61883 (South of Danville near Indiana state line)
Phone: 217-267-2124
Hours: M-F 8-5, Sat 8-noon

This is a large salvage yard with 5000 vehicles dating from 1939 to current. All makes available. Inventory list available.

Customers may browse the yard. In business since 1975.

MAX NORDEEN'S WHEELS MUSEUM
2 Miles North of Downtown Woodhull
WOODHULL, IL 61490 (25 miles southeast of Quad Cities off I-74)
Phone: 309-334-2589

Max Nordeen's Wheels Museum just north of Woodhull, IL.

Illinois

Hours: June, July, August Tues thru Sun 9-4. May, September, October open Sat & Sun only 9-4. Admission charged.

This is a privately owned museum containing the lifetime collection of its owner, Max Nordeen. Among the many items in the museum are some 25 cars including a rare 1942 Lincoln Continental Mark I Convertible, a 1947 Diamond-T semi-tractor, and a race car built by an inmate in the state penitentiary at Lincoln, Nebraska. There are other displays of auto related items, the Old West and Indian relics. Also shown are war items from the Civil War, World War I, World War II and the Korean War. Visitors are usually guided through the museum by Mr. Nordeen.

INDIANA

HISTORICAL MILITARY ARMOUR MUSEUM
2330 Crystal St
(North side of town)
ANDERSON, IN 46012 (30 miles northeast of Indianapolis on I-69)
Phone: 317-649-TANK
Hours: Tues and Thurs 1-4, Sat 10-4. Admission charged.

This museum is devoted primarily to military vehicles, especially tanks. They have vehicles from World War I through the present day and possess one of the largest collections of light tanks in the country. Also in the collection is a 1947 Cadillac limousine that was used by President Harry S Truman.

▼ AUBURN AREA
(On I-69 twenty miles north of Fort Wayne)

AUBURN-CORD-DUESENBERG MUSEUM
1600 S Wayne St
AUBURN, IN 46706
Phone: 219-925-1444
Hours: Daily 9-5. Closed Jan 1, Thanksgiving and Dec 25. Admission charged.

At one time the Auburn Automobile Company made luxury and exotic cars in the small city of Auburn. The memory of Auburn, Cord and Duesenberg motorcars is a major factor in the town's community life today. The museum preserving that heritage is located in the splendorous 1930 art deco national headquarters of the former auto maker. More than 100 antique, classic and special interest cars fill seven thematic exhibit galleries in this structure listed in the National Register of Historic Places.

Exhibits include superb examples of Cadillac, Packard, Lincoln, Rolls-Royce, Mercedes-Benz and many rare Indiana-built makes. Featured are the world's oldest Auburn, a 1904 Rear Entrance Tonneau; a 1932 Duesenberg Murphy Torpedo Convertible Coupe once owned by J. Paul Getty and a 1931 Cord L-29 front-drive Speedster. Visitors may see auto design and clay model studios, workers offices and classic cars in the magnificent factory showroom.

The museum, accredited by the American Association of Museums, offers ever-changing special exhibits, an

One of several Duesenbergs on display at the Auburn-Cord-Duesenberg Museum in Auburn, IN.

appealing museum store (The Duesy Shop), an automotive research library and full banquet and meeting facilities. Photography is permitted. The Auburn-Cord-Duesenberg Festival is held each Labor Day weekend, in a reunion of hundreds of Auburn, Cord and Duesenberg cars in motion.

NATIONAL AUTOMOTIVE AND TRUCK MUSEUM OF THE UNITED STATES

1000 Gordon Buehrig Place
(Adjacent to the Auburn-Cord-Duesenberg Museum)
AUBURN, IN 46706
Phone: 219-925-9100

Hours: Daily 9-5. Admission charged.

This museum is closely affiliated with the Auburn-Cord-Duesenberg Museum and occupies two of the remaining Auburn Automobile Co. buildings adjacent to the Auburn-Cord-Duesenberg Museum. The museum has a collection of over 100 trucks, busses, motor homes and similar vehicles. There are also automotive toys, models, automotive literature, signs, automobilia and a gift shop. Groups and clubs are welcome. Contact Angel Taylor, Administrator.

End of Auburn Area △

ANTIQUE AUTO & RACE CAR MUSEUM

Stone City Mall
(Hwy. 50/450 Exit off Hwy 37, southwest part of town)
BEDFORD, IN (65 miles southwest of Indianapolis on US 50 and SR 37)
Phone; 812-275-0556
Hours: Apr thru Dec M-Sat noon-6.

This museum is located in a former J. C. Penny building in one of Bedford's largest malls. It contains some 100 antique cars and race cars. Many of the race cars have been driven by well-known race drivers. There's Kyle Petty's Car No. 42 Pontiac "Mellow Yellow", several Kenyon Bros. midgets and Mel Kenyon's "Herbie" race car. Some of the Indy cars shown were driven by A. J. Foyt, Roger McCluskey, Rick Mears and other well-known drivers. Additional displays include antique household items and lots of picture of the local limestone quarries and mills. Car clubs welcome.

AUTO HEAVEN (Salvage)

103 W Allen St
BLOOMINGTON, IN 47401 (40 miles southwest of Indianapolis)
Phone: 800-777-0297 or 812-332-9401
Hours: M-F 8:30-5:30, Sat 8:30-noon.

This salvage yard has many 1967-69 CAMAROs, 1967-69 FIREBIRDs and 1966-69 TEMPEST/LEMANS. There are other collectibles among the nearly 1000 vehicles. Customers may browse the yard. In business since 1979.

BEARCREEK FARMS (Theme park)

8339 North 400 East
(Watch for signs on SR 67 east of its Jct with US 29)
RR 1, Box 180B
BRYANT, IN 47326
(On US 27 thirty five miles south of Fort Wayne)
Phone: 800-288-7630 and 219-997-6822
Hours: Daily Mar thru Dec. Admission charged.

This is a theme park with a days-of-yesteryear motif. There are rides, a county fair, live theater, restaurants, an old fort, guest accommodations, retail shops and The Tin Lizzie Museum. In the latter are some 20 antique cars, many of them Model T Fords, and displays highlighting the joys and agonies of driving such vehicles.

ELKHART (See South Bend/Elkhart Area)

FORT WAYNE FIREFIGHTERS MUSEUM

226 W Washington St
FORT WAYNE, IN 46852 (Northeast part of the state on I-69)
Phone: 219-426-0051
Hours: M-F 11-2. Admission charged

The museum building is located in Fire Station No. 3, which was constructed in 1893 to house horse-drawn

Indiana

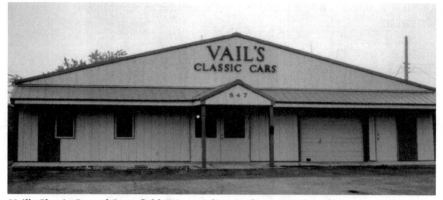

Vail's Classic Cars of Greenfield, IN specializes in the restoration of Mustangs.

fire equipment. On display is an 1848 L. Button Hand Pump, 1983 Amoskeag First Size Steamer, 1927 Ahrens-Fox, 1929 Ford Model A chemical fire truck, 1942 International Harvester fire truck built by the Fort Wayne Fire Department Fire Shop as well as a 1953 Cadillac ambulance. There are other artifacts and memorabilia. The fire museum has a cafe that serves lunch Monday thru Friday from 11-2. Edward W. Mahrt is the museum's President.

VAIL'S CLASSIC CARS (Restorer)
847 W Main St (US 40 West)
GREENFIELD, IN 46140 (20 miles east of downtown Indianapolis)
Phone: 317-462-7705
Hours: M-F 8-6, Sat 10-3.

This is a restorer specializing in MUSTANGs. They offer ground-up or partial restorations and sell restored Mustangs. They usually have 3 or 4 cars on their showroom floor for sale. They will also restore Mustangs and other cars belonging to customers. Vail's offers a

one-year/12,000 mile warranty on all vehicles restored and the company also sells NOS, used and reproduction parts for Mustangs. They do service work and have been in business since 1985.

COLLECTIBLE CLASSIC CAR MUSEUM OF HAGERSTOWN
403 E Main St
HAGERSTOWN, IN 47346 (East-central Indiana 45 miles east of Indianapolis just north of I-70)
Phone: 765-489-5598
Hours: M-F 1-5, admission charged.

Want to see your car displayed in a museum? Here's your chance. The museum will store and display your vehicle in a museum setting for a month or longer. A plaque identifies you and your car and a photo of your vehicle is retained for the museum's permanent collection. Because of this unique arrangement, the museum's collection of cars is ever-changing. There are several permanent cars in the collection and some of the cars on display are for sale. Fire trucks, motorcycles and even airplanes can be seen here. The facility is also available for social events, dances, parties, etc. Herman and Jane Rummel are the proprietors.

WEBB'S CLASSIC AUTO PARTS (Salvage)
5084 W State Rd 114 (8 miles north of Huntington)
HUNTINGTON, IN 46750
(23 miles southwest of Ft. Wayne)

Phone: 219-344-1714
Hours: M-F 8-5

Here's an 80-vehicle salvage yard that specialized in AMERICAN MOTORS products. AMX's and Javelins are a specialty but the other models of AMC are well represented. Webb's has new parts as well as used and can provide parts books and service manuals. Many parts are stored inside. Webb's also offers vehicle storage in a nearby facility. Escorted customers may browse the yard. In business since 1990. Jim Webb is the owner.

▼ INDIANAPOLIS AREA

INDIANAPOLIS MOTOR SPEEDWAY & HALL OF FAME MUSEUM
4790 W 16th St
SPEEDWAY, IN 46222
(A western suburb of Indianapolis)
Phone: 317-248-6747
Hours: Daily 9-5, except during May 9-6. Closed Dec 25. Admission charged.

This museum is inside the track of the famous Indianapolis Motor Speedway and displays many of the race cars that have raced here at the famous "Indy 500". More than 75 race cars are on display and many of them are winners including the 1911 Marmon "Wasp", the winner of the very first race. There is a large collection of racing memorabilia such as trophies, helmets, photo-

Many historic race cars are on display at the Indianapolis Motor Speedway Hall of Fame Museum.

97

graphs, etc. Video presentations of past races are shown and the museum has an extensive automotive library which is open by appointment. In addition to the race cars there is a sizeable number of antique cars, some of them made in Indianapolis.

Bus tours of the track are available and there is a Speedway-owned motel on the grounds and an 18-hole golf course, part of which is inside the track. The Hall of Fame was created in 1952 to perpetuate the names and memories of outstanding personalities in racing and in the development of the automotive industry. The names of those so honored are inscribed on a permanent trophy and watercolor portraits of living members are on display. There is a large gift shop offering official "Indy 500" souvenirs and many other items of interest. The "Indy 500" race is held annually on Memorial Day.

OLD CARS FOR FUN (Salvage)
505 S Tibbs (Southwest side of Indianapolis)
INDIANAPOLIS, IN 46225

Phone: 317-243-7777
Hours: M-Tues and Thurs-F 9-4:45, Sat 9-12:45.

This six-acre salvage lot has about 500 vehicles from the 1930s to the mid-1960s. Most are domestic makes; Packard, Hudson, Kaiser, Nash, Lincoln, Cadillac, Edsel and many others. There are some trucks. An inventory card is kept on each vehicle and yard personnel can tell quickly what parts still remain. In business since 1973.

WRIGHT'S AUTO SERVICE (Salvage)
102 S Shelby St
(South-central part of town)
INDIANAPOLIS, IN 46202
Phone: 317-638-4482
Hours: M-F 9-5.

An old salvage yard, in business since 1939, with vehicles from the 1930s to 1959. Many rebuilt parts available. Wright's also does mechanical work on older cars, including transmissions, engines and brakes. No body work.

End of Indianapolis Area △

▼ KOKOMO AREA

CITY OF FIRSTS AUTOMOTIVE HERITAGE MUSEUM
1500 N Reed Rd (US 31 North)
KOKOMO, IN 46901
Phone: 765-454-9999
Hours: Daily 10-5, admission charged.

You'll see between 80 and 90 antique vehicles in this new museum, including six Kokomo-built Haynes, one Kokomo-built Apperson and one of only two remaining Empire's in the world. There are also sizeable numbers of GM and Chrysler products—

The 1950s Diner on display at the Automotive Heritage Museum

Kokomo is a GM and Chrysler town. The museum has a replica of Elwood Haynes' first home and work shop in which he developed Indiana's first commercially successful automobile in 1894. There is a replica of a 1930s gas station and a pre-war diner. The museum has a nice gift shop and free parking. Dave Griffey is the Museum's CEO and Bob Gollner is the manager.

FAST LANE TOYS (Dealer)
4385 South 00 E/W (US 31 South)
KOKOMO, IN 46901
Phone: 765-455-0075
Hours: M-F 9-5, Sat 9-noon

Here is a small dealer with some very interesting antique vehicles. They carry between 20-30 cars in inventory, mostly domestic makes. Fast Lane will take trades, help find financing and arrange shipping. Drop in and see what they have.

ELWOOD HAYNES MUSEUM
1915 S Webster
KOKOMO, IN 46902-2040
(40 miles north of Indianapolis)
Phone: 765-456-7500
Hours: Tues thru Sat 1-4, Sun 1-5.
Free.

This was the home of Elwood Haynes, the inventor of Indiana's first commercially successful automobile. He made the first successful road test of his first car on July 4, 1894. Haynes was involved in the formation and operation of both the Haynes-Apperson Automobile Co. and later the Haynes Automobile Co., both of Kokomo. He was also the inventor of metal alloys, including stainless steel, Stellite and many other alloys used today in aircraft and high-heat applications. In the Haynes Museum is a 1905 Haynes automobile in which the driver sat in the back seat. There are other Haynes vehicles on display.

Indiana

The Elwood Haynes Museum, Kokomo, IN. (Listing on previous page.)

End of Kokomo Area △

STANDARD OIL MINI-MUSEUM
6th and South Sts
LAFAYETTE, IN 47901 (50 miles
northwest of Indianapolis on I-65)
Phone: 317-642-0280
Hours: Wed 1-5, Sat noon-8.

This is a restored and preserved 1928
Standard Oil Co. service station that has
been turned into a small museum. Its
glazed yellow brick exterior and Span-
ish-style architecture are original and
typical of such stations built all over the
country during the 1920s and 1930s.
Only seven stations of this particular
design remain in the world. The interior of the station is furnished and decorated as it was in the late 1920s and antique cars can be found in the two service bays awaiting "service".

DOOR PRAIRIE AUTO MUSEUM
2405 Indiana Av (US 35 South),
PO Box 1771

LaPORTE, IN 46350 (Northwest
corner of Indiana, 20 miles west of
South Bend just south of 1-94 and
the Indiana Toll Road.)
Phone: 219-326-1337
Hours: Apr 1 thru Dec 27 Tues-Sat
10-4:30, Sun noon-4:30

This is a new and magnificent three-
story auto Museum with antique autos
and other vehicles displayed on all three
floors. Upon arriving at the museum it
is recommended that visitors see the
video presentation on the first floor to
acquaint themselves with the museum.
There are about 50 vehicles in the collection including a number of Indiana-
built cars, such as the Duesenberg,
Studebaker, Cord and Auburn. Visitors
will also see a 1948 Tucker, 1910 Velie,
1903 Duryea, 1922 Ford Speedster and
a 1938 Mercedes Benz Roadster. Antique toys are on display and there is a
re-creation of a block of downtown

The three-story Door Prairie Auto Musum in LaPorte, IN displays some 50 automobiles, many of them Indiana-built.

LaPorte in the 1900s. The museum has an impressive gift shop. John Gardner is the Museum's Executive Director and Susan Boyd is the Assistant Director.

AUTO MARKET (Dealer)
650 S Pennsylvania St
MARION, IN 46953
Phone: 317-662-6320
Hours: M-F 8-5:30, Sat 9-1

You'll find some very nice vehicles here at Auto Market both on the lot and inside the showroom. There is a variety of makes and models with the best vehicles inside. This dealer takes trades, sells on consignment and can arrange transportation and financing. Drop by when you are in the area. Owner is Ron Collins.

HIGHWAY 135 AUTO PARTS
(Salvage)
Hwy 135 North at Squire Boone Rd
MAUCKPORT, IN 47142 (20 miles southwest of Louisville, KY on the Ohio River)
Phone: 800-428-2987 or 812-732-4352
Hours: M-F 8-6, Sat 8-3

Here's a salvage yard in the hills of southern Indiana that might have exactly what you are looking for. Highway 135 Auto Parts has a yard full of cars of mixed makes and models and light trucks from 1941 through 1971. If they do not have it, they will search for it. Customers may browse the yard and Stanley A. Kingsley, the owner, welcomes car clubs. In business since 1973.

THE JOHN DILLINGER HISTORICAL WAX MUSEUM
90 W Washington (Behind the Christian Church)
NASHVILLE, IN 47448 (35 miles south of Indianapolis on SR 36)
Phone: 812-988-1933
Hours: May thru Oct daily 10-5, Rest of year 1-5. Closed major holidays. Admission charged.

This museum preserves a very real, if regrettable, episode in American history, the 14-month reign of terror created by John Dillinger and his gang between his release from prison in May 1933 and his violent death on the streets of Chicago in July 1934. Dillinger was a native of Indiana born and raised in this part of the state. There are artifacts and memorabilia related to him and wax models of his gang members, his

101

Auto Market of Marion, IN deals in fine antique vehicles.

women, including Anna Sage, the "woman in red" who "fingered" him for the FBI. FBI agent, Melvin Purvis, who gunned him down, is also shown in wax. There are additional wax models of other notorious criminals of that era; "Pretty Boy" Floyd, "Baby Face" Nelson, "Ma" Barker and Bonnie and Clyde.

There are two antique cars in the museum, a 1934 Ford V-8 sedan and a 1933 Essex Terraplane 8 complete with fake bullet holes. These were not Dillinger's cars, but copies of the cars he favored as his get-away cars.

CANFIELD MOTORS (Salvage)
22-24 Main
NEW WAVERLY, IN 46961
(Between Logansport and Peru on US 24)
Phone: 219-722-3230
Hours: M-F 8-4, Sat by appointment.

An old, established salvage yard with two yards and several building special-

izing in American-made cars from the 1940s and up. Approximately 1000 vehicles total. Many orphans are available; Studebakers, Hudsons, Nash, Hudson and some pickup trucks. Customers may browse the yard and remove own parts. Bring your own tools and dress properly. In business since 1953. Robert Canfield is the owner.

WAYNE COUNTY HISTORICAL MUSEUM
1150 North "A" St
RICHMOND, IN 47374 (East-central part of the state on I-70)
Phone: 317-962-5756
Hours: Feb 7 thru second week in Dec; Tues-F 9-4, Sat-Sun 1-4. Closed major holidays.
Admission charged.

A fine county museum highlighting the history and progress of Wayne County, Indiana and displaying, among the many items of local interest, several of the 14 automobiles manufactured in

Richmond. These include a 1909 Richmond, a 1910 Wescott, a 1918 Davis and a 1920 Pilot. The museum has an interesting gift shop.

THE FABULOUS 50s MUSEUM AND AL'S HEARTBEAT CAFE
1541 W Tipton Av (U S 50 west)
SEYMOUR, IN 47274 (Midway between Indianapolis and Lousiville, KY on I-65)
Phone: 812-522-4574
Hours: Both museum and cafe M-F 11-9, Sat & Sun 10-10. Admission

charged to the museum.

The 1950s are on display at the Fabulous 50s Museum and on the menu at the 1950s decorated, neon and juke-box studded Heartbeat Cafe. In the museum is memorabilia from that fabulous era, the 1950s, including seven 50s cars. Other automobilia can also be seen. In the cafe is a 1950s pickup truck, all sparkling and new, and the lead item on the menu is the "Classic '57 Burger". Both the museum and cafe are new and clean. Rick Stultz and Albert Skaggs are the owners.

▼ SOUTH BEND/ELKHART AREA

BENDIX WOODS COUNTY PARK
32132 SR 2 (West of South Bend near LaPorte County line.)
NEW CARLISLE, IN 46552
Phone: 219-654-3155

This large county park was at one time the Studebaker Corporation's testing ground for its automobiles. A very unique landmark still remains in the park, an arboreal sign comprising approximately 8200 trees that spell out the word STUDEBAKER. The sign was planted in 1938 and is said to be the largest arboreal sign of its kind in the world. The park's Club House was the home of Studebaker's last president, Sherwood Egbert. A display on the Studebaker Company is on view in the Club House. Adjacent to the park to the east are several buildings and part of Studebaker's original test track which are in private hands and still in use.

The arboral sign spelling out the word "Studebaker" can still be clearly seen from above in Bendix Woods County Park.

Indiana

S. RAY MILLER ANTIQUE AUTO MUSEUM

2130 Middlebury St (Near the intersection of Middlebury St. and Industrial Parkway)
ELKHART, IN 46516
Phone: 888-260-8566
Hours: M-F 10-4, and on last weekend of the month noon-4. Admission charged.

This is a very fine privately-owned museum with about 40 fully restored automobiles, most of them pre-World War II and several of them classics. Many Indiana-made cars are in the collection such as Auburn, Cord, Duesenberg, Elcar, Marmon, Pratt-Elkhart, Sterling, Studebaker and Stutz. Of special interest is a 1930 Duesenberg J Murphy convertible once owned by Al Capone's lawyer and right-hand man, "The Barber" Factor, and a rare 1931 Studebaker Four Seasons Roadster. There is also an exceptionally large display of automobile radiator emblems.

NORTHERN INDIANA HISTORICAL SOCIETY MUSEUM

808 W Washington St
SOUTH BEND, IN 46601
Phone: 219-235-9664
Hours: Tues thru Sat 10-5, Sun 12-5. Closed holidays. Admission charged.

This museum records the pioneer era and the development of trades, crafts, farming and transportation in the St. Joseph River Valley. Some of the items on display are antique toys, early costumes and an outstanding exhibit on

the Studebaker family. The museum has no antique cars.

RUTHMERE MUSEUM

302 E Beardsley St
($^1/_2$ mile northeast of downtown Elkhart on SR 19)
ELKHART, IN 46514
Phone: 219-264-0330
Hours: First Tues in Apr thru Mid-Dec Tues-Sat tours at 11, 1 and 3. Also during July and Aug tours Sun at 3. Admission charged.

This was the magnificent Beaux-Arts home of A. R. Beardsley, a co-founder of Miles Laboratory. The home is lavishly furnished and decorated much as it was soon after it was built in 1908. In the garage are three antique cars, a 1912 Pratt, a 1916 Milburn Electric and a 1917 Cadillac. There is a souvenir and gift shop on the premises.

RV/MH HISTORY HALL OF FAME/ MUSEUM/LIBRARY

801 Benham Av
ELKHART, IN 46516
Phone: 219-293-2344 or 800-378-8694
Hours: M-F 9-4, free.

This unique museum displays antique recreational vehicles and motor homes. It is located in the center of a large RV/MH manufacturing area in northern Indiana and honors the manufacturers, suppliers, dealers, park and campground owners and others involved in this very specialized industry. The growth and development of the

These are some of the antique recreational vehicles and motor homes on display at the RV/MH Hall of Fame Museum in Elkhart, IN.

RV and MH industry is chronicled in photographs, displays and documents. The museum is an 15,000 Sq. ft. facility with more than a dozen vehicles, and this number is growing. There is also a growing library of RV/MH literature, books and historic documents.

STUDEBAKER NATIONAL MUSEUM

525 S Main St
SOUTH BEND, IN 46601
Phone: 219-235-9108 or 219-235-9714 or 24 hour info-line 219-235-9479
Hours: M-Sat 9-5, Sun noon-5.
Admission charged.

This museum displays about 70 vehicles, most of them made by the Studebaker Corporation of South Bend. There are also exhibits on the early industrial and commercial life of the South Bend area. Among the automobiles displayed is a 1900 Studebaker electric car, a 1927 Studebaker Commander, a 1928 Erskin, a 1956 Packard Predator, a 1962 Studebaker truck prototype, a 1937 cab forward bus, 1943 Weasel (a military vehicle made by Studebaker during World war II), a 1962 Studebaker GT Hawk and a 1963 Avanti. There is also a 1932 Rockne, made by Studebaker and named after the famous Notre Dame football coach, Knute Rockne. And, there is a one-of-a-kind

The Studebaker National Museum of South Bend, IN

Tippecanoe Place, the former home of Clement Studebaker, is now a fine-dining restaurant.

1934 Bendix prototype airflow automobile that was never put into production. The Studebaker National Museum has extensive archives on the Studebaker company.

TIPPECANOE PLACE
RESTAURANT (Historic home)
620 W Washington St
SOUTH BEND, IN 46601
Phone: 219-234-9077

This 40-room mansion, which is now a fine restaurant, was once the home of Clement Studebaker, one of the five brothers who ran the Studebaker Corporation in its heyday. Customers of the restaurant are free to wander through the interesting building which has four floors, an elevator and 20 fireplaces. Appropriate dress is required in the dining room.

End of South Bend/Elkhart Area △

IOWA

Iowans have been in the forefront of preserving their portion of the Old Lincoln Highway, America's first coast-to-coast road. The route began at Times Square in New York City and ended in San Francisco. Through Iowa the Lincoln Highway entered the state at Clinton on the east and exited at Council Bluffs, opposite Omaha, NE, on the west. Modern-day US 30 evolved from the Lincoln Highway and parallels sections of the old road. It is these sections that the Iowa members of the National Lincoln Highway Association hope to preserve. Most of the surviving sections of the old road have become local roads and some of them are unpaved. The Association is in the process of identifying these sections with replicas of the original red, white and blue highway signs that consisted of a capital letter "L" on a white field. Some of the signs are mounted on concrete posts of 1928 design. Another historic touch that the Association hopes to add are Burma-Shave signs along the route. Some of the sections of the highway will be widened to modern-day standards while other sections will be paved or repaved. Greene County, whose county seat is Jefferson, 40 miles west of Ames, has taken the lead in Iowa and preserved most of their section of the Lincoln Highway from the county's eastern border to it western

border. Citizens of Greene county are proud of the fact that their county was the first in Iowa to completely pave their section of the Lincoln Highway in 1924. The Greene County stretch of the highway is now acknowledged as an important site and listed on the National Register of Historic Places. The community of Nevada, IA, 8 miles east of Ames, has commemorated the Lincoln Highway since 1983 with a festival each August called Lincoln Highway Days. The Iowa chapter of the Lincoln Highway Association began in 1993 to promote an annual antique car rally along the length of the Lincoln Highway in conjunction with the Nevada festival and their own annual meeting in Ames. Participants begin the rally at either end of the Lincoln Highway and end up in Nevada for the festival.

BECKER'S AUTO SALVAGE
Highway 30 West
ATKINS, IA 52206 (10 miles west of downtown Cedar Rapids)
Phone: 319-446-7141
Hours: M-F 8-5, Sat 8-noon.

This is a 10-acre salvage yard, with many AMC's, Fords, Studebakers, Edsels, Chevys & more. Customers may browse the yard. In business since 1967.

The bill of sale of the 1949 Chrysler that Mamie and Dwight Eisenhower gave to Mamie's uncle as a surprise Christmas gift in 1948.

RON'S AUTO SALVAGE

24613 Butler Center Rd (3 miles south and 2 miles east of Allison)
ALLISON, IA 50602 (30 miles northwest of downtown Waterloo)
Phone: 319-267-2871
Hours: M-F 8-5, Sat 8-noon.

This is a large salvage yard of 15 acres with some 2000 vehicles ranging in age from 1949 to the mid-1980s. Most are mixed-make American-made cars and light trucks. Customers may browse the yard. The yard's owner, Ron Saathoff, pastures a heard of buffalo on his property near the highway as an attention getter. In business since 1965.

MAMIE DOUD EISENHOWER BIRTHPLACE

709 Carroll St
BOONE, IA 50036 (40 miles northwest of Des Moines)
Phone: 515-432-1896
Hours: June-Oct daily 10-5, Apr-May Tues-Sun 1-5, rest of year by appointment. Admission charged.

This modest home is the birthplace of Mamie Doud Eisenhower, wife of General, and later President, Dwight D. Eisenhower. The main floor of the home is furnished and decorated much as it was when Mamie lived here a a young girl. In the basement is a museum and library tracing the life of Mamie and her family history. In the garage are two antique cars. One is a 1949 Chrysler Windsor 4-door sedan that Mamie and Ike gave to Mamie's uncle, Joel Carlan, as a surprise Chistmas gift on Dec. 24, 1948. The other car is Mamie's 1962 Plymouth Valiant donated to the museum in 1996 by Charles "Bebe" Roboza of Florida, a friend of Richard M. Nixon's. Larry Adams is the museum's curator.

DUFFY'S COLLECTIBLE CAR CONNECTION (Dealer and museum)

250 Classic Car Court SW
CEDAR RAPIDS, IA 52404 (East-central part of state on I-380)
Phone: 319-364-7000
Hours: M-F 8:30-6, Sat 8-4:30. Admission charged to tour.

Duffy's Collectible Car Connection of Cedar Rapids, IA.

A large dealer of vintage automobiles with some 100 vehicles for sale and on display in a large, modern showroom. Walk down memory lane and view this car museum complete with restored cars from the 40s, 50s and 60s. View gas pumps, barber poles and wall murals. Most of the car are convertibles, hardtops and muscle machines. Financing can be arranged as well as transportation including exports. Appraisals also available and Duffy's takes trades.

NORM'S ANTIQUE AUTO SUPPLY (Salvage)
1921 Hickory Grove Rd
DAVENPORT, IA 52804
(Southeastern edge of state on the Mississippi River. One of the Quad-Cities)
Phone: 319-322-8388
Hours: M-F 9-5, Sat 9-noon.

A 150-car salvage yard with FORDS from 1917 to 1969, Chevrolets from 1923 to 1953, Chrysler products from 1929 to 1955, Durant products from 1923 to 1932, Packards from 1935 to 1952 and many GM products. Norm's also services speedometers, cables, starters, generators, distributors and rebuilds vacuum tanks. Customers may browse the yard. In business since 1967.

CLASSIC REACTION (Dealer)
100 S Locust St
DUBUQUE, IA 52003 (Eastern Iowa on the Mississippi River)
Phone: 319-588-6285
Hours: M-F 10-6, Sat noon-5

There are between 45 and 50 antique cars in this dealer's 11,000 sq. ft. showroom. Most are domestic cars and muscle cars in the affordable price range. An inventory list is available upon request. Classic Reaction will take trades, arrange financing and shipping and sell on consignment. Try to drop by on Thursday nights in the summer and join in their "Poker Run". This is a unique rally in which old car buffs are given a local route of five stops where they pick up one card each of a poker hand. The one who returns with the best hand wins a prize. Classic Reaction is owned by Larry Hill, a real friendly guy.

TERRY'S AUTO PARTS (Salvage)
Box 131
GRANVILLE, IA, 51022
(40 miles northeast of Sioux City)
Phone: 712-727-3273
Hours: M-F 8-5, Sat 8-1.

This 100-vehicle yard specializes in BUICKs from 1940 to 1984 including RIVIERAs from 1963 to 1984. Customers may browse the yard. In business since 1964.

CLASSIC AUTO RESTORATION & SALES (Restorer and dealer)
3695 Argyle Rd
KEOKUK, IA 52632
(Extreme southeaster tip of Iowa on the Mississippi River)
Phone: 319-524-2219
Hours: M-F 8-5

Here is a restorer that sells what he restores. He will also do a complete or partial restoration on your vehicle. Classic Auto has a large indoor show room facility and an outdoor lot where both restored and restorable vehicles are displayed. They specialize in 1950s and 60s American-made cars. The company takes trades, buys cars and arranges world-wide transportation. Larry May is the manager, Mike Jackson the sales manager.

NATIONAL SPRINT CAR HALL OF FAME & MUSEUM
Knoxville Raceway/County Fairgrounds (SR 14)
KNOXVILLE, IA 50138 (38 miles southeast of Des Moines)
Phone: 515-842-6176
Hours: M-F 10-6, Sat 10-5, Sun noon-5. Admission charged.

Legends of sprint car racing live at the National Sprint Car Hall of Fame & Museum. This fine three-story facility is on the second turn of the famous Knoxville Raceway. Most of the space is devoted to the Hall of Fame and Museum, but there are also 20 luxurious skybox suites overlooking the track. In the Hall of Fame one will find the names of outstanding drivers, owners, mechanics, officials, and members of the media who have contributed to the sport of sprint racing. In the museum more than 25 restored race cars are on exhibit along with big cars, midgets, engines, trophies, tools, helmets, uniforms, etc. The Skoal Racing Theater and Library/Archives Research Center houses archives and other historic documents, photographs, media reports, etc. related to sprint racing. Many such items are on display in the museum. There is a large museum gift shop offering die-cast toys, clothing, jewelry, artwork, books, videos and other collectibles.

▼ MASON CITY AREA

(north-central part of state off I-35)

KINNEY PIONEER MUSEUM
US Highway 18 West at
Mason City Airport
PO Box 421
MASON CITY, IA 50401
Phone: 515-423-1258
Hours: May 1 thru Sept 30 Wed,
Thurs, Fri & Sun noon-5. Admission charged.

This is a fine local museum displaying artifacts from pioneer days to the present, including an interesting exhibit on the composer Meredith Willson, a native of Mason City. There are several vintage cars in the museum including the world's only complete Colby Car. The Colby Car was made in Mason City from 1911 to 1914.

VAN HORN ANTIQUE TRUCK COLLECTION (Museum)
15272 North St
(Highway 65 North)
MASON CITY, IA 50401
Phone: 515-423-0550; off season,
515-423-9066
Hours: May 25 thru Sept 22 M-Sat
9-4, Sun 11-4. Admission charged.

You will see around 60 of the country's oldest and most rare antique trucks on exhibit and many displayed in setting of the era in which they were built. You will see restored trucks from 1908 to 1937. Other displays include an early gas engine collection, old farm implyments, tractors, crawlers, gas pumps, gas globes signs and equipment,

The World's only surviving Colby automobile is on display at Kinney Pioneer Museum, Mason City, IA.

Van Horn's Antique Truck Collection of Mason City, IA.

old country store items along with a gift shop and an old time coffee lounge. Free brochure upon request. Lloyd Van Horn is the museum's owner.

End of Mason City Area △

MEIER AUTO SALVAGE
US Hwy 75 North (Near county line)
SIOUX CITY, IA 51108 (West-central edge of the state on the Missouri River)
Phone: 712-239-1344
Hours: M-F 8-5, Sat 8:30-4.

There are about 1000 cars and pickups in this lot of mixed makes. Most are domestic. About 250 are from 1940s to 1960s and other vehicles to the present. Customers may browse the yard. In business since 1966.

OLSON LINN MUSEUM
Village Square
VILLISCA, IA 50864 (Southwest corner of the state on US 71)
Phone: 712-826-2756
Hours: June 1 thru Oct. 1, Sat noon-5 and Sun 1-5. Admission charged.

This museum has a fine collection of antique cars, trucks, buggies and farm equipment. Among the antique cars and trucks is a 1917 Allen, a 1917 Cole Cloverleaf Roadster, a 1918 Ford delivery van, a 1929 Ford Model AA truck, a 1910 Maxwell, a 1918 Sampson truck and a 1924 Star touring car.

The museum also owns and preserves the "Ax-Murder House" a short distance from the museum. This is the scene of one of Iowa's most famous unsolved mysteries. In 1912 eight people were axed to death in this house. Six were members of the family and two were neighbor children staying overnight. While at the museum inquire about the house and those interested in seeing it will be driven there in one of the museum's antique cars. Darwin Linn is the museum's owner.

SCHIELD INTERNATIONAL MUSEUM

805 W Bremer Av
WAVERLY, IA 50677 (15 miles north of Waterloo)

Phone: 319-352-8318
Hours: Memorial Day thru Labor Day Tues-Sun 1-5. Admission charged.

This is one of the few places in the U.S. where one can see a Pobeda automobile. The Pobeda (Victory) was made in the Soviet Union after World War II and was that nation's most popular car for more than a decade. This museum has a 1956 Pobeda 4 door sedan. They also have a Soviet-made tractor-crawler from the 1950s, and a 1957 Fendt (German) tractor, a 1912 Ford Model T and several other unique vehicles. Most of the items in the museum were collected by the museum's founder, industrialist Vern L. Schield. The museum is managed by Wartburg College.

The Schield International Museum of Waverly, IA has one of the few Soviet-made Pobeda automobiles in the U.S.

KANSAS

When US Highway 66 was the main route from Chicago to Los Angeles, a short stretch of it crossed the extreme southeastern tip of Kansas between the towns of Galena and Baxter Springs. In recent years these two communities have joined together to preserve this 10 mile stretch of the old highway for its historical value.

EISENHOWER CENTER (Historic home and presidential museum)
  200 SE 4th St
  ABILENE, KS 67410 (22 miles east

of Salina on I-70)
Phone: 785-263-4751
Hours: Daily 9-4:45; closed Jan 1, Thanksgiving and Dec 25.
Admission charged.

This is the site of the boyhood home of Dwight D. Eisenhower. The center consists of five main entities; the family home, the Eisenhower Museum, the Eisenhower Presidential Library, the Visitors Center and the Place of Meditation which is his final resting place and that of his wife, Mamie. Within these building is recorded the life and career of Eisenhower and members of his family. In the Eisenhower Museum are sev-

To the left is General Eisenhower's 1942 Cadillac 4-door sedan staff car used by him during and after World War II.

eral military vehicles and two antique automobiles. One automobile is a 1914 Rauch and Land Electric which was owned by Mamie Eisenhower's parents, Mr. & Mrs. John S. Doud. Eisenhower, as a young man, drove the car frequently when he came to visit. The other car is a 1942 Cadillac 4-door sedan used by Eisenhower in Europe as a staff car when he was commander of Allied forces there during World War II. Eisenhower used the car in the U.S. upon his return after the war and then it followed him back to Europe when he became Supreme Allied Commander in the early postwar years. When Eisenhower returned again to the U.S. the car remained in Europe and served his successor, Gen. Gruenther. In 1956 the car was declared surplus by the Army and by then it had its third engine and 200,000 miles on the odometer. A group of Eisenhower's friends bought the car, restored it and gave it to Ike. He, in turn, gave it to the museum.

WAGNER CLASSIC CARS (Restorer and dealer)

741 E Front St (2¹/₂ Mi south of I-70 off Hwy K-7)
BONNER SPRINGS, KS 66012 (Western suburb of Kansas City, KS)
Phone: 913-422 1955 or
800-755-0927
Hours: M-F 8:30-7, Sat 9:30-5:30

Willie Wagner, the owner of Wagner Classic Cars, not only restores antique car, but he sells what he restores. He also sells other vintage vehicles, specializing in GENERAL MOTORS vehicles, muscle cars and street rods. The good stuff is in their spacious showroom, a former Ford dealership building decorated in a 1960s motif. On an adjacent lot Wagner sells current model used cars.

Wagner's carries between 20 and 35 vintage cars in stock and can provide an inventory list upon request. They will help arrange financing, do repairs and partial restorations, provide appraisals, take trades, sell on consignment and will search for specific vehicles for customers. Car clubs are welcome.

BOB LINT MOTOR SHOP (Salvage)

101 S Main
DANVILLE, KS 67036 (40 miles southwest of Wichita on US 160)
Phone: 316-962-5247
Hours: M-F 8-5, Sat 8-noon.

This is an old, established salvage yard with about 70 vehicles of mixed makes and thousands of parts. A large selection of license plates is available as are wire wheels, radiators and transmissions. Some restoration work is done. An inventory list is available upon request. Customers may browse the yard. In business since 1953.

WALTER P. CHRYSLER BOYHOOD HOME & MUSEUM

102 W 10th St
ELLIS, KS 67637 (West-central part of the state at Exit 145 on I-70)
Phone: 785-726-3636
Hours: May-Sept M-Sat 9:30-4:30,
Sun 12:30-4:30. Oct-Apr
M-Sat 11-3, Sun 12:30-4:30.
Admission charged.

Walter P. Chrysler, founder of the Chrysler Corporation, spent most of his

115

Kansas

The Walter P. Chrysler Boyhood Home in Ellis, KS.

youth in Ellis and his boyhood home is preserved and open to the public. It is furnished much as it was when he lived here and his father worked for the railroad. The house is listed on the National Register of Historic Places. There is a museum on the grounds displaying additional items of interest related to Chrysler, his life in Ellis and the Corporation he founded. There are family photos and memorabilia as well as the desk Chrysler used during the later years of his business career. A 1924 Chrysler automobile, the first year of production for that marque, is on display in the museum. It was here in the Ellis railroad shops that Chrysler, as a young man, learned the metal-working trade before going east to work in the automobile industry. His wife, Della Forker Chrysler, was from Ellis and they were married here. The museum has a gift shop offering many Chrysler-related items and souvenirs.

WHEELS AND SPOKES CLASSIC AUTO DISPLAY (Museum and dealer)
383 Mopar Dr (Exit 159 at I-70 & US 183)
HAYS, KS 67601 (West-central part of state on I-70)
Phone: 785-628-6477
Hours: M-F 8-6, Sat 10-5. Closed holidays. Admission charged.

This establishment is both a museum and an antique car dealer with some 50 to 60 autos on display and with many of them for sale. Wheels and Spokes specializes in MOPAR vehicles, but also offers other makes. There are displays of license plates, hub caps, metal toys and a gift shop. Founded 1983.

VINTAGE TIN AUTO PARTS (Salvage)
4550-A Scotty Ln
HUTCHINSON, KS 67502 (40

miles northwest of Wichita)
Phone: 316-669-8449
Hours: Tues-Sat 9-6.

This is a large salvage yard with approximately 1200 vehicles, most of them American-made. Many of the vehicles are American orphans such as Packard, Nash, Hudson and DeSoto. There are also Chevys, Fords, Chryslers, Dodges, Plymouths, Oldsmobiles, Pontiacs and Cadillacs. Cars are from 1940 thru the 1970s. Customers may browse the yard. In business since 1948.

JIM'S AUTO SALES (Salvage)
Rt 2
INMAN, KS 67546 (15 miles northeast of Hutchinson on SR 61)
Phone: 316-585-6648
Hours: M-Sat 9-6. Sun by appointment.

This is an old yard with some 250 vehicles, most of them STUDEBAKERs from 1935 to 1966. There are also some Chrysler vehicles from the late 1930s to the mid-1970s and a few Fords and GM cars. Jim's has a large selection of NOS Studebaker parts from defunct Studebaker dealers. Most of the parts are for motors, transmissions, drivetrains, suspensions and instruments. Customers may browse the yard. In business since 1968.

REO ANTIQUE AUTO MUSEUM
100 N Harrison (Business Rt US 81)
LINDSBORG, KS 67456 (20 miles south of Salina off I-135)

Phone: 913-227-3252
Hours: Daily 1-4, donations accepted.

This is a privately-owned collection of about 30 antique cars of which about a dozen are REOs. Outstanding cars in the collection include a 1908 REO, a 1916 REO touring car, a 1923 REO Opera Coupe, a 1926 REO 4-door sedan and a 1929 REO Flying Cloud Coupe with golf club compartment. Other cars include a 1908 Buick, 1907 Cadillac Runabout, 1916 Metz Raceabout and a 1922 Hupmobile touring car. There is also a collection of antique machine tools. Q. A. Applequist is the owner.

HALL'S OLDSMOBILE SALVAGE
20849 F Road
SOLDIER, KS 66540 (40 miles north-northwest of Topeka)
Phone: 913-924-3748 and 913-924-3315.
Hours: M-Sat 8:30-5.

This yard, as the name implies, specializes in OLDSMOBILEs. They have some 1800 Oldsmobiles on 30 acres of flat Kansas farmland. Virtually every model of Oldsmobile is represented in this yard from 1936 to the present. There are also some 400 Chevys, Buicks, Pontiacs and Cadillacs from 1940 to 1972. Many of the parts are removed and stored in Hall's 5000 sq. ft. steel building. Hall's also offers NOS and new parts. Customers may browse the yard.

KENTUCKY

▼ BOWLING GREEN AREA

(South-central part of the state on I-65)

The General Motors Corvette asssembly plant, Bowling Green, KY.

GENERAL MOTORS CORVETTE ASSEMBLY PLANT (Plant tours)
I-65 Exit 28 at Louisville Rd
BOWLING GREEN, KY 42101
Phone: 502-745-8419
Hours: M-F tours at 9 and 1. Closed holidays and first two weeks of July. Free.

This plant offers one-hour guided tours showing how Chevrolet Corvettes are assembled. Every Corvette made since 1982 has been assembled at this plant. No cameras please.

NATIONAL CORVETTE MUSEUM
350 Corvette Dr (Exit 28 off I-65 just south of the GM Corvette Assembly Plant)
BOWLING GREEN, KY 42101
Phone: 502-781-7973 or 800-53-VETTE
Hours: Apr 1-Sept 30, daily 8-6; Oct 1-Mar 31 daily 8-5. Admission charged.

This is a fine 68,000 sq. ft. museum, opened in late 1994, that preserves and honors the history of the CORVETTE automobile from its beginning to the present. Many models of Corvettes are on display including the 1 millionth Corvette produced here in Bowling Green. The cars are displayed in authentic sets representing the stages of the Corvette's development. There are also exhibits on racing, design, building and marketing of the Corvette and its impact on the American auto industry. Guided tours available and there is free parking with ample bus and RV turn-around. The museum is available for parties, weddings, corporate functions, etc. There is a large gift shop offering Corvette clothing, jewelry, books and rare models.

End of Bowling Green Area △

PATTON MUSEUM OF CAVALRY & ARMOR
Building 4554
Fort Knox Military Reservation
FORT KNOX, KY 40121-0208
(20 miles south of Louisville on US 31W)
Phone: 502-624-3812 or 502-624-6350
Hours: May 1 to Sept 30 M-F 9-4:30, weekends and holidays 10-6; Oct 1 to Apr 30 M-F 9-4:30, weekends and holidays 10-4:30. Closed Dec 24, 25 and 31 and Jan 1. Free.

This museum is devoted to the memory of World War II General George S. Patton and to the U.S. Cavalry and armored units of all American wars. Among the many military vehicles on display is a caravan truck used by General Patton during World War II and the Cadillac sedan in which he was fatally injured in December 1945. Every July 4 a World War II battle re-enactment takes place near the museum using many of the museum's vehicles.

General George S. Patton was fatally injured in the back seat of this 1938 Cadillac limousine when it was involved in an automobile accident in Germany soon after the end of World War II.

119

LOUISIANA

**ARK-LA-TEX ANTIQUE AND
CLASSIC VEHICLE MUSEUM**
  601 Spring St
  SHREVEPORT, LA 71101
  Phone: 318-222-0227
  Hours: Tues-Sat 9-5, admission
  charged.

This new museum is in a handsome old three-story, 24,000 sq. ft. building that once was a Graham Bros. dealership and a Dodge dealership. The showrooms—that's right, plural—are on the first floor. The museum is also home to the Shreveport Firefighter's Museum. Altogether there are about 50 vintage cars, 4 fire trucks and more than a dozen motorcycles. Outstanding vehicles in the collection include a one-of-a-kind 1978 Hollenshead roadster with rumble seat made in the Philippines, a 1929 Marmon, a 1936 Pierce-Arrow and a rare MGKT of which only 100 were built. Many of the cars are on loan from local collectors so the exhibits rotate. Some of the cars are for sale. The museum participates in several annual antique car events, is available for parties and the like and has an impressive gift shop. Car clubs are welcome. The museum's director is Francene Miller.

MAINE

COLE LAND TRANSPORTATION MUSEUM

405 Perry Rd
BANGOR, ME 04401 (South-central part of the state on I-95)
Phone: 207-990-3600
Hours: May 1 thru Nov 11 daily 9-5. Admission charged.

This is a privately-owned museum displaying some 200 pieces of transportation equipment used over the years in Maine. Not only are there antique automobiles, but there are snow plows, tractors, trucks, railroad equipment, snowmobiles, bicycles, wagons and sleighs. The museum possesses one of the most extensive collection of early commercial vehicles in the country. Some of the vehicles of interest include a 1912 REO delivery truck, a 1913 Stanley delivery truck, a 1923 Packard Roadster, a 1923 American-LaFrance fire truck, a 1926 Mack cement mixer, a 1928 Buick Coupe, a 1933 GMC bus, a 1935 Linn snow plow, a 1936 International oil truck, a 1936 Chevrolet wrecker, a 1938 V-12 Lincoln, a 1941 Pontiac Streamliner Torpedo, a 1945 Willys Jeep, a 1946 King Midget and a 1953 Divco milk truck. There are various auto-related artifacts on display, and the museum has a gift shop with many interesting items for sale. Lowell G. Kjenstad is the museum's director.

BOOTHBAY RAILWAY VILLAGE (Museum)

3¹/₂ Miles North on SR 27
BOOTHBAY, ME 04537
(On the coast 35 miles northeast of Portland)
Phone: 207-633-4727
Hours: May 23-Oct 11 daily 9:30-5. Admission charged.

This is a museum village of approximately 30 buildings representing life in Maine as it was at the beginning of the 20th Century. Among the several building in the village is a blacksmith shop, a restored school house, a general store, a doll museum and a well-stocked gift shop. A steam train operates from the old station and rides of about 15 minute are offered thru the nearby woods. There is also an antique car museum with approximately 50 cars, many of which are Fords. In the car museum are displays of old gasoline engines, license plates, gas pumps and other automobile memorabilia. Museum founded 1963.

121

Maine

CLASSIC FORD SALES (Salvage)

PO Box 60 (Office)
EAST DIXFIELD, ME
(Western part of state on US 2)
Phone: 800-894-4300 or
207-562-4443
Hours: M-F 9-5

They call it "Ford Heaven" because it is high up on a mountain top and not easy to get to. Visitors who wish to visit the yard should phone first for directions. The yard is "located up the road a bit" at South Carthage. Upon arrival, though, visitors will see one of the largest FORD salvage yards in the world. There are more than 700 Fords here from 1949 through 1972 and later. Classic Ford Sales has many many T-birds, Fairlanes, Falcons, and can supply NOS parts as well as used. But, (guess what), no Mustangs! On the other hand Classic Ford Sales has a sizeable inventory of large Ford trucks beginning with the F100 series through tandem rigs. Visitors can browse the yard and Phil McIntyre, the owner, welcomes car clubs and groups. He says that if the numbers justify it, he'll prepare a cook out. Phil started the yard in 1992.

THE STANLEY MUSEUM

School St
KINGFIELD, ME 04947 (47 miles north-northwest of Augusta)
Phone: 207-265-2729
Hours: Tues-Sun 1-4. Closed all of April, all of Nov and Dec 25. Admission charged.

This museum, housed in a 1903 school building, honors the Stanley family of Stanley Steamer fame. There are three Stanley Steamer automobiles in the museum, a 1905, 1910 and 1916. Photos and memorabilia relate the history of this famous Maine family, especially Francis E. and Frelan O. Stanley, the inventive twin brothers who were the driving forces behind the Stanley Motor Carriage Company. Photography was also important to the Stanley family. They were the owners of the Stanley Dry Plate Co., the source of the family's wealth. Information on the company and its products are on display along with vintage cameras and photographs of local life in Maine at the turn of the century taken by Sister Chansonetta, who was an accomplished photographer.

The museum publishes a news letter 4 times a year containing historical and technical information on steam engines and newsbriefs of steam-related events. Susan S. Davis is the Executive Director.

COLLECTIBLE CARS AND PARTS (Salvage)

LIMESTONE, ME 04952 (North eastern edge of the state near the Canadian border)
Phone: 207-325-4915
Hours: M-Sat 8-5, Sun 8-2. Closed late Nov for the winter.

This is a very large salvage yard with some 5000 vehicles ranging in age from 1935 to the 1960s. All makes are represented and there are many light trucks. Mail orders welcome. Customers may browse the yard. In business since 1990.

An interior view of the Owls Head Transportation Museum, Owls Head, ME.

OWLS HEAD TRANSPORTATION MUSEUM

2 Miles South of Rockland on SR 73 at Knox County Airport
OWLS HEAD, ME 04854
(On Penobscot Bay 40 miles southeast of Augusta)
Phone: 207-594-4418
Hours: Apr-Oct daily 10-5. Rest of Year M-F 10-5, Sat and Sun 11-3. Closed Jan 1, Thanksgiving and Dec 25. Admission charged.

This is a large museum displaying one of the finest collection of antique cars, motorcycles, bicycles, buggies, engines and airplanes on the eastern seaboard. Among the more than 75 vintage cars displayed is a 1903 Mercedes Simplex, a 1906 Autocar, a 1914 Benz touring car, a 1912 Fiat Type 53A, a 1925 Citroen Torpedo, a 1929 Essex Super Six Boattail Roadster, and many other rare and unusual vehicles. There are also displays and photographs on early trans-portation in Maine from 1890 thru the 1920s. On the weekends during the summer various pieces of equipment are taken out of the museum and operated on the museum grounds. The Owls Head Museum is host to many clubs and events throughout the year.

SEAL COVE AUTO MUSEUM

Pretty Marsh Rd
SEAL COVE, ME 04674
(On the Ocean just southwest of Acadia Natl. Park)
Phone: 207-244-9242
Hours: June thru Sept daily 10-5. Admission charged.

This is a privately-owned museum with approximately 100 antique cars and 35 antique motorcycles. Some of the cars are extremely rare and many of them are of pre-World War I vintage. Some of the cars have been restored to world-class condition. Outstanding in

Maine

One of the many rare and unique vintage autos at the Seal Cove Auto Museum, Seal Cove, ME.

the collection is an 1899 DeDion Bouton, a 1905 Pierce-Arrow 40S Roadster, a 1913 Rolls-Royce Harden Silver Ghost, a 1904 Cadillac Surry Top Rear Entrance Tonneau, two Thomas Flyers, two Chadwicks, 12 early Fords and many other fascinating vehicles. There is also a 1914 FRP, the only surviving example of the nine manfactured. In the motorcycle collection is a 1911 Excelsior, a 1911 Pope, a 1913 Thor racing motorcycle, two early Indians, two early Yales and others. The museum also has a gift shop with many interesting auto-related items. This is the Richard Paine collection and the museum's president is Jim Homsher.

WELLS AUTO MUSEUM
Highway US 1
(Exit 2 off Maine Turnpike)
WELLS, ME 04090 (30 miles southwest of Portland)
Phone: 207-646-9064
Hours: Mid-June thru Sept daily 10-5; Memorial Day weekend thru Columbus Day weekend Sat & Sun 10-5. Closed rest of year. Admission charged.

This fine museum has a display of some 80 vehicles including New England's largest display of "Brass Era" cars. Included in the collection is a 1905 Grout Steamer, a 1907 Stanley Steamer

1912 Pathfinder from the collection of Brass Era autos at the Wells Auto Museum of Wells, ME.

Gentlemen's Speedy Roadster, a 1908 Baker Electric, a 1912 Pathfinder Armored Roadster, a 1918 Stutz Bearcat, a 1934 Chrysler Airflow, a 1935 Lagonda, a 1935 Bantam and a 1941 Chrysler Town & Country. There are displays of New England license plates, old toys, tools, hubcaps, nameplates and photos. There is also a exhibit of motorcycles, bicycles, nickelodeons, arcade picture machines, orchestrions, Regina Hexaphones and many more items. The museum has a well-stocked gift shop offering toys, jewelry, models, books and other auto-related items. Glenn Gould is the owner.

MARYLAND

US ARMY ORDNANCE MUSEUM
Building 2601
Aberdeen Proving Ground
ABERDEEN, MD 21005
(25 miles northeast of downtown
Baltimore)
Phone: 410-278-3602
Hours: Mon-Sun 10-4:45. Also
open 10-4:45 on Armed Forces Day,
Memorial Day, July 4 and Veterans
Day. Closed other holidays. Free.

This is a large Army museum displaying many pieces of equipment and items of war associated with the Army's Ordnance Department and the Aberdeen Proving Ground. Included in the collection of vehicles are several antique cars including Gen. John Pershing's 1917 Locomobile and German Kubelwagens and Schwimmwagens from World War II. Schwimmwagens are amphibious Volkswagons. The museum has a gift shop on the premises and free parking.

MARYLAND CLASSIC AUTO SALES (Dealer)
4001 Washington Boulevard
(Office)
4020 Washington Boulevard
(Showroom)
BALTIMORE, MD 21227

Phone 410-242-7327
Hours: M-F 8-6

If you like convertibles from the 1950s and 60s, you'll like this place. That is what they specialize in. Maryland Classic carries between 15 and 25 cars in stock and they're priced in the affordable range. They take trades, arrange financing and shipping and will pick up customers at the Baltimore Airport which is nearby. The company offers automobile storage and car clubs are welcome. The owner is Ivan Goldstein.

VOGT'S PARTS BARN (Salvage)
2239 Old Westminster Pike
FINKSBURG, MD 21048
(20 miles northwest of downtown
Baltimore on US 140)
Phone: 800-492-1300 or
301-876-1300
Hours: M-F 8:30-5, Sat 8:30-noon.

This is an old established salvage yard with some 2500 vehicles on 17 acres of land. They carry a generous mix of American-made vehicles and imports, including light trucks from 1935 to the 1990s. Vogt's has large selections of 1955-57 Chevys and 1960s Corvairs and Mustangs. The inventory is computerized and Vogt's will search other yards for specific parts. In business since 1956.

This is the attractive entrance to Vogt's Parts Barn on Old Westminster Pike.

POTOMAC GERMAN AUTO (Salvage)

4305 Lime Kiln Rd
FREDERICK, MD 21701
(40 miles west of Baltimore on I-70 and I-270)
Phone: 301-831-1111
Hours: M-F 8-5

A salvage yard of over 600 vehicles specializing in MERCEDES BENZ from 1965 to present. Many parts are dismantled and stored in an indoor warehouse. Many new parts available. Computerized inventory list available. Customers may browse the yard. In business since 1982.

SMITH BROTHERS AUTO PARTS (Salvage)

2316 Snydersburg Rd
HAMPSTEAD, MD 21074
(25 miles north-northwest of downtown Baltimore on SR 30)
Phone: 301-239-8514 or
301-374-6781
Hours: M-F 8-5, Sat 8-4.

There are approximately 400 to 500 cars of all makes in this salvage yard ranging in age from 1935 to the 1980s. Smith Brothers has any Ford driveline parts. Customers may browse the yard.

FIRE MUSEUM OF MARYLAND, INC.

1301 York Rd
LUTHERVILLE, MD 21093 (a northern suburb of Baltimore)
Phone: 410-321-7500
Hours: May-Oct Sat-Sun; June, July, Aug W-F; Apr-Nov group tours.
Admission charged.

This is one of the largest fire museums in the United States with a collection of more than 40 pieces of hand-pulled, horse-pulled and motorized apparatus on permanent display. There is a 1917 Mack pumper, a 1920 Seagrave pumper, a 1924 American-LaFrance ladder truck, a 1928 Mack firetruck, a 1935 Stutz pumper, a 1941 American-LaFrance Foamite pumper and others. Numerous hand-operated pieces of equipment are shown along with other

Maryland

firefighting items. Visitors may send a similated fire alarm over an antique fire alarm telepraph system. The museum was founded in 1971 by Stephen G. Heaver, Sr., and his son Steve, Jr.

One of the many fire engines at the Fire Museum of Maryland. See listing an previous page.

CHUCK'S USED AUTO PARTS (Salvage)

4722 Saint Barnabas Rd
MARLOW HEIGHTS, MD 20748
(A southeastern suburb of Washington, DC)
Phone: 301-423-0007
Hours: M-F 8-5, Sat 8-2.

This yard specializes in CORVETTEs and late model GENERAL MOTORS cars and trucks. They have about 250 vehicles in the yard with many of them restorable. Chuck's will also locate specific parts from other sources. Customers may browse the yard. In business since 1981.

PETRY'S JUNK YARD (Salvage)

800 Gorsuch Rd
WESTMINSTER, MD 21157
(30 miles northwest of Baltimore on SR 9)
Phone: 301-876-3233 or 301-848-8590
Hours: M-Sat 8-5. Sun by appointment.

This yard specializes in all makes of cars and light trucks from the 1940s thru the 1970s and has a total of about 400 to 500 vehicles. An inventory list is available upon request. Customers may browse the yard. Towing service available. In business since 1967.

MASSACHUSETTS

BELLINGHAM AUTO PARTS
(Salvage)
206 Mechanic St
BELLINGHAM, MA 02019
(30 miles southwest of downtown
Boston near the Rhode Island
state line)
Phone: 508-966-1230 or
508-966-9721
Hours: M-F 9-5, Sat 9-2:30.

This is an old salvage yard with about
2000 vehicles on 7 acres of land. Most
of the vehicles are current models, but
there is a respectable number of vintage
vehicles both domestic and foreign. This
is one of the few salvage yards in the
nation that offers parts for PLAYBOY
automobiles. The owners were Playboy
dealers during that marque's short life.
The yard has many Hudsons and other
orphans such as Nash, Essex and
Packards. Customers may browse the
yard. In business as a salvage yard since
the 1960s. Edward T. Moore is the
owner.

▼ BOSTON AREA

BOSTON DUCK TOURS
(Amphibious vehicle rides)
790 Boyleston St (Office)
Prudential Center, Huntington Av
side (Point of departure)
BOSTON, MA 02199
Phone: 617-723-DUCK
Hours: Apr-Nov daily 9 am to half
hour before sunset. Departures
every 30 minutes. Admission
charged.

Down the streets of Boston you go in
this World War II-era amphibious vehicle
and then into the Charles River. That's
the thrill of it - going both on land and
water in the same vehicle. The driver tells
you the history of the vehicles and about
the landmarks you pass. During World
War II these vehicles were called DUKWs
(pronounced "ducks") and were used
extensively to ferry men and material
from ship to shore in many parts of the
world. Nowadays they are heated,
equipped with cushioned seats, painted
brightly and inspected regularly by the
Coast Guard for safety to make an ideal
fun-vehicle for the whole family. Duck
rides are available in other parts of the
country but this is the only one in New
England. Ducks are still used for serious
business too. In the blizzard of 1978 they
were pressed into service in the Boston
area to rescue stranded citizens.

Massachusetts

MUSEUM OF TRANSPORTATION
15 Newton St in Larz Anderson
Park
BROOKLINE, MA 02146 (A
southern suburb of Boston)
Phone: 617-522-6547 and 617-522-
6140 (recording)
Hours: Tues-Sun 10-5. Closed
Thanksgiving and Dec 25. Admission charged.

There are about 25 vintage cars on display in the 1888 carriage house of the former home of the famous diplomat, Larz Anderson. Changing exhibits reflect the influence of the automobile on various periods of American history and with various themes. Many of the permanent cars are from the turn-of-the-Century. The earliest car is from 1899. Other cars of various eras are on loan from private owners. The Museum hosts an annual car auction, Concours d'Elegance and many car club events.

Other displays in the museum highlight the lives of the famous Anderson family and there are exhibits telling of the early life in the Brookline area. The museum also has an interesting and pleasant gift shop.

End of Boston area △

STEVENS AUTO WRECKING
(Salvage and dealer)
160 Freeman Rd
CHARLTON, MA 01507 (10 miles
southwest of Worcester on I-90)
Phone: 508-248-5539 or
508-832-6380
Hours: M-F 8-5, Sat 8-2:30.

A large salvage yard of approximately 3000 vehicles with cars and trucks from the 1930s to the 1980s. The heaviest concentration is from the late 1940s to the early 1970s. Vehicles are of mixed makes and models with some imports. Stevens also offers used and reconditioned cars for sale. Customer may browse the yard. In business since 1958. Freddie Stevens is the owner.

CORVETTE MIKE NEW ENGLAND
10 Water St
PLYMOUTH, MA 02360 (On the
coast 30 miles SE of Boston)
Phone: 508-747-VETT
Hours: M-F 9-7, Sat 9-5.
Sun noon-5 (Phone first)

Corvette Mike is only "A big block from the Rock", Plymouth Rock, that is, in downtown Plymouth. As the name implies, the company specializes in Corvettes and offers low mileage, late model vehicles as well as vintage machines. The company carries about 30 cars in inventory, aids in financing, does appraisals, sells on consignment, takes trades, offers leases and searches for desired vehicles. There is a small gift shop and Corvette Mike has an annual car show on the premises. Mike Vietro, the owner, welcomes car clubs.

STEPHEN PHILLIPS MEMORIAL TRUST HOUSE (Museum)
34 Chestnut St
SALEM, MA 01970
(15 miles northeast of Boston on Massachusetts Bay)
Phone: 978-744-0440
Hours: Memorial Day weekend thru Oct 31, M-Sat 10-4:30.
Admission charged.

This is the mansion of a family of prosperous sea captains. The main house is decorated with early American furniture, Chinese porcelains, colonial portraits and other fine furnishings. In the carriage house are 10 wagons, dating from 1840, and 3 antique automobiles that once belonged to the family. The autos are a 1924 Pierce-Arrow, a 1936 Pierce-Arrow limousine and a 1929 Model A Ford.

HERITAGE PLANTATION (Museum)
Grove and Pine Sts off SR 130
SANDWICH, MA 02563
(West end of Cape Cod)
Phone: 508-888-3300
Hours: Mid-May thru Mid-Oct daily 10-5. Admission charged.

A museum founded by J. K. Lilly III to display some of his family's collection of Americana. Housed in a Shaker round stone barn are some 35 vintage autos including President William Howard Taft's 1909 White Steamer, a 1922 American-made Rolls-Royce, a 1912 Mercer Raceabout, a 1915 Stutz Bearcat and a 1930 Duesenberg once owned by Gary Cooper. Tours of the estate are available in a jitney. An automotive library is open by appointment and there is a souvenir and gift shop on the grounds. In the other buildings are displays of American handicrafts, art, firearms, flags, model soldiers and many other items. The grounds are lavishly decorated with trees, shrubs and some 10,000 rhododendrons.

INDIAN MOTORCYCLE MUSEUM
33 Hendee St
(Exit I-291 at Saint James St)
SPRINGFIELD, MA 01139
Phone: 413-737-2624
Hours: Mar-Nov daily 10-4, rest of year daily 1-5. Closed Jan 1, Thanksgiving and Dec 25.
Admission charged.

This is a museum devoted to INDIAN Motorcycles, the first gasoline-powered motorcycles to be manufactured in the United States. It is located in the last building owned by the company. The Indian Motorcycle Company began manufacturing here in Springfield in 1901 and continued until the company went out of business in 1953. Many examples of Indian motorcycles are on display including some of the earliest models and models used by American paratroopers in World War II. There is also a large display of toy motorcycles and motorcycle memorabilia. One display highlights the history of women on wheels. The Indian Motorcycle Company, at various times, also manufactured outboard motors, airplane engines and automobiles. A 1927 Indian automobile is on display. The museum has a gift shop.

Here's how to get to the Yankee Candle Car Museum.

**THE YANKEE CANDLE
CAR MUSEUM**
Rt 5
SOUTH DEERFIELD, MA 01373
(Western part of the state on I-91)
Phone: 413-665-2020
Hours: Daily 9:30-6. Closed
Thanksgiving and Dec 25.

Here is one of the finest car museums in the east. Some 80 restored vehicles are on display on a rotating basis because many of them are on loan from local collectors. There are pre-World War I brass-era cars, muscle cars, exotics, sports cars, vehicles from the 1930s and 1940s and many post-World War II cars. There's a VW Beetle once owned by Jerry Seinfeld and a 1966 Ghia 450SS that belonged to Johnny Carson. In most museums the "do not touch" signs are everywhere, but not here. Visitors can sit in a Ferrari or Rolls-Royce and have their picture taken. The Yankee Candle Car Museum has a large gift shop offering logo accessories, models, clothing, prints, books and, of course, candles. Steve Smith is the museum's manager.

Adjacent to the museum is the Yankee Candle Company's large retail store which offers thousands of candles and other related items. The store is 100,000 sq ft and has perpetual displays of Christmas decoration and gifts.

**LONGFELLOW'S WAYSIDE
INN OF SUDBURY**
US Hwy 20 West and
Wayside Inn Rd
SUDBURY, MA 01776 (22 miles
west of downtown Boston)
Phone: 508-443-1776
Hours: Inn open daily 9-6. Gristmill
open Apr-Nov daily 9:30-5.
Schoolhouse open May-Oct daily
11:30-5. Donations requested.

This is an old restored inn made famous by Henry Wadsworth Longfellow who composed his poem "Tales of a Wayside Inn" while sitting by the Inn's fire place. The Inn offers lodging and meals and there are a number of interesting and historic outbuildings on the grounds including the Martha-Mary Chapel, a gristmill and Mary Lamb Schoolhouse. In the 1920s the Inn was abandoned and in decay when Henry Ford came to its rescue and restored it once more into a working inn. Ford restored the gristmill and moved to the property a schoolhouse from Sterling, MA which he believed to be the original schoolhouse immortalized in the McGuffey Reader classic "Mary Had a Little Lamb". Others, however, have since doubted the authenticity of this schoolhouse in relation to the McGuffey classic.

Nevertheless, Henry Ford and his wife, Clara, loved the Wayside Inn and visited it often and attended many of its square dance parties, an activity Henry and Clara loved. In 1939 Henry Ford build the Martha-Mary Chapel and named it after his mother and his wife's mother. After restoring the Wayside Inn, Ford went on to create his famous Ford Museum and Greenfield Village complex in Dearborn, MI.

MICHIGAN

**BARTNIK SALES & SERVICE
(Salvage)**
6524 Van Dyke
(Intersection of SR 53 and SR 81)
CASS CITY, MI 48726
(35 miles east of Bay City)
Phone: 517-872-3541
Hours: M-F 8-5:30, Sat 8-5.

This salvage yard has approximately
375 cars and trucks. They specialize in
vehicles mostly from the 1960s and
1970s. There is a mix of makes and
models. Most are domestic. Mail orders
welcome. Customers may browse the
yard. In business since 1955.

SUPER AUTO PARTS (Salvage)
6162 Lapeer Rd
CLYDE, MI 48049
(15 miles west of Pontiac)
Phone: 810-982-6895
Hours: M and W-Sat 11-5.

This yard has about 600 vehicles,
mostly from the 1950s and 1960s. There
are some 1970s models, also. Vehicles are
of mixed makes and body styles. Customers may browse the yard. In business
since 1940. It is suggested that visitors
phone for directions to Super Auto Parts.

**TOWNE & COUNTRY MOTORS
(Dealer)**
78927 North SR 51
DECATUR, MI
(25 miles west of Kalamazoo)
Phone: 616-423-3131
Hours: Apr-Oct M-F 9-8, Sat 9-6,
rest of year M-Sat 9-5.

MUSCLE CARS and STREET RODS
are what Towne & Country Motors is
all about. But, you will see a few classics
and antique vehicles, too, in their showroom. This fast-growing company carries about 50 cars in inventory and sells
cars world-wide. They can provide an
inventory list, take trades, do repairs,
arrange financing, and will search for
specific vehicles for customers. Greg
Gorzelanny, the owner, says car clubs are
welcome any time. Your contact man at
Towne & Country is Dave Peters.

▼ DETROIT AREA

During the first half of the 20th
Century Detroit emerged as America's
automobile capital... a title which it
retains to this day. Many cities contended
for the honor, but it was here that the
big names and survivors in the very

competitive early automotive industry assembled. By doing so, they propelled Detroit into one of America's great industrial centers. As a result, the city and its suburbs abound with historical automotive sites. Here are the international headquarters and major factories of the automotive giants, the homes of many of the famous personalities of the industry, their monuments, their museums, their philanthropic works and their graves. One need travel just a few blocks in the city in any direction to run into a street, a park, a school or a building bearing an historical automotive name. Visitors will dart about the city on the Edsel Ford Freeway, the Chrysler Freeway and the Fisher Freeway. They will encounter the Henry Ford Hospital, Henry Ford Centennial Library, Henry Ford High School, Henry Ford Junior High School, Henry Ford Elementary School, General Motors Tech., the General Motors Building and Dodge Brothers State Parks.

CHRYSLER HISTORICAL MUSEUM
(Under construction)
Featherstone and Squirrel Rds
(Off I-75 and SR 59)
AUBURN HILLS, MI
(A northern suburb of Detroit just east of Pontiac)
Phone: 248-512-2698 (Chrysler Public Relations Dept.)

Watch for this one! It is going to be big and will open sometime in 1999. The Chrysler Corporation is building a state-of-the-art 35,000 sq ft museum in Auburn Hills to feature the long history and many achievements of the corporation. There will be about 75 cars in the collection with between 40 and 50

on display at any one time. The museum will have its own restoration shop, a theater, archives and research department, a gift shop and a court yard. The company says it will be the first, dedicated, on-site museum built by a U.S. automaker.

AUTOMOTIVE HALL OF FAME
21400 Oakwood Blvd (Adjacent to the Henry Ford Museum)
DEARBORN, MI 48124 (Southwestern suburb of Detroit)
Phone: 313-240-4000
Hours: Memorial Day-Oct 31, daily 10-5; rest of year Tues-Sun 10-5. Closed Thanksgiving, Dec 25 and Jan 1. Admission charged.

The Automotive Hall of Fame is designed to be a visitor attraction and educational resource. It celebrates accomplished people of the worldwide motor vehicle industry for the purpose of inspiring others, especially young people, to higher levels of achievement in their own work and lives. It is a unique "people place" of innovation and inspiration where interactive experiences and one-on-one demonstrations are entertaining and enlightening.

Some of the several hundred names that will be found in the Hall of Fame are Gordon M. Buehrig, designer of the Auburn, Cord and Duesenberg cars; Elmer Wavering, inventor of the car radio and the alternator; John W. Koons, Sr. of Falls Church, VA, the world's largest Ford dealer; Ralph Teetor, a blind engineer and inventor of cruise control and Soichiro Honda, founder of the Honda automotive empire. (See photo on following page.)

Michigan

The Automotive Hall of Fame in Dearborn, MI is a place of innovation and inspiration.

DETROIT HISTORICAL MUSEUM
5401 Woodward Av
DETROIT, MI 48202
Phone: 313-833-1805
Hours: W-F 9:30-5, Sat-Sun 10-5
closed major holidays except Easter.
Admission charged, except free on Wednesday.

This is a large city museum tracing the growth of the Detroit area from pre-Columbian days to the present. Among the many exhibits is a reconstruction of early Detroit streets and stores, an historic model railroad, a gallery of historic costumes and a collection of antique cars. About 12 cars are on display and are rotated regularly because the museum has a very extensive collection of antique vehicles. Many of the museum's vehicles are rare and one-of-a-kind. The museum has a gift shop.

DETROIT PUBLIC LIBRARY—NATIONAL AUTOMOTIVE HISTORY COLLECTION
5201 Woodward Av
DETROIT, MI 48202
Phone: 313-833-1000
Hours: Library open Tues and Thurs-Sat 9:30-5:30, Wed 1-9. The National Automotive Historic Collection's hours Tues, Thurs-Sat 1-5, Wed 5-9. Both closed on major holidays. Free.

The National Automotive Historical Collection (NAHC) contained within this library has the largest public automotive archive collection on the North American Continent. They have hundreds of thousands of books, magazines, manuals and documents covering such subjects as company histories, products, people, progress, events, racing, restoring, advertising, servicing, court cases, novels, parts manuals, chronologies, cartoons, calendars, posters, business records and music. They also have 183,000 photographs. The collection is open to the general public interested in automotive history. A reference service is offered and the collection publishes "Wheels, Journal of the National Automotive History Collection". The NAHC is supported, in part, by Chrysler, Ford, General Motors and donations from other sources.

THE FISHER MANSION
(Historic home)
383 Lenox Av
DETROIT, MI 48215
Phone: 313-331-6740
Hours: Mansion open during summer Tues-Sun, rest of year F-Sun with tours at 12:30, 2, 3:30 and 6. Restaurant open during summer Tues-Sun, rest of year F-Sun for lunch and dinner.

This was the magnificent riverfront home and estate of Lawrence Fisher, founder of the Fisher Body Co. and President of Cadillac Motors. Completed in 1927, the Fisher Mansion is remarkable for its ornate stone and marble work, wood crafted doors and archways, stained glass windows, Art Deco tile work, exquisite chandeliers and black walnut parquet floors. Over

The Fisher Mansion, former home and estate of Lawrence Fisher, founder of Fisher Body Co. and President of Cadillac Motors.

Michigan

The Edsel & Eleanor Ford House, Grosse Pointe Shores, MI.

200 ounces of gold and silver leaf decorate the ceilings and moldings. On the water front is an enclosed dock for visitors who choose to arrive by boat. The Mansion is the home of the Bhaktivedanta Cultural Center which is inspired by the spiritual teachings of His Divine Grace A. C. Bhaktivedanta Swami Prahudapa. The Center was established by Alfred Brush Ford, great-grandson of Henry Ford and Elisabeth Reuther Dickmeyer, daughter of United Auto Workers Union President, Walter Reuther who jointly purchased the estate in 1975. Inside the mansion is "Govinda's" a fine dining gourmet vegetarian restaurant.

**EDSEL & ELEANOR FORD HOUSE
(Historic home)**
   1100 Lake Shore Rd

GROSSE POINTE SHORES, MI 48236 (A northern suburb of Detroit)
Phone: 313-884-4222
Hours: Tours offered Tues-Sun at 1, 2, 3 and 4. From April thru Dec 31 Tues-Sat 10-4, Sun noon-4. Admission charged.

This was the 60-room lake-front mansion and estate of Henry Ford's only son, Edsel, his wife Eleanor and their four children. The house was begun in 1926 and completed in 1929. Edsel Ford lived here until his death in 1943 and his wife lived on in the house until 1976. The house is decorated much as it was when the Fords lived in it with fine furniture, oriental rugs, oil painting, crystal chandeliers and English walnut paneling. The grounds are well landscaped and can be toured. There is a tea room open to the public and in the Gate Lodge Garage is Mrs. Ford's 1952 custom-made Lincoln Town Car. The Edsel & Eleanor House hosts an annual antique car event called the "Eyes of the Classics" which celebrates automotive design and art, past, present and future.

HENRY FORD HOME "FAIR LANE" (Historic home)

University of Michigan-Dearborn Campus off US 12
DEARBORN, MI 48128-1491
(An eastern suburb of Detroit)
Phone: 313-593-5590
Hours: Tours offered all year Sun 1-4:30, and from April thru Dec M-F 10, 11, 1, and 2. Pool Restaurant open M-F 11 am to 2 pm. Estate closed Jan 1, Easter and Dec 25. Admission charged.

This was the home and estate of Henry Ford, founder and owner of the Ford Motor Co. Henry Ford was born in Dearborn and as he made his fortune he brought his home town along in the shadow of his success by building within the city limits the huge Rouge River factory complex and other Ford manufacturing facilities, the World Headquarters of the Ford Motor Co., the Henry Ford Museum and Greenfield Village, and ultimately his own home and estate, "Fair Lane". The house and grounds are open to the public and appear much as they did when the Ford family live here and entertained such world renowned people as President Herbert Hoover, Charles Lindbergh, the Duke of Windsor, Thomas Edison, Harvey Firestone and John Burroughs. The estate reflects the mechanical genius of Ford in that the main house has its own

"Fair Lane", Henry and Clara Ford's home in Dearborn, MI.

Michigan

phone system, a private laboratory, a water piano and a vacuum tube-operated hair dryer. On the grounds is a 20 car garage, a four-story power house and a dam with a small hydroelectric station. There are dining facilities on the ground that offer food prepared according to some of Clara Ford's favorite recipes. Each July "Henry Ford Day" is held here and each Christmas the mansion and grounds are decorated for the holiday season.

HENRY FORD MUSEUM & GREENFIELD VILLAGE

20900 Oakwood Blvd (Village Road & Oakwood Blvd)
DEARBORN, MI 48124
Phone: 313-271-1620
Hours: Daily 9-5. Closed Thanksgiving and Dec 25. Greenfield Village buildings closed Jan-Mar. Admission charged, group discounts available.

Henry Ford Museum & Greenfield Village is the world's largest indoor-outdoor museum spanning over 90 acres. Holdings include more than one million objects and 25 million historical papers. Henry Ford founded the museum and village in 1929 to show how far and fast America has come in technological achievements. In a brief moment of history, America was transformed from a farming society to a manufacturing society. Visitors are invited to take a look back at 300 years worth of American resourcefulness and innovation.

Nothing in the 20th Century has changed the face of American culture and lifestyle as much as the invention of the automobile. The most popular exhibit at the museum, "100 Years of the Automobile in American Life", showcases this transformation. It features a highway of 100 cars and trucks, part of the museum's 160-vehicle collection that is perhaps the finest in the world. Among the significant vehicles are the only existing 1886 Duryea Motor Wagon, the first production car in America; five presidential limousines, including the one in which President John F. Kennedy was assassinated in 1963; and an astonishing array of many makes and models significant to auto history, including one-of-a-kind concept cars. The exhibit also includes car memorabilia and cultural milestones of America's automotive past, including a classic 1946 diner, a tourist cabin, an original Holiday Inn room and a McDonald's sign flashing "15-cent Hamburgers" from 1960.

The Newest exhibit, "The Story of the Champion: Locomobile's Old 16", is a permanent multi-media experience that highlights the car that was pivotal in American automobile history— Locomobile's Old 16. Old 16 sped to victory at the race for the Vanderbilt Cup in 1908. The exhibit experience, designed to capture the excitement and intensity of the sideline of the race, employs a variety of techniques including lighting, graphics and sound blended with film. A major feature of the exhibit is a film produced by Academy Award-winning producer Sue Marx.

"Henry's Story" traces Henry Ford's development as an innovator and explores the impact of his work on his own life and on the world. Among featured artifacts are the 1886 Quadricycle, his

The Henry Ford Museum, Dearborn, MI.

first "horseless carriage", a huge Highland Park engine, one of the nine that powered the Ford Highland Park, Michigan plant from 1912 to 1930; Ford's watch repair tools, and a spinning wheel that was a gift from Mohandas Gandhi.

The 81-acre Greenfield Village is adjacent to the Henry Ford Museum. This collection of buildings celebrates the resourcefulness of, and tells the stories of, famous and not-so-famous Americans. In Greenfield Village you will find buildings and homes in which America's greatest inventions—the auto, airplane and light bulb—were developed. Part of its charm is in the incongruous conjuncture of famous inventors; only in Greenfield Village do the Wright Broth-

ers live around the corner from Thomas Edison's laboratory!

MOTORSPORT HALL OF FAME MUSEUM

43700 Expo Center Dr [Southwest corner of I-96 and Novi Rd (exit 162) at the base of the water tower] **NOVI**, MI 48375 (A northwestern suburb of Detroit) Phone: 248-349-7223 Hours: Daily 10-5. Admission charged.

This Hall of Fame, located in Novi's spacious Expo Center, honors outstanding personalities in auto, motorcycle, airplane and boat racing. Some of those honored in the museum include "Can-

The Motorsports Hall of Fame honors many famous racing personalities and has race cars on display.

nonball" Baker, Gen. Jimmy Doolittle, A. J. Foyt, "Big Daddy" Don Garlits, Phil Hill, Bill Muncey, Barney Oldfield and Richard Petty. The museum has several race cars, boats and motorcycles on display and plans to accumulate more. Vehicles of note on display include Bobby Unser's 1964 and 1965 Novi race cars, Kenny Bernstein's Budweiser funny car, Mark Donohue's 1970 Lola and Tom Kendall's 1990 Chevy Intrepid IMSA GTP race car. The museum has a gift and souvenir shop which offers many items of interest to racing fans.

Ron Watson is the company's president.

OAKLAND UNIVERSITY'S MEADOW BROOK HALL
(Historic home)
Walton Blvd & Adams Rd 3 miles west of Oakland University campus. **ROCHESTER**, MI 48063 (A northern suburb of Detroit) Phone: 810-370-3140

Hours: Guided tours daily at 1:30 and M-Sat at 10:30-5, July-Aug and daily during the Holiday Walk; Sun 1-5, rest of year. Closed holidays except in December when the mansion is decorated for the Christmas season. Admission charged.

This 100-room mansion was built in 1929 at the cost of $4 million by Matilda Rausch Dodge Wilson, the widow of John Dodge, the automotive pioneer. The home is lavishly decorated with needlepoint draperies, hand-carved paneling, priceless art treasures and a sculptured ceiling in the dining room. There are 24 fireplaces, a great hall, a ballroom and the grounds are beautifully landscaped.

PLYMOUTH HISTORICAL MUSEUM
155 S Main St
PLYMOUTH, MI (Western suburb of Detroit)

Meadow Brook Hall, the Dodge-Wilson mansion in Rochester, MI.

Phone: 313-455-8940
Hours: W, Thurs & Sat 1-4, Sun
205. Admission charged.

The Plymouth Historical Museum reflects the early history of Plymouth, MI with replicas of turn-of-the-century store fronts, period furniture, clothing and other "Then and Now" exhibits, many of which are hands-on displays. The museum has the world's only surviving Alter car manufactured in Plymouth in 1916-17.

End of Detroit Area △

▼ FLINT AREA (40 miles northwest of Detroit)

Flint is very much an automotive town, especially when it comes to General Motors. GM's founder, William Crapo Durant, was born in Flint and is honored by having one of the city's main plazas named in his honor, "The Durant Plaza". Other entities in Flint are also named in honor of Durant.

When I-69 enters Flint's city limits its name changes to Chevrolet-Buick Freeway and when I-475 enters, it becomes United Auto Workers (UAW) Freeway.

THE ALFRED P. SLOAN, JR.
MUSEUM
1221 E Kearsley St (In the Flint
Cultural Center Mall)
FLINT, MI 48503
Phone: 810-760-1169
Hours: M-F 10-5, Sat-Sun noon-5.
Closed holidays. Admission
charged.

This large museum honors the man who was the president of General Motors from 1923 to 1946, during which time General Motors became No. 1 in

143

The Alfred P. Sloan, Jr. Museum, Flint, MI.

the automotive industry. The museum has about 100 automobiles, including the world's largest collection of GM's experimental cars. Only about half of the collection is on display at any one time. Included in the collection is a reproduction of a 1904 Buick (Buick's first production year), a 1908 Buick Model 10 roadster, a 1914 Marr Cycle Car, a Flint-made 1915 Monroe roadster, a 1917 Stanley Steamer, a 1930 Marquette, a 1951 Buick XP-300, a 1956 Centurion sedan and many other unique and rare cars. There is an exhibit honoring William Crapo Durant, the founder of Gen-eral Motors Corp. and a native of Flint. The museum hosts a "Summer Auto Fair" each June and is the site of many other auto-related activities. There are displays of carriages, a large doll collection and an exhibit on health and the workings of the human body complete with a transparent anatomically correct manikin. A generous amount of information on the history and growth of Flint and Genesse County is on display and a large archive collection is available and open by appointment. The museum has a gift and souvenir shop with many interesting items for sale.

End of Flint Area △

VAN ANDEL MUSEUM CENTER OF THE PUBLIC MUSEUM OF GRAND RAPIDS
272 Pearl St NW
GRAND RAPIDS, MI 49504
(West-central part of the Lower Peninsula)
Phone: 616-456-3977

Hours: Daily 9-5 including holidays. Admission charged.

This fine city museum encompasses many subjects; the history of the city and surrounding areas, its rise as a manufacturing center, especially in the area of furniture manufacturing. In-

One of the antique cars at the Van Andel Museum is this 1913 Studebaker suspended from the ceiling.

cluded in the museum's collection are several automobiles including a Grand Rapids-built 1932 DeVaux convertible, a Grand Rapids-built 1920 Lorraine Touring Car, a 1904 Queen Runabout and a 1913 Studebaker which is suspended from the ceiling. There's an area of the museum called "Furniture City", a planetarium, a working carousel that the kiddies can ride, a cafe and a gift shop.

GILMORE-CLASSIC CAR CLUB OF AMERICA MUSEUM
6865 Hickory Rd
HICKORY CORNERS, MI 49060
(15 miles northeast of Kalamazoo)

Watch for the red barns. That's Gilmore-Classic Car Club of America Museum.

145

Phone: 616-671-5089
Hours: First Saturday in May thru last Sunday in Oct daily 10-5. Admission charged.

Here is a large museum consisting of seven red barns in a rural setting with approximately 300 cars on exhibit. The museum is closely associated with The Classic Car Club of America and is the site of nine classic car activities each summer. There are a number of Packards on display from 1905 to 1956, Cadillacs from 1903 to 1965, and Rolls-Royces from 1909 to 1938. The museum has a London double-decker bus and an extensive library of automotive literature, which is open by appointment. Other exhibits include the Walt Disney Gnomemobile movie set, steam toys and collections of brass lamps, horns and two collections of over 1000 hood ornaments.

RANDY HALLMAN SPECIALTY CARS (Restoration and dealer)
N 3792 US 2
IRON MOUNTAIN, MI 49801
(Western end of the Upper Peninsula on the Wisconsin state line)
Phone: 906-774-5897
Hours: M-F 8-5, Sat 9-noon, other times by appointment.

This is a restoration shop with the showroom. In the showroom are some 25 antique vehicles offered for sale, some, but not all, of them restored here. Hallman takes trades, offers appraisals, arranges financing and shipping, and delivers in their own truck.

In the restoration end of the business Hallman does partial or ground-up restorations and specializes in V-8 FORDs from 1932 to 1953.

Several of the antique REO automobiles on display at the R. E. Olds Transportation Museum in Lansing, MI.

R.E. OLDS TRANSPORTATION MUSEUM

240 Museum Dr
LANSING, MI 48933 (South-central part of the state)
Phone: 517-372-0529
Hours: M-Sat 10-5, Sun noon-5.
Closed Jan 1, Easter, Thanksgiving and Dec 25. Admission charged.

This is a large city-owned museum preserving the history of Lansing, and honoring automotive pioneer, Ranson E. Olds, a local resident who developed both the OLDSMOBILE and REO lines of automobiles. Some 30 vehicles are on display including many vehicles made by Olds' companies. The earliest vehicle is an 1897 Olds Motor Wagon; there are also 1901 and 1904 curved dash Oldsmobiles, a 1906 REO, a 1926 Star, the first Oldsmobile Toronado from 1966 and a Grand Rapids-made Bates automobile. The museum is housed in the former Bates Company administration building. Other exhibits include engines, a large collection of automobile wheels, machinery, vintage automobile advertising, a Lansing-built bicycle carriage and photos and memorabilia of the Olds family and home. There is a gift and souvenir shop in the museum.

SCHULTZ'S AUTO SALVAGE

10101 N Belsay Rd
MILLINGTON, MI 48746 (17 miles northeast of Flint)
Phone: 517-871-3165
Hours: M-Sat 9-5.

This salvage yard has about 500 vehicles and specializes in GENERAL MOTORS products from the mid-1960s and up. Customers may browse the yard.

Towing service available 24 hours. In business since 1978.

DODGE BROTHERS HOME MARKER (Historic site)

N Fifth St and Burns St
NILES, MI 49120 (Southwest corner of Michigan, just north of South Bend, IN)

John and Horace Dodge were born in Niles but their home no longer exists. It is, however, marked with a plaque noting its location. The brothers who founded the Dodge Brothers Motor Car Company learned the machinist trade here and went on to found, in 1914, the company that bore their name. They quickly acquired a reputation for producing a fine automobile and then, in 1920 just eleven months apart, died while still young men. Walter P. Chrysler bought their company in 1928 and Dodge has been a part of the Chrysler line ever since.

VICKSBURG CLASSIC CAR SALES

13562 Portage Rd (Just north of Vicksburg on Portage Rd)
VICKSBURG, MI 49097 (10 miles south of Kalamazoo Airport)
Phone: 616-649-1900
Hours: M and W 9-8, Tues, Thurs, F 9-6, Sat 9-4.

Vicksburg Classic Car Sales specializes in MUSCLE CARS, but carries some specialty cars and trucks too. You'll also find Corvettes, Mercedes-Benz and other quality cars. The company has a large selection. They take trades, help arrange financing, do appraisals and arrange shipping. Stop by and take a look.

147

▼ YPSILANTI AREA (10 miles southeast of Ann Arbor)

PRESTON TUCKER HOME
110 N Park
YPSILANTI, MI

This was Preston Tucker's home at the time he developed his first Tucker automobile. The car was hand-built by Tucker and several associates in the large carriage house behind the home. The home and carriage house are in private hands now so please drive by only and do not disturb the residents.

**YPSILANTI AUTOMOTIVE
HERITAGE COLLECTION and
MILLER MOTORS HUDSON
(Museum)**
110-12 E Cross St

(In historic Depot Town)
YPSILANTI, MI 48198
Phone: 734-482-5200
Hours: Thurs-F 2:30-6, Sat 10-4, Sun noon-5.

This museum is in the building of a former Hudson dealership and tends to favor Hudson automobiles and other cars with a Ypsilanti connection. There are many displays in the museum highlighting Ypsilanti's automotive history which is considerable for a town of its size. For example, Ypsilanti is the home of the famous Willow Run Plant, built by Henry Ford during World War II to mass produce B-24 bombers on an assembly-line basis. After the war Kaiser-Fraser automobiles were made at

A 1946 Hudson convertible on display at the Ypsilanti Automotive Heritage Collection. The convertible top mechanism was manufactured in Ypsilanti.

the Willow Run Plant. After Kaiser-Fraser passed into history the huge Willow Run plant continued to manufacture automotive components under a variety of owners and co-owners. One of the cars on display in the museum was built at Willow Run; the 1969 Chevrolet Corvair Monza. The museum also has information on Preston Tucker, a Ypsilanti native, and producer of the Tucker automobile. In the museum's collection is a fiberglass Tucker used in the movie "Tucker, The Man and His Car".

End of Ypsilanti area △

UPPER PENINSULA OF MICHIGAN: FORD INDUSTRIAL COMPLEX

During the 1920s Henry Ford invested heavily in the western sector of the Upper Peninsula of Michigan and created a small industrial empire to provide his huge network of factories in the Detroit area with wood products, iron ore, coal, limestone and silica. Much of that industry has declined today, but some of the old buildings and industrial sites can still be seen. Some are still operating businesses while others are abandoned. Visitors interested in seeing a particular side should inquire locally as to its location and accessibility.

The cities and operations involved in the Ford industrial complex are:

ALBERTA: A sawmill. The town of Alberta was named after Alberta Johnson, the wife of one of Henry Ford's brothers-in-law.

BIG BAY: A sawmill. Ford built a hotel named "Big Bay Lodge" in the 1920s which was later sold and renamed. Parts of the movie "Anatomy of a Murder" were filmed in the hotel. An exclusive residential area existed outside Big Bay known as "The Huron Mountain Club" where many Ford executives lived.

IRON MOUNTAIN, WI: A factory producing finished wood parts for Ford vehicles.

ISHPEMING: The "Blueberry" Iron Mine.

KINGSFORD: A sawmill, a hydroelectric plant, an automobile assembly plant and a chemical plant making charcoal briquettes out of sawdust.

L'ANSE: A large lumber operation including a sawmill and a factory producing wood parts for Ford vehicles. This was also the site of Ford's main dock facilities.

MICHIGAMME: The "Imperial" Iron Mine.

MUNISING: A sawmill.

PEQUAMING: At one time Ford owned this entire town. Located here was a sawmill and Ford's private summer home, known as "The Bungalow". He visited the area frequently. Today "The Bungalow" is a bed and breakfast inn.

SIDNAW: The site of Ford's first lumbering operation in the Upper Peninsula.

149

MINNESOTA

POLK COUNTY MUSEUM
US 2 East
CROOKSTON, MN 56716 (Northwestern part of the state on US 2)
Phone: 218-281-1038
Hours: Late May thru mid-Sept daily noon-5. Donation requested.

This is a local museum consisting of several buildings displaying hundreds of historical items representing life in the area during the late 19th Century and early 20th Century. Included in the displays are about half a dozen antique cars, several pieces of antique farm machinery and a Conestoga wagon.

BRINDLEY'S AUTO SALVAGE
Hwy 65 (Between Glennville and Gordonsville)
GLENNVILLE, MN 56036 (South-central Minnesota 12 miles south of Albert Lea)
Phone: 800-584-9458 or 507-448-2905
Hours: Flexible to suit visitors. Please phone.

This yard has been around since 1954 and is full of fine post-war vehicles, some 2500 in all. Half of them are between the 1930s and 1960s. There are orphans such as Willys, Hudsons, Nashes and Packards.

Convertibles and station wagons are plentiful. Old tractors, trucks and commercial vehicles can also be found at Brindley's. The yard is run by a father and son team, Dwaine and Shane Brindley. Customers may browse the yard.

AL'S AUTO PARTS (Salvage)
SR 10 East
(Four miles east of town)
GLYNDON, MN 56547 (Five miles east of Fargo, ND off I-94)
Phone: 218-498-2797
Hours: M-F 10-5, Sat noon-5, best to phone first.

Need a part for your Hupmobile, Crosley, Nash, Studebaker, Kaiser, Fraser or Hudson? If so, call Al's. He's got 'em on his 40-acre lot. Al's also has mnay vintage Fords, Chryslers and GM vehicles. There are some light trucks too, especially from the 1950s and 1960s. Al's was started in 1955 by Al Gardner and is now run by his son, Randy. Randy says car clubs are welcome to come and visit.

MINNESOTA'S MACHINERY MUSEUM
HANLEY FALLS, MN 56245 (Southwestern part of the state on SR 23)
Phone: 507-768-3522 or

507-768-3580
Hours: May thru Sept W-M 1-5,
closed Tues. Donations requested.

This is a six-acre complex comprising a large new museum building, a camp ground and parking. The museum building is full of vintage machinery and pioneer household items. Included in the displays are about a dozen antique cars, mostly American-made, from 1929 to the 1970s. Most of the cars are on loan from local collectors, so the displays change from time-to-time. During the second weekend in August each year when the town celebrates the Threshing Show and Old Timers Reunion some 50 to 70 vintage cars are on display in and around the museum. The museum also has a gift shop.

JOE'S AUTO SALES (Salvage and dealer)

5849 190th St East
HASTINGS, MN 55033 (22 miles southeast of downtown Saint Paul)
Phone: 800-359-0970 or 612-437-6787
Hours: M 9-noon and 1-5, Tues thru F noon-5, Sat 8-noon.

This yard has some 1000 vehicles and specializes in FORD and MERCURY cars and LIGHT TRUCKS. The ages of the vehicles range from 1939 to 1983 with the heaviest concentration being between 1955 and 1975. There is, however, a decent inventory of 1950-1955 Fords. Customers may browse the yard. Many parts are disassembled and stored inside and NOS parts are available too. Joe's does repair work, rebuilds some

parts and offers used and rebuilt cars for sale. In business since 1966.

CEDAR AUTO PARTS (Salvage)

1100 Syndicate St
JORDAN, MN 56011
(20 miles southwest of Minneapolis on US 169)
Phone: 800-755-3266 or 612-492-3300
Hours: M-F 8-6, Sat 8-2.

This yard has about 750 vehicles of various makes from 1949 to the present with many 1950s and 1960s vehicles. CORVETTEs are a specialty and there are a number of special interest cars and 4 X 4s. Other services offered include complete body work, transmission rebuilding, rebuilt parts and some new parts. Customers may browse the yard. In business since 1973.

DOUG'S AUTO PARTS (Salvage)

US 59 North
MARSHALL, MN 56258
(Southwestern corner of the state on US 59 and SR 23)
Phone: 507-537-1487
Hours: M-F 8-5.

This salvage yard of some 200 vehicles specializes in FORDs from 1932 to 1948 and CHEVROLETs from 1937 to 1968. They also have a good selection of big Ford and Chevy trucks from 1932 and up. There are other makes and years of vintage cars in the yard, and a complete line of new sheet metal panels is offered. In business since 1974.

▼ MINNEAPOLIS/SAINT PAUL AREA

ELLINGSON CAR MUSEUM
(Museum and dealer)

20950 Rogers Dr (Northwest of downtown Minneapolis off I-94 at the Rogers exit)

ROGERS, MN 55374 (Northwestern suburb of Minneapolis)

Phone: 612-428-7337

Hours: Museum, M-Sat 10-5, Sun 10-5; dealership M-Sat 10-5.

Admission charged to the museum.

This is a new educational museum covering the whole spectrum of the American automobile from its inception to current times. The museum's collection is arranged in chronological order beginning with the early teens. Unique settings have been devised to display the cars. For example, the cars of the 1930s are parked in a high school parking lot of the 1940s simulating cars that high school students might have owned in the 1940s. The 1950s display is a used car lot and the 1960s display is a replica of the Twin Cities Raceway dragstrip. Most of the cars are "everyday" cars that ordinary people drove. Other displays include operating juke boxes, a doll collection and a re-creation of a 1950s-era television repair shop. The Minnesota Historical Society assisted the museum by providing numerous photographs and correct-for-the-era signs, billboards and other memorabilia. The museum has a nice gift shop and Clarabelle's Ice Cream Parlor which is open Sat and Sun, and Memorial Day through Labor Day. In the

Yesterday's Auto of Minneapolis offers a selection of about 35 antique vehicles for sale from this multi-story location.

152

same building, and under the same management, is an antique vehicle dealership offering an average of about 40 cars for sale of mixed makes and years. The dealership will take trades, search for specific vehicles and help customers with financing and transportation. Ellingson's has its own restoration shop, but it is not open to the public.

YESTERDAY'S AUTO (Dealer)
2800 Lyndale Av South
MINNEAPOLIS, MN 55408

Phone: 612-872-9733
Hours: M-F 10-5, Sat 10-2.

This dealer of antique vehicles carries an average inventory of about 35 vehicles of mixed makes and models. They usually have a good selection of classic American, British cars and light trucks. Yesterday's Auto, which is owned and operated by Al Hagen, can arrange transportation and financing and provide appraisals. There is also a gift shop on the premises.

End of Minneapolis/Saint Paul Area △

**WINDY HILL AUTO PARTS
(Salvage)**
9200 240th Av NE
NEW LONDON, MN 56273
(40 miles southwest of Saint Cloud on SR 23)
Phone: 612-354-2201
Hours: Daily 8-5

This is a very large salvage yard covering 150 acres with some 7,000 vintage vehicles plus newer vehicles. Most are American-made cars and trucks from 1915 to the mid-1980s. There is also a good selection of military trucks. Customers may browse the yard and remove their own parts. In business since 1966. Finding the yard is not easy. You may want to phone for directions. Allan Bajari is the owner.

PINE RIVER SALVAGE
SR 371 North
PINE RIVER, MN 56474 (Near the geographic center of the state 30

miles north of Brainerd)
Phone: 800-642-2880 or
218-587-2700
Hours: M-Sat 8-6, Sun by appointment.

This salvage yard has over 3500 vehicles of mixed makes and body styles from 1940 to the 1980s. Mail orders welcome. Please send SASE. Customers may browse the yard.

SLEEPY EYE SALVAGE CO.
2 Miles South on SR 4
SLEEPY EYE, MN 56085 (38 miles west-northwest of Mankato)
Phone: 507-794-6673
Hours: M-F 8:30-6, Sat 8-4.

There are some 600 vehicles of mixed makes and models in this yard from the years 1937 to 1977. Towing available. Mail orders welcome. Customers may browse the yard. In business since 1968.

Minnesota

HOOKED ON CLASSICS (Dealer and restorer)

701 Jefferson Av SW (SR 25)
WATERTOWN, MN 55388
(25 miles west of Minneapolis/
Saint Paul)
Phone: 612-446-1950 or
612-955-2706
Hours: M-F 9-5, Sat 10-4, Sun
noon-4.

Classics, muscle cars, street rods, sports cars, restorables - all these can be found at Hooked on Classics. And, if you pick a restorable, the company can give you a partial or complete restoration job in their in-house restoration shop. Normally some 250 vehicles are available to choose from and the company can provide an inventory list. Hooked on Classics takes trades, helps arrange financing and shipping, provides appraisals, will search for the vehicle of your heart's desire and is well known for handling estate sales both in cars and parts. Daryl Kirt, the owner, welcomes car clubs and interested groups.

VALLEY MOTORS (Dealer)

1773 Mobile Dr (Hwy 61 South)
WINONA, MN 55987 (120 miles
southeast of Minneapolis/Saint
Paul on the Mississippi River)
Phone: 888-452-0859 or
507-452-0859
Hours: M-F 8-6, Sat 9-4

It is very pretty country in this part of Minnesota—on the Mississippi River. Here you will find Valley Motors, a dealer in affordable vintage vehicles. They carry about 40 cars in stock at all times in their indoor showroom and on an adjacent lot. Valley Motors provides many services; they do repairs, help arrange financing, offer appraisals, sell on consignment, take trades, provide an inventory list and will search for the vehicle of your choice. Also on display, and mostly for sale at Valley, is a nice assortment of automobilia; signs, books, models, etc. Free soda pop is always available and Tom Thorson, the owner, puts out free coffee and cookies for car clubs and groups when he knows they are coming by.

MISSISSIPPI

IMPERIAL PALACE AUTO COLLECTION

850 Bayview
BILOXI, MS 39530-1701
Hours: Daily 9 am to 11 pm.
Admission charged.
Phone: 800-436-3000

Here is part of one of the greatest auto collections in the world. Together with the main collection at the Imperial Palace Hotel in Las Vegas, NV, this collection of cars represents the best there is to see in the world of antique vehicles. Over 100 classic, special interest, exotic and historic vehicles are on display. And, as in Las Vegas, many of them are ex-celebrity cars. This is a

"must see" for car buffs visiting the area.

The Imperial Hotel is a huge resort complex offering gambling, fine dining, luxurious rooms and suites, top entertainment, a movie theater and space for meetings and conventions. The auto collection is on the second floor of the parking facility.

CLASSIQUE CARS UNLIMITED (Storage, appraiser, parts and museum)

PO Box 249 (Mail address)
   5 Turkey Bayou Rd (Location)
LAKESHORE, MS 39558
(Southern part of state on the Gulf near the Louisiana state line)
Phone: 800-543-8691 and
            228-467-9633
Hours: M-F 9-6, Sat by appointment.

This is a very unique operation that sells parts for 1960s, 1970s and 1980s LINCOLNs and THUNDERBIRDs and stores customers' cars in a climate-controlled storage facility. In a private museum are cars from the Karen A. Williams collection, many of which belonged to famous people. The museum, however, is open by invitation only.

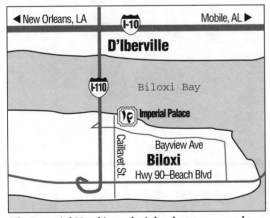

The Imperial Hotel is on the inland waterway and can been seen as one crosses the I-110 bridge.

MISSOURI

R & R SALVAGE
US 60
AURORA, MO (25 miles southwest of Springfield on US 60. Mail address Rt 2 Box 195G, Verona, MO 65769)
Phone: 800-426-HEMI(4364) or 417-678-5551
Hours: M-Sat 8-5.

This is claimed to be the world's largest MOPAR salvage yard. There are 2000 Chrysler-made vehicles in this yard ranging in age from the early 1950s to the late 1970s. There are considerable numbers of vehicles with B-bodies from the late 1960s and E-bodies used in Plymouth Barracudas and Dodge Chargers. R & R's yard covers 75 well-groomed acres and cars are segregated as to marque. Some restorable cars are available as are some parts for Hemi and 440 engines. Customers may browse the yard and remove some parts themselves. In business since 1976.

▼ BRANSON AREA

DUCK RIDES
(Amphibious vehicle tours)

In Branson, Missouri's music city, there are two companies that offer "Duck Rides". Rides, that is, in World War II-era amphibious vehicles known then as DUKWs (pronounced "ducks"). These vehicles were used extensively during the war to ferry men and supplies from ship to shore. Today they have other

It is a unique experience to be on a Ride The Ducks amphibious vehicle as it enters Table Rock Lake.

uses like taking people on amphibious joy rides. The companies offering these tours pick up passengers at their office locations and elsewhere around town, proceed through the streets of Branson and into Table Rock Lake. The "captain" narrates the history of the area and tells about the ducks during the 70-minute tours which includes a pass thru the Wilderness Safari Animal Park. The ducks are Coast Guard approved and well-equipped for safety on both land and lake.

The companies offering Duck Rides are:

RIDE THE DUCKS
2320 W SR 76W
BRANSON, MO 65616
Phone:417-334-5350
Hours: Mar-Dec Daily 8-dusk, closed Thanksgiving.

WATER DUCKS, INC.
1838 W SR 76W
BRANSON, MO 65616
Phone: 417-336-2111
Hours: Please phone.

End of Branson Area △

SMITH'S CLASSIC CARS (Dealer)
1636 Scott St (Business U.S 60)
DEXTER, MO 63841 (Southeastern corner of the state)
Phone: 314-624-0010
Hours: M-F 8-5, Sat vary.

Smith's Classic Cars carries between 20 and 30 antique vehicles for sale at all times in their spacious indoor showroom. Many of the vehicles are affordable cars from the 1950s and 1960s. An inventory list is available. Smith's will take trades, help arrange financing and transportation, do appraisals and sell on consignment. Car clubs are always welcome and each year, in July, an antique car auction is held here. Sherm Smith is the owner.

This is Smith's Classic cars of Dexter, MO.

Some 60 vintage cars are on view at Auto World Museum along with trucks, tractors, fire trucks and many other items of interest.

AUTO WORLD CAR MUSEUM
1920 N Bluff St
(Business US 54 North)
FULTON, MO 65251 (22 miles east-southeast of Columbia, MO)
Phone: 573-642-2080
Hours: Daily 10-4, closed Thanksgiving, Dec 25, Jan 1 and Easter.
Admission charged.

Here is one of the finest antique car collection in the Midwest. More than 60 vintage and special interest cars are on display in this former Walmart store. The oldest vehicle is an 1895 Haynes, only one of two surviving models. That's just one of nine pre-war - World War I that is - vehicles. Other cars of interest include a 1910 Kelsey 3-Wheel, a 1922 Wills St. Claire, a 1926 Pierce-Arrow 7-Passenger Touring Car, a Canadian-built 1930 Ford Roadster, a 1931 Marmon V-12 sedan, a 1941 Lincoln Mark 1 and a 1981 DeLorean.

Also on display are vintage fire trucks, tractors, model trains, Hit and Miss engines, old tools, a miniature carnival and lots of auto-related memorabilia. Convention space and meeting rooms available with ample free parking. The museum has a fascinating gift shop with many items of interest to old car buffs. Carmen W. McIntire is the museum's Executive Director.

J & M VINTAGE AUTO (Salvage)
Hwy B West (2 miles west of town)
GOODMAN, MO 64846
(20 miles south of Joplin)
Phone: 417-364-7203
Hours: M-Sat 8-5

This salvage lot has some 1200 cars and pickups from 1930 thru 1968. Mail orders welcome. Customers may browse the yard. Other services offered include towing and repair work. In business since 1973.

This 1941 Chrysler Royal 2-door coupe was purchased by Harry S Truman while he was still a Senator and used by him in Washington, DC throughout most of World War II.

HILLSIDE AUTO SALVAGE
Rt. 4 Box 179B
JOPLIN, MO 64801 (Southwest corner of the state on I-44 near the state line)
Phone: 417-624-1042
Hours: Tues-Sat 8-dark

This 200-vehicle yard specializes in FORDs from 1941 and in CAMAROs, CORVETTEs and FIREBIRDs from their first years of production thru 1981. Customers may browse the yard. In business since 1989.

HARRY S TRUMAN HISTORICAL SITES
INDEPENDENCE, MO
(An eastern suburb of Kansas City)

Independence, MO was the home of President Harry S Truman and several sites significant to his life and presidency are located within the city and are known collectively as the Harry S Truman Historic Sites. At two of these are automobiles that either belonged to him or were used by him as president.

At the Harry S Truman Library and Museum on the northeast edge of town at US 24 and Delaware St. are three cars: a 1941 Chrysler Royal 2-door purchased by Truman in Nov. 1940 and used by him in Washington, DC throughout most of the war when he was Senator and Vice President; a 1941 Chrysler Windsor 4-door sedan also purchased in Nov. 1940 and driven by his wife, Bess, throughout the war; and a 1945 Lincoln Cosmopolitan limousine which was one of the White House fleet cars during his presidency.

At the Truman Home on the corner of Truman Rd. and Delaware St. is a 1972 Chrysler Newport 4-door sedan. As one may guess, Truman was a "Chrysler man". This was the last car Truman purchased and his wife drove it until her death in 1982. It is still parked in their garage as it was on the day Bess died, and has 18,000 miles on the odometer. The car is kept cleaned, waxed and in running order.

159

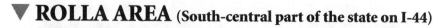

▼ ROLLA AREA (South-central part of the state on I-44)

MEMORYVILLE, U.S.A. (Museum, restorer, dealer)
US 63 North of Junction with I-44
ROLLA, MO 65401
Phone: 314-364-1810
Hours: M-F 9-6, Sat-Sun 9-5.
Closed Jan 1, Thanksgiving and Dec 25. Admission charged to museum.

This is a large antique car museum, restoration facility and art gallery. In the car museum there are some 60 cars on display including a 1902 Holsman, a 1907 Cadillac, a 1917 Army truck, a 1926 Stutz, a 1932 Mercedes and a 1937 Rolls-Royce P-3. Some of the cars are for sale. Other displays in the museum include works of art, antique engines, a variety of storefronts representing early 20th century Rolla and a large gift shop. Automobile storage and maintenance services are offered. Memoryville's restoration shop is one of the largest in the country and does partial to complete frame-off restorations on their own vehicles and those of others.

ROUTE 66 MOTORS (Dealer)
12661 Old Highway 66
(Exit 189 from I-44)
ROLLA, MO 65401
Phone: 314-265-5200
Hours: M-Sat 9-5.

This antique vehicle dealer offers a general line of affordable vehicles from their covered lot just off the Interstate on Old Highway 66. They carry about 35 vehicles in inventory most of the time and have an interesting Nostalgia Gift Shop. Route 66 Motors sells cars on consignment, does appraisals, takes trades, searches for specific vehicles for customers and provides an inventory list. Car clubs are welcome. Wayne Bales is the owner.

End Of Rolla Area △

PATEE HOUSE MUSEUM
12th & Penn Sts
SAINT JOSEPH, MO 64503 (45 miles north of Kansas City on the Missouri River)
Phone: 816-232-8206
Hours: Apr-Oct M-F 10-5, Sun 1-5. Feb-Mar. and in Nov Sat 10-5, Sun 1-5. Admission charged.

This is a fine local museum located in an elegant old hotel built in 1858 which is registered as a National Historic Landmark. The museum has many displays on the early history of the area including exhibits on the Hannibal-St. Joseph railroad, a "Gay Nineties" house, Pony Express artifacts and memorabilia on the famous outlaw, Jesse James. There is also a display of about a half dozen antique autos including an electric car built in St. Joseph. There are several restored buggies and wagons and a 1920s service station.

Singer Bobby Darin's 1960 custom-built Dream Car on display at the National Museum of Transport.

Patee House served as Headquarters for the Pony Express in 1860. Next door is Jesse James Home Museum where the outlaw was killed Apr 3, 1882. Now featured are artifacts found in his grave when it was exhumed for DNA tests in 1995 which proved that the body buried there actually was Jesse James.

▼ SAINT LOUIS AREA

NATIONAL MUSEUM OF TRANSPORT

3015 Barrett Station Rd
SAINT LOUIS, MO 63122-3398
Phone: 314-965-7998
Hours: Daily 9-5. Closed Jan 1, Thanksgiving and Dec 25. Admission charged.

This is a large county-owned museum, established in 1944, displaying a wide spectrum of transportation equipment. There are displays of locomotives and rail cars, aircraft, streetcars, buses, trucks, horse-drawn vehicles, boats and some 35 automobiles. Autos of interest include a 1901 St. Louis (built in St. Louis), a 1907 Anderson, a 1906 Model N Ford, a Chrysler turbine car and singer Bobby Darin's 1960 custom-built Dream Car. Many smaller exhibits are also in the museum all dealing with transportation.

End of Saint Louis Area △

Missouri

VERSAILLES AUTO SALVAGE
SR 52 at County Rd T (1.5 miles west of town)
VERSAILLES, MO 65084 (35 miles west-southwest of Jefferson City)
Phone: 314-378-6278
Hours: M-F 8-5, Sat 8-noon.

This is a large salvage lot with some 1900 vehicles, mostly American-made. The yard specializes in 1964 1/2 to 1973 MUSTANGs and CHEVELLEs. Other cars are available from the postwar era to the present. Customers may browse the yard. In business since 1988.

MONTANA

MONTANA AUTO MUSEUM

1106 Main St (In the former
Montana State Prison Complex)
DEER LODGE, MT 59722
(30 miles north of Butte on I-90)
Phone: 406-846-3111 or
406-846-3114
Hours: June-Aug daily 8 am-8 pm,
Sept-Nov and Feb-May schedule
varies. Closed Thanksgiving, Dec 25
and Jan 1. Admission charged.

You will find this unique museum
inside the walls of the former Montana
State Prison. There are 120 cars, light
trucks and other antique vehicles plus
some motorcycles, fire trucks and lots
of automobilia. The museum has an
extensive collection of old automobile-
related photographs and a large license
plate collection. Many of the cars are on
loan so the exhibits change from time-
to-time. The museum's vehicles partici-
pate in two annual events, the "Powell
County Prison Break Run" each June
and the "Chamber of Commerce Territorial Days". There is a nice gift shop and
free parking. Andrew Towe is the director of the former Prison Complex and
Jim Haas in the museum's curator.

▼ KALISPELL AREA
(30 miles southwest of Glacier National Park)

FENDER'S RESTAURANT
(Theme restaurant)

On US 93 (North of town)
KALISPELL, MT 59901
Phone: 406-752-3000
Hours: Daily 11 am to 11 pm

This is a unique restaurant with antique automobiles as its theme. Over the
entrance to the restaurant is a canopy
which is actually the hood of a 1941
Ford truck and the two front fenders of
the truck, painted red, are on either side
of the doorway. The story of these truck
parts and the reason for the restaurant's
name are printed on the menu. Inside
the restaurant, the walls are covered
with photos and memorabilia relating
to antique automobiles. In one part of
the restaurant there are booths made
from old car bodies. (See photo, next
page.) Customers actually dine inside
the automobiles and some of the seats
are complete with head rests.

The restaurant has a lounge, casino
and banquet rooms.

163

Montana

One of the booths in Fender's Restaurant made from old car bodies.

WISHER'S AUTO RECYCLING
(Salvage)
  2190 Airport Rd
  KALISPELL, MT 59901
  Phone: 406-752-2461
  Hours: M-F 8:30-5:30, Sat 8:30-1.

A salvage yard with some 1200 vehicles of mixed makes from 1950 to the late 1980s. Inventory list available at no charge. Services offered are towing, frame work, mechanical and body work and painting. In business since 1963.

End of Kalispell Area △

MEDICINE BOW MOTORS
(Salvage)
  5120 US 93 South
  MISSOULA, MT 59801 (West-central part of state on I-90)
  Phone: 406-251-2244
  Hours: M-F 8:30-6, Sat by appointment.

This company specializes in FORDs from 1946 to 1951. There are approximately 500 cars in the yard, about 75% of them Fords. The others are GM (20%) and Chrysler (5%). Medicine Bow has a good selection of pickups and light trucks. The company can also supply rebuilt flathead engines, lake pipes, spotlights, hubcaps, lowering kits and chassis for 1955-57 Chevrolets. Most of the inventory is computerized and visitors may browse the yard. In business under current management since 1993.

Medicine Bow Motors of Missoula, MT.

MIRACLE OF AMERICA MUSEUM
58176 US 93 South
POLSON, MT 59860 (Northwestern Montana at the south end of Flathead Lake)
Phone: 406-883-6804
Hours: Memorial Day thru Labor Day M-Sat 8-8, Sun 2-6. Rest of year M-Sat 8-5. Reasonable admission charged.

This museum has a wide selection of displays that includes something for everyone. Displays include military vehicles and weapons, logging equipment, pioneer and Indian artifacts, toys, dolls, musical instruments, old signs, posters, cowboy items, boats, farm equipment, horse-drawn vehicles and about a dozen antique cars and another dozen antique motorcycles. Miracle of America Museum has been called "Montana's Smithsonian" because of its wide variety of displays. Photo on following page.

DANIELS COUNTY MUSEUM AND PIONEER TOWN
7 County Rd
SCOBEY, MT 59263 (Northeastern corner of the state on SR 13)
Phone: 406-487-5965
Hours: Memorial Day thru Labor Day daily 12:30-4:30. Admission charged.

This is a restored pioneer town portraying early 20th-century homestead life in this part of Montana. There are many period antiques, furnishings, pieces of farming equipment, clothing and the like from that era. Also on display in the restored town are some 50 antique cars and trucks. Some of the vehicles are permanent but most are on loan from local collectors so the display is ever-changing. Each June, during Scobey's Pioneer Days Festival, a Threshing Bee is held at the museum. There is also a gift shop on the premises.

The entrance to the Miracle of America Museum, Polson, MT.

FLATHEAD SALVAGE AND STORAGE
495 SR 82
SOMERS, MT 59932 (Northwest part of the state at the north end of Flathead Lake)
Phone: 406-857-3791
Hours: M-F 8:30-5:30, Sat 9-1:30.

This is a 600-vehicle salvage yard and a storage facility for antique cars. The salvage yard specializes in vintage vehicles from 1932 to 1950 and in later models from 1970 and up. Towing service is available and customers may browse the yard. In business since 1984.

NEBRASKA

CARHENGE (Curiosity)
US 385 North
(2.5 miles north of Alliance)
ALLIANCE, NE 69301 (Northwest corner of the state)
Phone: 308-762-1520 (Alliance Chamber of Commerce)

This is an automotive interpretation of the famous Stonehenge monument in England. Old car bodies, mostly from the 1960s, have been up-ended and partially buried in a large circular pattern similar to the stones at Stonehenge. The rear ends of the cars have been buried so that the headlights all point skyward. Other car bodies have been placed horizontally across pairs of partially buried cars. Carhenge can be seen from the highway and visitors are free to park and wander around the site.

PLAINSMAN MUSEUM
210 16th St
AURORA, NE 68818
(70 miles west of Lincoln on I-80)
Phone: 402-694-6531
Hours: April 1 to Oct 31 M-Sat 9-5, Sun 1-5; rest of year daily 1-5.
Closed Jan 1, Easter, Thanksgiving and Dec 25. Admission charged.

This museum, consisting of two large buildings, is devoted to preserving the local and regional heritage of the plains. There are exhibits on the plains Indians, the early explorers and the first set-

This is Carhenge, Nebraska's version of the famous Stonehenge monument in England.

167

Part of the antique car collection at the Plainsman Museum, Aurora, NE.

tlers. In the museum are period homes including an original log cabin, a Sod house, a Victorian house and a prairie chapel. The homes are equipped with period furnishings. There are also about 20 antique autos and trucks including a 1908 Brush 2-passenger roadster, a 1908 Chalmers 5-passenger touring car, a 1908 Sears, a 1928 Willys, a 1932 Cadillac 4-door sedan and other automotive displays and memorabilia. Mrs. Gwen Allen is the museum's director.

EASTERN NEBRASKA AUTO RECYCLERS (Salvage)
Mile Marker 351 on US 34
ELMWOOD, NE 68349
(22 miles east of Lincoln)
Phone: 402-994-4555 and
402-475-1135
Hours: M-F 9-6, Sat 9-4.

There are approximately 1500 cars and trucks of mixed makes in this lot including many 1940s models. Other cars range in age up to the 1980s. Some cars are restorable. Towing and mechanical repair services offered and customer may browse the yard. In business since 1980.

OSINTOWSKI'S REPAIR (Salvage)
Rt 1, Box 107
GENOA, NE 68640
(70 miles northwest of Lincoln)
Phone: 402-678-2650
Hours: M-Sat 8-8.

This salvage lot of approximately 250 vehicles specializes in MOPAR products from the 1950s thru the 1970s and PONTIACs from the 1960s and 1970s. There are other makes of vehicles in the yard, mostly from the 1960s. Custom-

This rare 1903 American automobile is on display at the Stuhr Museum in Grand Island, NE.

ers may browse the yard. Towing available. In business since 1984.

STUHR MUSEUM OF THE PRAIRIE PIONEER

Junction US 281 and US 34
GRAND ISLAND, NE 68801
(90 miles west of Lincoln on I-80)
Phone: 308-385-5316
Hours: May-Oct 15 daily 9-5. Main building and Fonner Rotunda open Oct 16 thru Apr 30 M-Sat 9-5, Sat 1-5. Closed Thanksgiving and Dec 25. Admission charged.

This is a very large museum with some 50 buildings spread out over 200 acres of the Nebraska prairie. In the main two-story museum are many displays on the culture and times of the early settlers, an art gallery, a gift shop and a short orientation film narrated by the late Henry Fonda, a native of Grand Island. Within the complex is "Railroad Town", a completely reconstructed town depicting a typical Nebraska small town in the late 1800s and early 1900s. In the town is the house where Henry Fonda was born. Of interest to car buffs is the "Antique Farm Machinery and Auto Exhibit" building which houses some 200 vehicles of all types. Most of the autos are Fords and Chevrolets, with other cars of interest such as a 1903 American, a 1913 Overland touring car, a 1916 Pullman touring car, a 1922 Velie roadster and a 1926 Hudson two-door sedan.

HASTINGS MUSEUM
1330 N Burlington (US 281)
HASTINGS, NE 68901 (15 miles south of I-80 Interchange)
Phone: 402-461-4629 or
800-508-4629
Hours: M-Sat 9-5, Sun and holidays 1-5. Closed Jan 1, Thanksgiving, from noon on Dec 24 and all day Dec 25. Admission charged.

This museum has extensive displays on natural history, pioneer history, local Indian tribes, a 50-seat planetarium and a 200-seat IMAX large-screen-format theater. Among the many and varied exhibits are some dozen antique autos, most of them pre-World War I. Included in the collection is a 1903 Cadillac, a 1909 Sears Motor Buggy, a 1910 Brush and a 1912 Rauch and Lang Electric. There are also collections of clocks, coins, guns and dishes. The museum has an interesting gift shop.

PHELPS COUNTY HISTORICAL MUSEUM
US 183 North
HOLDREGE, NE 68949 (South-central part of the state 65 miles southwest of Grand Island)
Phone: 308-995-5015
Hours: M-Sat 10-5, Sun 1-5, closed major holidays.
Donations requested.

This is a local museum that traces the history of Phelps County from its pio-

neer days to the present. Included in the many displays are about a half dozen antique vehicles including a restored 1916 Ford Model T, a rare 1914 Republic truck, a 1920 Federal truck, a restored 1952 Buick and an old Dodge truck that was converted into a water-well driller. There are also horse-drawn vehicles on display and Cushman motor scooters. Harry Stuart is the director.

WARP PIONEER VILLAGE (Museum)
Junction of US 6/34 and SR 10
MINDEN, NE 69859 (South-central part of state 43 miles southwest of Grand Island)
Phone: 800-445-4447 or
308-832-1811
Hours: Daily 8-sundown.
Admission charged.

This is a very large museum and village complex with the main theme being "See How America Grew". Thousands of items are displayed in chronological order so that the visitor can see the progress and developments thru the years. There are displays of farm equipment, airplanes, toys, bicycles, motorcycles, electric lighting, musical instruments and an unusual exhibit of seven generations of rooms including kitchens, living rooms and bed rooms. There are also some 350 antique cars most of which are pre-1930. Unique among the automobiles is an 1897 Milwaukee steam car, a 1911 Little, a 1915 Woods Electric, a 1918 Case open touring car, a 1918 Franklin air-cooled brougham and a 1924 Meteor funeral car. To the rear of the large museum building is a

Watch for the unique signs that lead to the Harold Warp Pioneer Village.

SANDHILLS MUSEUM
440 Valentine St
(US 20)
VALENTINE, NE
69201 (North-central part of the state near the South Dakota border)
Phone: 402-376-3293
Hours: Memorial Day thru Labor Day daily 9-noon and 1-6. Rest of year by appointment. Admission charged.

This museum has a variety of exhibits including some 16 vintage cars. Included is a 1901 Locomobile steamer, a 1909 Maxwell, a 1912 Austro Daimler, a 1916 Paterson touring car and a 1924 Flint. Other displays include guns, hub caps, tools, machinery, mills, jukeboxes, Regina music boxes, household items and freak animals. Mrs. G. M. Sawyer is the curator.

pioneer village which includes a 19th-century general store, a Pony Express station, a railroad depot, a working steam powered carousel and several other interesting buildings. A part of the complex, and adjacent to it, are a motel, restaurant and campground. In the museum is a gift shop with many interesting items.

NEVADA

These two restored antique GMC trucks are part of the sizeable collection of antique vehicles at the Ponderosa Ranch.

PONDEROSA RANCH

100 Ponderosa Ranch Dr (SR 28)
INCLINE, NV 89450 (North end of Lake Tahoe)
Phone: 702-831-0691
Hours: May-Oct daily 9:30-5.
Admission charged.

This is a western theme park build around the original television set of the ranch house on the long-running television show "Bonanza". The "Bonanza" house is open to the public. Other buildings in the park consist of an old time saloon, general store, mystery mine, museum, petting zoo, playground, kiddyland and other attractions. Over 50 antique cars and trucks are parked around the grounds and in sheds. At the northern end of the park is a significant collection of military vehicles in an open lot. Antique cars of interest include a restored 1912 Cadillac touring car, a 1927 Essex boat-tail roadster, a 1913 Oakland touring car, a Czech-made 1931 Tatra limousine, a 1917 Autocar paddy wagon, a 1927 Whippet 4-dr sedan, a 1915 Pierce-Arrow Doctor's Car, a 1912 IHC Highwheeler and a 1916 Studebaker hearse. The park has several restaurants and gift and souvenir shops.

AUTO EXHIBITION HALL (Museum)
Laughlin's Riverside
Resort Hotel & Casino
LAUGHLIN, NV
(Southernmost tip of Nevada
on the Colorado River)
Phone: 800-227-3849 or
702-298-2535
Hours, Auto Exhibition Hall: M-F 9
am-10 pm, Sat-Sun 9 am-1 pm

This fine collection of antique
vehicles will be found on the third floor
of Laughlin's Resort Hotel & Casino.
There are some 70 cars in the collection
including an 1886 Benz replica, a
DeLorean, Rolls-Royces, Duesenbergs,
a Muntz and many other interesting
cars. There is also a collection of vintage motorcycles. Some of the cars are
on loan and a few are for sale. One car
of note is their 1965 Mustang, a one-off
prototype reportedly built by Ford
Motor Co. for the James Bond film
"Goldfinger". It is painted with gold-
fleck paint. Mark Osborn is the
museum's curator.

▼ LAS VEGAS AREA

CLASSIC & COLLECTIBLE CARS (Dealer)
3111 S Valley View, Suite W-103
LAS VEGAS, NV 89102
Phone: 702-873-2222
Hours: M-F 10-5, Sat 10-2.

This antique car dealer offers a wide
variety of collectible cars from their indoor showroom. Most cars are in the
affordable range and there is an average of some 20 vehicles on display at all
times. An inventory list is available. The
company will buy cars, sell on consignment, take trades, arrange transportation and do appraisals. Owners are
Michael and Larry Nicholl.

GR8AUTO (Dealer)
3744 Boulder Hwy
LAS VEGAS, NV 89121
Phone: 702-457-4000
Hours: M-Sat 10-6

There is a nice mix of clean and rust-
free vintage vehicles here at Gr8auto in
the affordable range that most people
can appreciate. The company carries
about 40 cars in inventory at all times
in their showroom and on an adjoining
lot. They take trades, sell on consignment, arrange financing, search for specific vehicles and do appraisals. Tom
Calabrese is the owner and likes to see
car clubs come by.

IMPERIAL PALACE AUTO COLLECTION
Imperial Palace Hotel
Fifth Floor of the Parking Terrace
3535 Las Vegas Blvd South
LAS VEGAS, NV 98109
Phone: 702-731-3311
Hours: Daily 9:30 am-11:30 pm.
Admission charged.

This is truly one of the world's great
car collections. The Imperial Palace Collection has some 700 of the finest automobiles in existence with about 200 on

173

display in their spacious museum. The cars are rotated constantly so the displays are ever-changing. The vehicles in the museum are arranged in a gallery-like setting. One can view Duesenbergs, Mercedes, Rolls-Royces, Cadillacs, a Tucker, a 1910 Thomas Flyer, a 1907 Franklin Type D Landaulet, a 1932 Stutz convertible and many other rare and historic vehicles. Within this collection is literally a room full of Duesenbergs. The Duesenberg Room holds the world's largest collection of Model J Duesenbergs and the museum is constantly looking for more of them. There is also a collection of cars belonging to U.S. Presidents lined up in what the museum calls "President's Row". In addition to cars there are antique fire trucks, buses, motorcycles, horse-drawn carriages and many exhibits of auto memorabilia. A large gift shop sells a wide variety of auto-related items and an automotive library, containing some 500 pieces, is open to the public.

The Imperial Palace in Las Vegas, NV has one of the world's great auto collections with numerous celebrity cars and an outstanding collection of Duesenbergs.

Outstanding in the collection are the large number of celebrity cars, some of which are:

- Max Baer's Duesenberg
- Jack Benny's 1910 Maxwell
- James Cagney's 1930 Duesenberg
- Al Capone's 1925 Packard Dual Windshield touring car and his 1930 Cadillac
- Enrico Caruso's 1920 Hudson
- Cecil B. DeMille's 1931 Cadillac V-12 Towncar
- Jack Dempsey's 1926 McFarlan
- Father Divine's Duesenberg
- President Dwight D. Eisenhower's 1952 Chrysler Imperial limousine parade car
- W. C. Field's 1938 Cadillac
- Emperor Hirohito's 1935 Packard
- Adolph Hitler's custom-built 1939 770K Mercedes-Benz
- President Herbert Hoover's 1929 Cadillac
- Howard Hughes' 1954 Chrysler
- President Lyndon Johnson's 1964 Cadillac limousine
- President John F. Kennedy's 1962 bubbletop Lincoln limousine
- Liberace's 1981 Zimmer
- Gen. Douglas MacArthur's 1942 Packard 120 Clipper Custom
- Tom Mix's 1937 Cord
- Marilyn Monroe's 1955 Lincoln Capri convertible
- Claretta Petacci's 1939 Alfa Romeo.

This is one of the cars in the Liberace Museum, his Bicentennial Rolls-Royce.

She was Mussolini's mistress and he gave her this car.
- King Pradjadhipok's (of Siam) 1928 Delage limousine
- Elvis Presley's 1976 Cadillac
- President Franklin D. Roosevelt's 1936 Ford convertible with hand controls and his 1936 unrestored 1936 Cadillac complete with bullet holes...the result of an assassination attempt
- Billy Rose's Duesenberg
- Lord Rothschild's 1930 Cadillac
- President Harry S Truman's 1950 Lincoln
- Paul Whiteman's Duesenberg
- Phillip W. Wrigley's Duesenberg

Not all of these cars will be on display at any one time. They are often on tour or in storage.

KEN'S AUTO WRECKING (Salvage)
5051 Coppersage St
LAS VEGAS, NV 89115
Phone: 702-643-1516
Hours: M-F 10-4, Sat 10-1.

This salvage lot has about 360 vehicles and specializes in AMC products from 1953 thru 1980, THUNDERBIRDs from 1958 to 1978 and CHRYSLER products from 1956 to 1980. Ken's also rebuilds motors for restorations. Customers may browse the yard. In business since 1979.

K & L AUTO WRECKING (Salvage)
4540 Hammer Lane (Northeast side of town)
LAS VEGAS, NV 89115
Phone: 702-644-5544
Hours: M-F 8-5, Sat 8-3.

Nevada

This six-acre 700-vehicle yard specializes in CHEVROLETs and PONTIACs from 1953 thru 1972. In addition there are some Fords also in the lot. Most of K & L's business comes from walk-in customers visiting Las Vegas. Customers must be escorted thru the lot and K & L personnel will remove all parts. In business since 1984.

LARRY'S AUTO WRECKING (Salvage)

4160 Studio St (Just off I-90 near Nellis Air Force Base)
LAS VEGAS, NV 89115
Phone: 702-644-1671
Hours: M-F 8-5, Sat 8-noon.

This salvage yard has about 600 vehicles of both domestic and imported makes. All vehicles are 10 years old or older and many are rust-free thanks to the dry Nevada climate. Many items such as glass, taillights, engines and electrical components have been removed and are stored inside. Customers must be escorted thru the yard and Larry's personnel will remove parts. In business since 1987.

THE LIBERACE MUSEUM

1775 E Tropicana Av
LAS VEGAS, NV 89109
Phone: 800-626-2625 or 702-798-5595

Hours: M-Sat 10-5, Sun 1-5, closed Jan 1, Thanksgiving and Dec 25. Admission charged.

This museum is devoted to the memory of the late entertainer, Liberace. Among the many items on display that belonged to this popular showman are about half a dozen of his personal cars including a customized Duesenberg covered with rhinestones. Most of the cars were used in his performances. There is also a collection of rare pianos and Liberace's elaborate costumes. The museum has an elegant gift shop selling many Liberace-related items including copies of some of his glitzy jewelry.

SOUTHWEST AUTO WRECKING (Salvage)

4510 E Smiley Rd
LAS VEGAS, NV 89115
Phone: 800-267-1609 or
702-643-1771
Hours: M-F 8-4:30, Sat 8-2:30.

This is a very large salvage yard with some 4500 vehicles; most of which are domestic makes from the 1980s and up. Southwest is a good source for glass and can offer new sheet metal panels and accessories. Customers may browse the yard. In business since 1981. Jon Berry is the general manager.

End of Las Vegas Area △

WHISKLY PETE'S HOTEL-CASINO

Off I-15 at the Nevada/California state line
PO Box 19119

PRIMM, NV 89019-9119
Phone: 800-FUN-STOP
Hours: Open 24 hours a day,
7 days a week.

176

The Bonnie & Clyde death car is on display at Whiskey Pete's Hotel-Casino 24 hours a day, 7 days a week.

In the lobby of this Hotel-Casino is the famous "Bonnie and Clyde" death car, a 1934 Ford V-8 four-door in which the two notorious outlaws were ambushed and killed. The car is original and unrestored and has 167 bullet holes in it.

NATIONAL AUTOMOBILE MUSEUM: The Harrah Collection

10 Lake St South (Near downtown Reno)
RENO, NV 89501
Phone: 702-333-9300
Hours: M-Sat 9:30-5:30, Sun 10-4, closed Thanksgiving and Dec 25.
Admission charged.

This is one of the most famous automobile collections in the world. It was begun by the late Reno businessman William F. "Bill" Harrah, who collected and restored antique, classic and special interest autos for over 40 years in his own collection and restoration shop in nearby Sparks, NV. After Harrah's death a generous selection of the most rare and unique vehicles were donated to the National Automobile Museum (The Harrah Collection). Today there are over 220 cars in the museum which are displayed in galleries and period street scenes depicting each quarter of the 20th Century. The visitor will see a 1911 Maxwell (Bill Harrah's first collector car), a 1906 Adams Farwell, a famous 1907 Thomas Flyer that was the winner in the 1908 New York to Paris race, a 1911 Franklin Averell Special that got 83.5 miles per gallon, a 1913 K-R-I-T that used a swastika on its radiator emblem, a Tucker and many cars that once belonged to famous people. The museum also has a multimedia theater, changing exhibits, a restaurant and a world-renowned automotive research

The National Automobile Museum, Reno, NV.

library, which is accessible only by correspondence. There is an interesting and well-stocked gift shop with many antique car-related items.

Some of the celebrity cars on display at the National Automobile Museum are:

- Jack Benny's 1923 Maxwell
- James Dean's 1948 Mercury used in his most famous movie "Rebel Without a Cause"
- Douglas Fairbank's and Mary Pickford's 1928 Model A Ford
- Don "Big Daddy" Garlits' "Wynn's Charger" dragster
- Bill Harrah's "Jerrari", a 4-WD Jeep Wagoner with a Ferrari engine
- Rust Heinz's (of the H. J. Heinz family) custom-built 1938 Phantom Corsair
- Al Jolson's 1933 V-16 Cadillac All-Weather Phaeton
- John F. Kennedy's 1962 Lincoln convertible
- Ed "Big Daddy" Roth's 1961 "Beatnik Bandit" hot rod
- Frank Sinatra's 1961 Ghia
- Lana Turner's 1941 Chrysler
- John Wayne's 1953 Corvette that he gave to his friend Ward Bond

NEW HAMPSHIRE

**LANE'S GARAGE & AUTO BODY
(Salvage)**
SR 106
LOUDON, NH 03301
(7 miles northeast of Concord)
Phone: 603-783-4752
Hours: M-F 8-6, weekends by
appointment.

This salvage yard handles all makes
of cars from 1930s thru 1960s. Some are
restorable or can be used for parts cars.

**LUSSIER'S CORVETTE CITY
(Dealer and parts)**
1000 2nd St
MANCHESTER, NH 03102
(Southern New Hampshire, 60
miles north of Boston, MA)
Phone: 800-GET-A-VETTE or
603-623-1771

Hours: M-Thurs 9-8, F 9-6,
Sat 9-5, Sun noon-5.
Closed major holidays.

This is a large dealer specializing in
all years of CORVETTEs and MUSCLE
CARS. There are as many as 80 vehicles
in inventory at any one time in Lussier's
indoor showroom and adjacent lot.
Lussier's welcomes other makes of antique vehicles as trade-ins. They sell cars
on consignment, can provide an inventory list and have a computerized "Vehicle Locating Service". They can also
arrange financing, transportation and
do appraisals. Lussier's has a full service
department and offers parts for Corvettes and muscle cars. Car clubs are always welcome. The owner is George
Lussier and Kevin Mills is the General
Manager.

NEW JERSEY

SPACE FARMS ZOO AND MUSEUM
218 County Rd 519 (in
Beemerville)
BEEMERVILLE, NJ 07461
(Northern tip of the state)
Phone: 973-875-5800
Hours: May thru Oct daily 9-5.
Admission charged.

This 100 acre complex houses a zoo
with over 500 animals, including a petting zoo, an agricultural museum with
antique farm equipment, sleighs, wagons and Indian artifacts, and an antique
car museum. In the car museum are
some 50 vintage cars, mostly pre-1940,
and a collection of antique motorcycles
and bicycles. Vehicles of interest include
a 1903 Orient, a 1906 Buick Roadster, a
1907 International Auto Buggy, a 1911
Ford Torpedo Runabout, a 1925 Jewett
sedan, a 1928 Marmon Roosevelt, a
1931 Kissel 4-door sedan, a 1931 Willys-
Knight Victorian Coupe and a 1954
Kaiser Darrin. The museum also has a
well-stocked gift shop and a picnic area.

BLACK TIE CLASSICS
(Dealer and restorer)
Milford and Atlantic Av
BERLIN, NJ 08009
(A New Jersey suburb of Camden)
Phone: 609-768-1900
Hours: M-F 9-7, Sat 9-5.

You can buy an antique car here, or
have one restored, or both. Black Tie
Classics has an inventory of about 35
vintage vehicles of mixed makes for sale
and can provide partial or total restorations. They sell on consignment, take
trades, provide an inventory list, arrange
financing and shipping, do appraisals,
search for specific vehicles and rent auto
storage space. They will also lease cars
and, for special occasions, provide a
driver. John J. Bertino, the owner, says
car clubs are always welcome.

COBWEB COLLECTIBLES
(Literature & ephemera)
9 Walnut Av
CRANFORD, NJ 07016
(5 miles west of Elizabeth off
Garden State Pkwy, exit 137)
Phone: 908-272-5777
Hours: M-Sat 11-5. Please phone
ahead, shop is sometimes closed
when the owner is attending swap
meets, etc.

This collectibles store has a large
stock of auto memorabilia such as
books, postcards, toys, gasoline globes
and promotional material. They also
have a collection of auto related sheet
music, and offer advice and expertise in
this unique field.

THE STABLE, LTD. (Dealer)
217 Main St
GLADSTONE, NJ 07934 (25 miles
east of downtown Newark)
Phone: 908-234-2055
Hours: M-F 9-6, Sat 9-5

JAGUARS... and other fine European cars are the big thing at The Stable. You'll find between 50 to 60 top-quality vintage machines here to choose from. An inventory list is available upon request. The company does its own service work and service work for others, and they stand behind their work. The Stable will take trades, sell on consignment, provide appraisals, assist in arranging financing and shipping, search for specific vehicles, lease cars and provide storage. Car clubs are most welcome. Tom Rossiter is the president.

KUSER FARM MANSION AND PARK (Historic home)
390 Newkirk Av
HAMILTON, NJ 08610
(Eastern suburb of Trenton)
Phone: 609-890-3630
Hours: May thru Nov Thurs-Sun 11-3; Feb thru Apr Sat-Sun 11-3. Last tour starts at 2:30 pm. Free.

This is the 22-room summer "Country Home" and estate of the late Fred Kuser, a prominent businessman. The Kuser family was instrumental in forming the Fox Film Corporation which, after a merger, became 20th Century-Fox. The Kuser family also manufactured the Mercer Motor Car along with the Roebling family.

Most of the mansion's rooms are open to the public including Kuser's private projection room. Scattered throughout the mansion are photos and memorabilia of the Mercer Motor Car Company. The formal gardens and the many buildings on the 22 acres can be visited on the outside by taking the self-guided walking tour. Call regarding holiday closings and the 30+ educational events and attractions, in addition to the Victorian Christmas house tour and an outside Winter Wonderland for children of all ages.

GOLDEN CLASSICS (Museum & Dealer)
1165 SR 88 West
LAKEWOOD, NJ 08701 (18 miles
southwest of Long Branch)

Golden Classics of Lakewood, NJ.

Phone: 732-370-2323
Hours: M, Thurs & F 9-9, Tues,
W & Sat 9-6.

This is one of the largest antique car dealers on the east coast offering up to 150 classic, exotic and antique cars for sale in their new, modern showroom. All of their cars are kept indoors. Celebrity cars are sometimes available. Golden Classics buys cars, sells on consignment, arranges financing and transportation and has a substantial business in leasing antique cars. The company has a facility for light restoration work and an interesting gift shop. They also have about 5 antique car auctions a year and about 10 car shows. Nick Demartino is the president and Mark Demartino is the vice president.

ANTIQUE CARS, PARTS AND TRAINS (Dealer, parts, literature)

Second and Broad Sts
MILLVILLE, NJ 08332
(South-central part of the state
35 miles west of Atlantic City)
Phone: 609-825-0200
Hours: Summer M-Sat 9-6,
Winter M-Sat 9-5.

This dealer specializes in the buying and selling of CORVETTEs. They also offer replacement parts and literature on those vehicles, take trades, arrange transportation and do appraisals. In addition to antique cars, the company buys and sells Lionel and American Flyer model trains and offers automobilia, a general line of antiques, books and model cars.

OLD TIME AUTOS, INC./MEMORY LANE (Dealer, restorer, parts)

800 N Blackhorse Pike
WILLIAMSTOWN, NJ 08094
(15 miles SE of Camden off
Atlantic City Expressway)
Phone: 609-875-5500
Hours: M-F 10-7, Sat 10-6

There is over 100 vintage vehicles here at Old Time Autos, both in their showroom and on an adjacent lot. Cars are of mixed makes and models from the 1920s and up, and are in the affordable category for the average collector. An inventory list is available. The company does service work and partial or full restorations and carries a large inventory of used parts. They take trades, sell cars on consignment, assist in financing, offer appraisals and search for desired vehicles. Car clubs are welcome. Check with Gary Senior, the owner.

NEW MEXICO

 New Mexico is one of the states that has made an effort to preserve parts of historic highway US 66. I-40 parallels US 66 in many places and the old stretches of US 66 are currently being used as frontage roads, especially in eastern New Mexico near the Texas state line. In Gallup the city fathers have made efforts to preserve many of the old buildings along the section of US 66 that ran thru their town. This is being done both for historical preservation and because the buildings and road are often used by the movie and TV industries as filming locations.

NORTH 54 SALVAGE, INC.
US 54 North
PO Box 387
ALAMAGORDO, NM (South-central part of the state 80 miles

north of El Paso, TX)
Phone: 800-624-4941
Hours: M-F 8-5

It is hot and dry in this part of the country and car parts, along with many other things, last a long time. You will find that true with parts from North 54 Salvage. They have about 2000 vehicles on their 25-acre lot from the late 1930s to the mid 1970s. They have a goodly number of convertibles, hardtops, wagons and pickups. North 54 Salvage also has hard-to-find early air conditioning parts from the 1950s. Furthermore, there's an inventory of large trucks and military vehicles from the 1950s and 1960s. Customers may roam the yard and remove their own parts with permission. Important! Wear proper attire for tall grass and desert conditions. George Smith and his pretty daughter, Amy, run the show here, partner!

▼ ALBUQUERQUE AREA

DISCOUNT AUTO PARTS (Salvage)
4703 Broadway SE
ALBUQUERQUE, NM 87105
Phone: 505-877-6782
Hours: M-F 8-5:30, Sat 8-1.

This is a large salvage yard with approximately 1400 vehicles specializing in VOLKSWAGENs from day-one to the present. New Volkswagen parts also offered. Customers may browse the yard.

New Mexico

J & R VINTAGE AUTO MUSEUM
(Museum and dealer)
3650A SR 528 (1/2 mile south of Hwy 44 on Hwy 528)
RIO RANCHO, NM 87124 (A northern suburb of Albuquerque)
Phone: 505-867-2881
Hours: Summer M-Sat 10-6, Sun 1-5, winter M-Sat 9-5, Sun 1-5.
Admission charged to the museum.

Here is an interesting place. In the front of the building is a large automobilia store selling die cast models, books and many other auto-related items. In the back is a 60-car museum, and out further—in the back yard—are vehicles awaiting restoration by J & R's own restoration shop. Of the cars on display about 40 of them are for sale. As the cars come and go, the display is ever-changing. On permanent display are some rare machines such as a 1926 Wills-St. Claire and a 1917 White. Cushman motorscooters and construction equipment can also be seen in the museum. Car clubs are always welcome here and the manager is Bobby Roy.

End of Albuquerque Area △

DEMING LUNA MIMBRES MUSEUM
301 S Silver St
DEMING, NM 88030 (Southwest corner of the state on I-10)
Phone: 505-546-2382
Hours: M-Sat 9-4, Sun 1:30-4.
Closed Thanksgiving and Dec 25.
Donations requested.

This museum contains exhibits pertaining to the history of the southwest and the Mimbres Indians. In the museum can be seen pioneer artifacts such as clothing, household items, quilts, dolls, mounted animals, room furnishings and a re-creation of a 19th-century funeral home. Artifacts from the Mimbres Indians include pottery, clothing, baskets, tools and weapons. The museum also has a small collection of antique vehicles including a Model T Ford, a 1907 REO, an American LaFrance fire truck and 1943 World War II fire truck. They plan to expand in this area and eventually build a separate building housing transportation equipment.

WAR EAGLE AIR MUSEUM
2012 Airport Rd
(Exit 11 from I-10, go west)
SANTA TERESA, NM 88008
(A western suburb of El Paso, TX)
Phone: 505-589-2000
Hours: Tues-Sun 10-4.
Admission charged.

This is a fine and spacious air museum dedicated to preserving and restoring military aircraft from the World War II and Korean War eras. Mixed in with the museum's many aircraft and other displays are more than a dozen antique autos of interest. Included in the auto collection is a 1935 Auburn

This is the War Eagle Museum's immaculately restored 1936 Packard Super 8 Roadster.

Boattail, a 1908 Overland, a 1958 Cadillac Biaritz, a 1942 Cadillac torpedo body, a 1936 Packard Super 8 Roadster and others. All of the cars are in running condition. The War Eagle Museum has a large gift shop offering auto-related, air-related and military-related items. Bob Magruder is the gift shop manager and Skip Trammell is the director of the museum.

CALLAHAN'S AUTO MUSEUM
    410 Cedar St
    TRUTH OR CONSEQUENCES,
    NM 87901 (65 miles north-
    northwest of Las Cruces on I-25)

Phone: 505-894-6900
Hours: Daily 9-5, but please phone ahead. Donations requested.

This is a privately-owned museum displaying the auto collection of Bill and Betty Callahan along with cars on loan from others. Included in the collection is a 1927 Packard, 1928 Dodge, 1928 Ford Model A touring car, 1928 Durant, 1935 De Soto Airflow and a 1950 Chrysler limousine once used by the Governor of New Mexico. Other displays include a large collection of toy cars and busses and other items of automobilia.

NEW YORK

TUCKER'S AUTO SALVAGE

On US 11 (Just east of its Junction with SR 122)
BURKE, NY 12917 (Northeastern corner of the state near the Canadian border)
Phone: 518-483-5478
Hours: M-F 8-5, Sat 8-noon.

There are over 1000 vehicles in this upstate New York salvage yard including many STUDEBAKER cars and trucks. The other vehicles in the lot consist of a variety of makes from post-WW II to current. Many parts have been removed and are stored in a warehouse. Some NOS parts are available and Tucker's does mechanical repairs, body work & sand-blasting. Customers may browse yard. In business since 1973.

CORVETTE AMERICANA
HALL OF FAME (Museum)

SR 38 South (3 miles south of Cooperstown)
COOPERSTOWN, NY 13326 (50 miles west of Schenectady at the southern end of Lake Otsego)
Phone: 607-547-4135
Hours: June 28 thru Labor Day daily 9:30-8; Feb 12 thru June 27 and after Labor Day to Nov 30 daily 9:30-6. Closed Thanksgiving and rest of year. Admission charged.

This 30,000 sq. ft. museum traces the history of the CORVETTE automobile from its beginning to the present. The museum has 35 Corvettes displayed in chronological order and each car is built into a color co-ordinated Hollywood-type set of a famous American landmark such as Mt. Rushmore, the Alamo, Gateway Arch and Niagara Falls. At each display there is a multi-media show with music, TV, movies, sports, news events, commercials and personalities corresponding with the year of the car. Visitors walk thru a time tunnel and into time capsules representing a particular year. The museum has a large display room featuring every Corvette sales brochure, postcard, plastic model, magazine, ad, promo model and owner's manual ever made. There are also memorabilia displays of pop culture celebrities such as the Beatles, James Dean, Marilyn Monroe and others. Yet another room is an old-time theater displaying cars featured in the Corvette-oriented movies "Corvette Summer" and "Death Race 2000". Behind the theater is a re-creation of the famous Indy 500 racetrack with Corvette pace cars of 1978, 1986 and the Indy Festival car of 1990.

The Indy Festival car is one of the displays at the Corvette Americana Hall of Fame in Cooperstown, NY.

CLASSIC CAR CENTER (Dealer)
5110 Camp Rd
HAMBURG, NY 14075 (Southern suburb of Buffalo)
Phone: 716-649-6400 or 716-662-3160 or 716-445-1811
Hours: M, W & F 1-9, Tues, Thurs & Sat 10-6\

There are four showrooms full of cars at this vintage car dealer. They carry about 60 cars in inventory at all times and can provide an inventory list to interested parties. Cars are a general mix from the brass era to the latest exotic. Classic Car Center will take trades, sell on consignment, arrange financing and transportation, provide appraisals and search for specific vehicles. The company sponsors two auctions annually, one in the spring and one in the fall. Terry Young, the owner, says car clubs are always welcome.

AMERICAN MUSEUM OF FIREFIGHTING
125 Harry Howard Av
HUDSON, NY 12534 (26 miles south of Albany on the Hudson River)
Phone: 518-828-7695
Hours: Daily 9-4:30. Free.

This is one of the largest fire fighting museums in the U.S. with 68 engines on display including a 1922 REO Speedwagon, a 1924 LaFrance Brockway Torpedo, a 1925 Ford Model T19 and a 1928 Ahrens-Fox. There are also displays of horse-drawn and manually operated firefighting equipment, uniforms, speaking trumpets, badges and a fine collection of oil paintings, prints and lithographs.

THE FRANKLIN D. ROOSEVELT LIBRARY, MUSEUM & HOME
Albany Post Rd
HYDE PARK, NY 12538 (Halfway between New York City & Albany on the Hudson River)
Phone: 914-229-9115 or 914-229-2502 (Sat & Sun)
Hours: May thru Oct daily 9-5, rest of year Thurs-M 9-5. Closed Jan 1, Thanksgiving, Dec 25. Admission charged.

This is the home and 200-acre estate of President Franklin D. Roosevelt. It is now a National Historic Site with a presidential library and a museum. Among the many belongings of the President on display is a 1938 Ford 4-door convertible with special hand controls that he used to get around this estate and the local area. Roosevelt's legs were crippled by polio when he was a young man and he could not use them to drive.

▼ LONG ISLAND (East of New York City area)

THE HIMES MUSEUM OF MOTOR RACING NOSTALGIA
15 O'Neil Av
BAY SHORE, NY 11706 (Central part of Long Island, south shore)
Phone: 516-666-4912
Hours: Daily 9-9. Donations requested

This fine museum honors motor racing, especially in the Long Island area. On display are about two dozen midget race cars, sprints and stock cars including a Kurtis-Kraft midget driven by Mario Andretti. There are also several antique automobiles, motorcycles, boats, toys, pedal cars and racing memorabilia such as helmets, uniforms, trophies and photographs. The museum has small gift shop.

ONLY YESTERDAY CLASSIC AUTOS, INC. (Dealer)
24 Valley Rd
PORT WASHINGTON, NY 11050

(Western part of Long Island on the north shore.)
Phone: 516-767-3477 or 800-270-1960
Hours: M-F 10-6, Sat 10-5

If you are interested in cars with a pedigree, this is the place. Only Yesterday Classic Autos, Inc. handles only top quality and finished cars, mostly from the 1930s through the 1960s. They have between 15 and 18 of these beauties on display at all times in their 1950s-decorated showroom. An inventory list is available. The company takes trades, sells on consignment, arranges transportation and financing, does repairs and detailing, provides appraisals, arranges leases and will search for vehicles they do not have on the floor. The owner, Chuck Spielman, is an avid Corvette lover and has 4 of his personal cars, all national prize winners, on display in the showroom. There is a small gift shop and car clubs are always welcome.

UNIQUE CORVETTES, INC. (Dealer and restorer)
226 Belle Mead Rd
SETAUKET, NY 11733 (Central part of Long Island)
Phone: 516-751-8388
Hours: M-F 9-6, Sat 9-5

This company specializes in selling and restoring CORVETTES from 1953 to the present. They have a spacious 11,000 sq ft facility with some 35 to 45 Corvettes for sale in their showroom at all times. An inventory list is available upon request. Unique Corvettes arranges financing and transportation, does appraisals, sells on consignment, takes trade and offers leasing. They have an annual car show at their establishment each summer called the "Summer Sizzle". Car clubs are welcome to visit at any time. Contact Bob or Jason Scorsone.

End of Long Island △

BRITISH AUTO (Salvage)
600 Penfield Rd
MACEDON, NY 14502 (15 miles east-southeast of Rochester)
Phone: 315-986-3097
Hours: M-F 8-5.

This interesting salvage yard specializes in BRITISH-MADE cars only from 1950 to the present. In the yard one will find Austins, Austin-Healys, Jaguars, Jensens, Lotuses, MGs, Triumphs, TVRs, English Fords and others. There are some 700 cars total and the company has parts from another 400 dismantled vehicles. British Auto has new and NOS parts, imported parts, a parts locator service and a complete repair service. In business since 1975.

▼ NEW YORK CITY AREA

WALTER P. CHRYSLER HOME
US Merchant Marine Academy
Steamboat Rd
KINGS POINT, NY 11024
(West end of Long Island on the north shore)
Phone: 516-773-5387
Hours: Daily and weekends 9-4:30.
Closed federal holidays. Free.

The US Merchant Marine Academy was built on the former estate of Walter P. Chrysler in 1942 during World War II. The mansion was left intact and remains on the grounds of the Academy. It can be seen by visitors during the general tour of the Academy.

NEW YORK CITY FIRE MUSEUM
278 Spring St (Between Varick and Hudson Sts)
NEW YORK, NY 10013
Phone: 212-691-1303
Hours: Tues-Sun 10-4.
Closed major holidays.
Admission charged.

New York

This museum occupies a renovated 1904 firehouse located in Manhattan's Soho area. It displays one of the most comprehensive collections of fire-related art and artifacts from the 18th century to the present, including beautifully preserved hand- and horse-drawn and motorized pieces of apparatus, toys and models, fire engine lamps, presentation silver, oil painting, Currier and Ives and other prints, and an important collection of fire insurance marks. There is a museum store offering a wide range of imaginative gifts for people of all ages.

VINTAGE CAR STORE OF NYACK (Dealer)

40 Lydecker (Foot of High Av)

NYACK, NY 10960 (Northern suburb of New York City on west bank of Hudson River at the Tappan Zee Bridge)
Phone: 914-358-0500
Hours: M-F 9-5, Sat 9:30-5, Sun noon-5.

The town of Nyack is a huge antique center for metropolitan New York City so it is an ideal location for an antique car dealership like Vintage Car Store of Nyack. Here, in a big warehouse, can be found between 40 and 60 vintage cars of various makes and models. Many of the vehicles are quality cars such as Cadillacs, Ferraris, Jaguars, etc. An inventory list is available upon request. On display, but not for sale, is a magnificent collection of automobile art, prints, photos and other related automobilia. Vintage Car Store of Nyack can arrange financing and transportation, takes trades, sells on consignment, provides appraisals, leases cars, offers limited storage and will search for that special car you have always wanted. Gary Blankfont is the owner and extends a standing invitation to car clubs to come and visit.

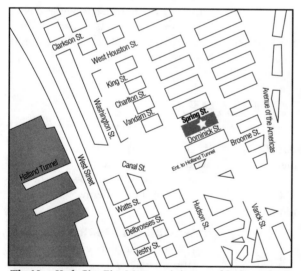

The New York City Fire Museum is just one block north of the entrance to the Holland Tunnel.

End of New York City △

At the Old Rhinebeck Aerodrome antique planes and cars perform together in a weekly air show.

NORTHEAST CLASSIC CAR MUSEUM

24 Rexford St (SR 23)
NORWICH, NY 13815
(38 miles northeast of
Binghamton on scenic SR 12)
Phone: 607-334-AUTO
Hours: Daily 10-5.
Admission charged.

Take the scenic drive along SR 12 and the Chenango River and you will come to the town of Norwich. There you will find this first class museum with a first class display of more than 50 classic automobiles. Most of the cars are meticulously restored quality vehicles and are fully operational. There are Duesenbergs, Packards, a Cord, Auburn, Pierce-Arrow, Hupmobile, La Salle plus the world's largest collection of FRANKLIN luxury cars. There is also a collection of MGs from the 1930s to the 1950s and an extensive collection of Stanley Steamers. For information about the museum contact Michael Tobey.

OLD RHINEBECK AERODROME (Museum)

44 Stone Church Rd
RHINEBECK, NY 12572
(Halfway between New York City and Albany)
Phone: 914-758-8610
Hours: May 15 thru Oct daily 10-5.
Weekend air shows mid-June to mid-Oct at 2 and 4. Admission charged.

This museum complex is devoted primarily to antique airplanes from the 1900s to the late 1930s. The buildings of the complex are situated around a World War I-style aerodrome and every weekend in the summer air shows are performed over the aerodrome. Integrated into this unique scene are some 30 antique automobiles, several antique motorcycles and a World War I French Renault tank. Some of the vehicles take part in the air show. When not participating in the air shows, the planes and vehicles can be seen sitting around the field, or in their hangars or in the museum. Old Rhinebeck has a gift and souvenir shop with many interested items related to the museum's overall theme.

BOB & ART'S AUTO PARTS
(Salvage)
2641 Reno Rd
SCHODACK CENTER, CASTLETON-ON-HUDSON, NY 12033 (10 miles south of Albany)
Phone: 518-477-9183
Hours: M-Sun 1-5.

This salvage yard has about 1000 vehicles from the late 1940s to the late 1960s, and specializes in AMC products to the 1980s, especially Ramblers. There are also some Hudsons, GMCs, Fords and Chrysler products. Customers may browse the yard. In business since 1958.

ADLER'S ANTIQUE AUTOS, INC.
(Salvage)
801 SR 43
STEPHENTOWN, NY 12168 (20 miles southeast of Albany near the Connecticut border)
Phone: 518-733-5749
Hours: M-Sat 8:30-5. Closed Dec to March.

There are approximately 625 vehicles in this yard that specializes in CHEVROLET cars and trucks from the 1940s thru the 1970s. There is particularly good coverage from 1947 to 1954 on Chevys and GMC trucks. Services offered include towing, restoration and consultation. In business since 1979. Bob Adler is the owner.

MUSEUM OF AUTOMOBILE HISTORY
321 N Clinton St (Downtown Syracuse)
SYRACUSE, NY
Phone: 315-478-2277
Hours: W-Sun 10-5. Admission charged.

You will not find any antique cars here but you will find about everything else related to old cars. This museum has some 10,000 automobilia items on display. They include oil paintings, toys, games, letters, sheet music, gas station collectibles, stamps, greeting cards, car accessories, photos, signs, posters, banners, pedal cars, hub caps, auto-graphs, clocks, design renderings, folk art, trophies… got the picture? This is a fun place to visit. All this glorious stuff was put together by Walter Miller, an automotive literature dealer of long standing.

M & G VINTAGE AUTO
(Restorer and dealer)
1 SR 17
TUXEDO PARK, NY 10987

(30 miles north-northwest of Manhattan on I-84)
Phone: 800-631-8990 or 914-753-5900
Hours: M-F 7:30-6

This company specializes in the restoration of MGs from 1945 to the 1980s. They are the world's largest parts suppliers for MG automobiles. They also do service work and sell cars in their indoor showroom. Parts catalog available.

▼ WEEDSPORT AREA (20 miles west of Syracuse off I-90)

HALL OF FAME AND CLASSIC CAR MUSEUM, D.I.R.T. MOTORSPORTS
1 Speedway Dr (Adjacent to the Cayuga County Fairgrounds)
WEEDSPORT, NY 13166
Phone: 315-834-6667 or 315-834-6606
Hours: M-Thurs & Sat 10-5, F 10-9, Sun noon-7. Admission charged.

This fine museum honors the sport of dirt track racing and the people associated with it. There are several race cars on display, several muscle cars and several dozen antique cars. Race cars of note include Gary Balough's "Batmobile" and Will Cagle's "No. 24 Coupe". The museum has a Finders Network that assists people in locating, buying and selling antique cars. In the "Classic Corral", adjacent to the main building, are vintage cars for sale. A

Kruse International Collector Car Auction is held here each year in July, and in August a large car show called "The Northeast Classic Motorsports Extravaganza", is held. The museum has a large gift and souvenir shop that offers a wide assortment of apparel, souvenirs and limited collector items. Jack Speno is the museum's curator.

NASH AUTO PARTS (Salvage)
Pump Rd
WEEDSPORT, NY 13166
Phone: 800-526-6334 or 315-252-5878
Hours: M-F 9-5, Sat 9-1.

This salvage yard has all makes of cars from 1920 to current totalling some 3000 vehicles. They also offer a parts locating service, NOS and NORS parts, bead blasting and cleaning. Customers may browse the yard. In business since 1952.

End of Weedsport Area △

NORTH CAROLINA

This is the Estes-Winn-Blomberg Antique Car Museum and two of its fine old cars.

**ESTES-WINN-BLOMBERG
ANTIQUE CAR MUSEUM**
Biltmore Homespun Shops/Grove
Park Inn
Macon Av
ASHEVILLE, NC 28804
(West-central part of state on
I-40 and I-29)
Phone: 828-253-7651
Hours: Apr thru Dec M-Sat. 10-5,
Sun. 1-5. Rest of year by request.
Free.

This auto museum is part of the
Biltmore Homespun Shops, a complex
of buildings, adjacent to the luxurious
Grove Park Inn, housing a historic
woollen mill started by Mrs. George W.
Vanderbilt in 1901 to preserve the Old
World wool manufacturing skills of the
local people. In the auto museum are
22 autos including a 1916 Overland, a
1926 Cadillac, a 1926 Pontiac, a 1928
Chandler, a 1932 Chevrolet coupe and
a 1950 MGTD.

 CHARLOTTE AREA

BACKING UP CLASSICS, INC.
(Museum and dealer)
4545 Hwy 29 (Concord)

HARRISBURG, NC 28075
(12 miles northeast of Charlotte)
Phone: 704-788-9494

This is Backing Up Classics of Harrisburg, NC.

Hours: M-F 9-5:45, Sat 9-5, Sun 10-5. Admission charged.

This museum specializes in antique, classic, special interest, race and muscle cars of the 1950s, but there are vehicles from other decades also. The main display of vehicles, consisting of about 50 vehicles, changes twice a year because the museum has more vehicles than can be displayed at one time. Some of the cars are for sale. In the museum's collection of race cars is a 1997 Ford Thunderbird driven by Mark Martin and a midget racer driven by Ken Schrader. Backing Up Classics offers appraisals, storage and has an automotive- and NASCAR-oriented gift shop. The company president and founder is Allan Miles.

all four of the Hendrick teams. The teams' racing shop is adjacent to the museum and a 40 ft window is provided in the dividing wall so that visitors to the museum can view the work going on in the shop. The chassis shop is also open to the public.

In the museum are a number of race cars, race trucks, concept cars and movie cars along with race cars of the past. Technical displays tell of the working parts of a race car and an exploded display shows how the frame and body of race cars are constructed. There is a huge trophy display, uniforms, photographs and lots more. A 2000 sq ft gift shop offers almost everything imaginable in the way of race-oriented souvenirs and gifts. Chuck Mack is the museum's director.

HENDRICK MOTORSPORT MUSEUM & GIFT SHOP

4400 Papa Joe Hendrick Blvd (Directly west of the Charlotte Motor Speedway)
HARRISBURG, NC 28075
(12 miles northeast of Charlotte)
Phone: 704-455-0342
Hours: M-F 8:30-5, Sat 9-2, Free.

This 25 acre complex is the home of

NORTH CAROLINA AUTO RACING HALL OF FAME

119 Knob Hill Rd
MOORESVILLE, NC 28117
(Northern suburb of Charlotte)
Phone: 704-663-5331
Hours: M-Sat 9-5, admission charged.

The mission of this fine museum is to celebrate and enhance the rich heri-

195

tage of Motor Sports and to commemorate those who have made outstanding contributions to it. Those so honored, of course, are highlighted in this museum. There are about 35 race cars on display representing all types of auto racing, some driven by famous drivers. Other features of the museum are the Goodyear Mini-Theater and an Indy car simulator. An art gallery displays works of some of the more famous motorsports artists and some of their works are on sale in the gift shop. Incorporated within the museum are race shops and a race-themed restaurant.

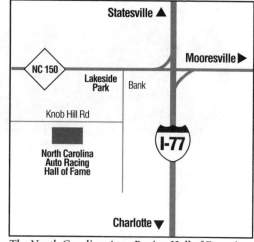

The North Carolina Auto Racing Hall of Fame is easily accessible from I-77 north of Charlotte.

NOSTALGIC CARS, INC. (Dealer)
I-85 at Sam Wilson Rd Exit,
PO Box 668054
CHARLOTTE, NC 28266
(Southwest edge of state near the state line)
Phone: 704-393-1957
Hours: M-F 9-5, Sat 9-1

This dealer is just 10 minutes from Charlotte-Douglas International Airport. They specialize in CHEVROLETS but offer vehicles of other makes, too. Nostalgic takes trades, arranges financing and transportation, sells on consignment and searches for specific vehicles. Stop by and take a look. Their motto is "Let's make a deal".

End of Charlotte Area △

C. GRIER BEAM TRUCK MUSEUM
117 N Mountain St
CHERRYVILLE, NC 28021 (30 miles northwest of Charlotte)
Phone: 704-435-3072
Hours: Fri 10-5 and Sat 10-3. Free.

This unique truck museum was established by C. Grier Beam, founder of Carolina Freight Express, one of the nation's largest trucking firms. The museum has more than a dozen restored trucks on display including a 1926 Chevrolet tractor, a 1935 International tractor, several White trucks and a 1947 Mack EF tractor with a 1946 Fruehauf trailer with a sleeping compartment in the front. These sleeping compartments were later discontinued for safety reasons. The museum has a small gift and souvenir shop.

The C. Grier Beam Truck Museum of Cherryville, NC.

AMERICAN LaFRANCE MUSEUM
11710 Statesville Blvd
CLEVELAND, NC 27013
(Midway between Winston-Salem
and Charlotte on US 70)
Phone: 704-278-6200
Hours: Tues and Thurs 1-4:30.
Tours available. Free.

Here is one of America's premier builders of firefighting equipment - and they have been at it since 1832. Their informative and interesting museum, an adjunct to their factory in Cleveland, traces that history and has on display many of their historic vehicles. The oldest piece of equipment in the museum is an 1858 Button & Blake (a forerunner to the American LaFrance Co.) Hand Pumper. Then, there is a pair of steamers, a 1904 and a 1911 model. Motorized vehicles begin with their 1911 "Type 5" Double Tank Combination vehicle and continues up through the 1960s. Of interest to car buffs is a 1911 American LaFrance Roadster com-

American LaFrance's 1911 "Type 5" Double Tank combination fire truck. One of only 48 made before being replaced by an updated model.

memorating the short time, before World War I, that the company made automobiles. Highlighted in the museum are some of the company's major contributions to the firefighting profession such as the first rotary-steam fire engine, the invention of the screw-driven extension ladder and the development of the piston steam engine. The museum has an extensive archive on the company's history and a gift shop.

MORRISON MOTOR CO. (Dealer)

1170 Old Charlotte Rd
CONCORD, NC 28027 (20 miles northeast of Charlotte)
Phone: 704-782-8812 or 704-782-7716
Hours: M-F 8-6, Sat 8-1

Here is a dealer that handles affordable collector cars. Most are domestic makes and models. Their average inventory of vintage cars is around 30 and a list of cars for sale is available. Morrison takes trades, arranges financing and searches for that special car you have always wanted. Jimmy Morrison, the owner, likes it when car clubs visit. He says they are "good people".

RICHARD'S AUTO SALES & SALVAGE

SR 49 (12 Miles southwest of Ashboro)
DENTON, NC 27239 (32 miles south of Winston-Salem)
Phone: 336-857-2222
Hours: Tues-F 10-5, Sat 8-1. M, call.

This large lot has some 2500 cars and trucks, mostly from the 1950s thru the 1970s with some vehicles from the 1930s and 1940s. Many cars are whole and re-storable. Customers may browse the yard and remove their own parts. This business may be for sale. It is suggested that visitors phone first. Richard Keller is the owner.

CARL SANDBURG NATIONAL HISTORIC SITE

Little River Rd
FLAT ROCK, NC 28731 (22 miles south of Asheville)
Phone: 704-698-5627
Hours: Daily 9-5, closed Dec 25.
Admission charged.

This is the home of the late poet-historian Carl Sandburg. Among his many belongings are two vehicles he owned at the time of his death in 1967; a 1951 Ford tractor and a 1962 Jeep. The Jeep was given to Sandburg as partial payment for writing the script of the movie "The Greatest Story Ever Told".

HAWK'S HILL
(Car collector community)

SR 18 North (Hawk's Hill Community nine miles north of Lenoir)
1 Pheasant Run (Sales office)
LENOIR, NC 28645 (50 miles west of Winston-Salem near Pisgah National Forest)
Phone: Sales office 704-754-2870
Hours: Phone sales office for appointment.

Golfers cluster together in golfing communities, so why don't car collectors cluster together in car collector communities? Well, it is happening in

North Carolina. They call Hawk's Hill housing development "America's First Community for the Car Collector". Instead of a golf course the community center piece is an elegant garage/club house combination. In the garage part of the structure are lifts, compressed air, tools and most everything it takes to service, and tinker with, old cars. In the club house part there is a greatroom, fire place, full kitchen and guest rooms upstairs. The wooded lots are big, one acre and up; plenty of room for your own multi-car garage. At the time of this writing all but 5 of the original 23 lots have been sold, but the developers, Al & Pat Witt, long-time antique car buffs, plan expansions. They also plan and help organize rallies, car shows, tech sessions, functions with car clubs, etc. To find Hawk's Hill proceed up SR 18 from its junction in Lenoir with U.S. 321 past Cedar Rock Country Club (on the right) three more miles to Hawk's Hill (also on the right). Drive in and take a look.

THUNDERBIRD BARN (Salvage)
2919 Eklin Hwy
NORTH WILKESBORO, NC 28659 (55 miles west of Winston-Salem)
Phone: 910-667-0837
Hours: M-F 9-5, Sat 9-noon.

This is a small salvage yard with about 50 vehicles, all THUNDERBIRDs, from 1958 thru 1969. Customers may browse the yard. In business since 1988.

RICHARD PETTY MUSEUM
Branson Mill Rd (Adjacent to the Richard Petty race car shops)
RANDLEMAN, NC 27217 (15 miles south of Greensboro)
Phone: 910-495-1143
Hours: M-Sat 9-5. Closed Thanksgiving and Dec 25. Admission charged.

This museum traces the racing careers of Lee Petty and his son, Richard Petty, from the late 1940s to the present. The walls of the museum are loaded with trophies won by this fascinating father and son racing duo. Also in the museum are several of Richard Petty's famous race cars along with many items of racing memorabilia. There is a 25-minute movie covering the racing career of Richard Petty. The museum is located on the grounds of Lee Petty's home and members of the Petty family are often in the area. The museum has a gift shop with many racing-related items for sale.

NORTH CAROLINA TRANSPORTATION MUSEUM; SPENCER SHOPS NATIONAL HISTORIC SITE.
411 S Salisbury Av
SPENCER, NC 28159 (35 miles south of Winston-Salem on I-85)
Phone: 704-636-2889
Hours: Apr thru Oct M-Sat 9-5, Sun 1-5; Nov thru Mar Tues-Sat 10-4, Sun 1-4. Closed major holidays. Donations accepted.

This is a large museum, housed in the former repair shops of the Southern Railroad. Featured in the main museum building are displays of the various modes of transportation used thru the history of North America from canoes,

North Carolina

The Spencer Shops of the Southern Railroad, built in 1907, are now a museum complex housing the North Carolina Transportation Museum and this 1935 Ford, The North Carolina Highway Patrol's first car.

to Conestoga wagons, to railroads, to airplanes. Included, of course, are automobiles. In the car collection there is a 1913 model T Ford depot hack, a 1912 Hupmobile, a 1921 Lincoln Roadster and a 1935 Ford Highway Patrol car. There is also a major display on the evolution of the automobile. An operating antique steam train takes visitors, for a small fee, on a tour of the complex, which includes a restored roundhouse.

MARKET FIRE HOUSE MUSEUM
Salem Square in the "Old Salem" District
WINSTON-SALEM, NC 27102
(North-central part of the state)

Phone: 910-721-7300
Hours: M-Sat 9-5, Sun. 12:30-5, closed Thanksgiving, Dec 24 and 25. Admission charged.

This fire museum is in 2 of the 63 restored buildings in the historic "Old Salem" district of Winston-Salem. Included in the museum, along with a wide variety of fire fighting displays, are several antique firetrucks including the two earliest firetrucks used in North Carolina. Other buildings in the "Old Salem" district include a visitor's center, a boys' school, a tavern, a silversmith shop, a tobacco shop, a shoemaker's shop, a bakery, a Moravian church and cemetery and several restored private homes.

NORTH DAKOTA

WALKER'S GARAGE (Salvage)
SR 49 (3 miles north of Beulah)
BEULAH, ND 58523
(60 miles northwest of Bismarck)
Phone: 701-873-4489
Hours: M-F 8-5, Sat 8:30-3

This is one of the few salvage yards in the country with a significant number of EDSELs. Walker's has about 200 of them among their total inventory of some 3000 vehicles. Leroy Walker, the yard's proprietor, is known in some circles as "King of the Edsels". He and his yard have been featured on ABC and CNN television shows. The other vehicles in the yard are mainly American-made cars, trucks, busses and tractors from 1946 to current. There are a few pre-war vehicles also. Walker's does repair work and some restoration.

EAST END AUTO PARTS (Salvage)
75 10th Av East
DICKINSON, ND 58601
(95 miles west of Bismarck on I-94)
Phone: 701-225-4206
Hours: M-F 8-5, Sat 8-noon

This 1200-vehicle salvage yard has cars and trucks from the 1930s to the 1980s. They specialize in CHEVROLETs, FORDs, DODGEs and IMPORTS. Towing service and inventory list available. Customers may browse the yard. In business since 1963.

PIONEER VILLAGE AND MUSEUM
2005 Burdick Expw East
(On the fairgrounds)
MINOT, ND 58702
Phone: 701-839-0785
Hours: May thru Sept Tues-Sun 10-6, rest of year by appointment. Admission charged.

This museum complex consists of 10 buildings and has displays primarily on the history of the local area. There is a pioneer home, an old schoolhouse, blacksmith shop, courthouse, church and in one building a display of tractors, buggies, an old firetruck and about a half dozen antique cars. Cars of interest include a 1909 Model T Ford, a 1919 Oakland and a 1920 Buick. The museum has no gift shop. Harvey Teets is curator.

North Dakota

These two Model A Ford replicas are side-by-side in the Bonanzaville car museum. The car on the left is a Shay Reproduction and on the Right is a Classic Reproduction made in ND.

BONANZAVILLE, USA (Museum complex)
1351 W Main St
(Junction of I-94 and US 10)
WEST FARGO, ND 58078
(Western suburb of Fargo)
Phone: 701-282-2822
Hours: Village and museum open June thru late Oct daily 9-5; rest of the year the Village is closed, but the museum is open Tues.-F 9-5. Admission charged.

This large museum complex consists of more than 45 buildings on a 15 acre site. The Village is a reconstructed pioneer town representing life in North Dakota during the "Bonanza" farm era. The Regional Museum has extensive exhibits on Indian culture and early pioneer life in the Red River Valley and the northern Great Plains. There is a train depot with a steam locomotive, railroad snowplow, coach car and caboose. Separate buildings house airplanes, telecommunications equipment, farm machinery, horse-drawn vehicles and antique cars. Some 80 antique cars and 40 pieces of farm machinery are on display. Noteworthy among the cars is a 1903 Ford, a 1904 Holzman, a 1908 Brush, a 1914 Detroit Electric, a 1924 Studebaker and a 1956 Ford Thunderbird. There are also displays of hubcaps, license plates, mechanic's tools and machinery and a small automotive library. An annual festival called "Pioneer Review Days" is held here during the third week in August. Bonanzaville has a large and well-stocked gift and souvenir shop. Margo Lang is the administrative manager.

OHIO

▼ AKRON AREA

ARLINGTON AUTO WRECKING
(Salvage)
445 N Arlington St
AKRON, OH 44305
Phone: 216-434-3466
Hours: M-F 8-5, Sat 8-4

This salvage yard has about 500 vehicles of mixed makes and specializes in both used and new standard transmissions and hard-to-find drivetrain parts. Customers may browse the yard. In business since 1942.

GOODYEAR WORLD OF RUBBER
(Museum)
1201 E Market St
AKRON, OH 44316

Phone: 216-796-7117
Hours: M-F 8:30-4:30, closed holidays. Free.

This is the Goodyear Tire & Rubber Company's museum on the history of rubber and on the company's founder, Charles Goodyear. There are extensive displays on the uses of rubber in automotive tires, various industrial and commercial products, and in such diversified applications as moon-landing vehicles and artificial hearts. There is a replica of a rubber plantation and a reproduction of Charles Goodyear's workshop as well as photographs of him, some of his personal belongings and explanations of his contributions to the rubber industry.

End of Akron Area △

CANTON CLASSIC CAR MUSEUM
Market St at 6th St SW
CANTON, OH 44702 (20 miles south of Akron)
Phone: 330-455-3603
Hours: Daily 10-5. Admission charged.

This museum is on the historic Lincoln Highway in an old Ford/Lincoln dealership building that closed in 1929. The museum has about 40 restored vintage and classic cars including a rare 1914 Benham roadster, a 1922 specially designed Packard Twin-6 built for the

The Canton Classic Car Museum of Canton, OH.

used in the movie "Those Daring Young Men in Their Jaunty Jalopies" and a 1931 12-cylinder Marmon. Some of the other cars in the collection were made in Ohio. There is a celebrity car, Amelia Earhart's 1916 Pierce-Arrow. Other displays include early police and fire department memorabilia, gasoline and steam engines, antique auto signs and post cards. There is also an automotive-oriented gift shop and the museum is handicapped accessible.

Greer Steel family, a 1922 Holmes (made in Canton), a 1928 Lea Francis

▼ CLEVELAND AREA

FREDERICK C. CRAWFORD AUTO-AVIATION MUSEUM
10825 East Blvd
CLEVELAND, OH 44106
Phone: 216-721-5722
Hours: M-Sat 10-5, Sun noon-5. Closed major holidays. Admission charged.

This large museum, owned and operated by the Western Reserve Historical Society, has about 125 cars. Noteworthy cars include an 1895 Panhard et Levassor, an 1898 Winton, a 1909 Simplex, a 1913 Austro-Daimler, a 1932

Peerless V-16 all-aluminum prototype sedan with body by Murphy, a 1936

Part of the fine collection of antique and historic automobiles at the Frederick C. Crawford Auto-Aviation Museum in Cleveland, OH.

Ford made of stainless steel, a 1981 Aston Martin Lagonda and "Chitty-Chitty-Bang-Bang II", 1 of 4 originals built in the 1920s that later inspired the movie car of the same name. Other displays include aircraft, motorcycles, bicycles and other transportation-related items. The museum has an automotive library, a restoration shop in which visitors can watch restorations in progress, a turn-of-the-century street of shops and an interesting gift store.

ROCK AND ROLL HALL OF FAME AND MUSEUM
    E 9th St & Erieside Av
    CLEVELAND, OH 44114
    Phone: 216-781-7625

Hours: Memorial Day-Labor Day W-Sat 10-9, Sun-Tues 10-5:50, rest of year daily 1-5:30 (closed W). Closed Thanksgiving and Dec 25. Admission charged.

This museum, as the name implies, honors individuals and groups who are well-known in the field of Rock and Roll. Among the many items on display are several automobiles. They include Janis Joplin's Porsche, the Rock and Roll band, Z Z Top's, custom-built "Eliminator" and three European cars which are hanging from the ceiling with a unique Rock and Roll history of their own. Other vehicles belonging to Rock & Roll celebrities have been shown in the museum from time to time.

End of Cleveland area △

▼ COLUMBUS AREA

DEL-CAR WRECKING (Salvage)
    5501 Westerville Rd
    WESTERVILLE, OH 43081
    (Northeastern suburb of
    Columbus)
    Phone: 614-882-0220
    Hours: M-F 8-5

This 12-acre salvage yard has 1300 vehicles and specializes in American-made cars and trucks from 1963 to the present. An inventory list is available. In business since 1971.

MOTORCYCLE HERITAGE MUSEUM
    33 Collegeview Rd (I-270 exit 27)
    WESTERVILLE, OH 43081
    (Northeastern suburb of
    Columbus)
    Phone: 614-891-2425
    Hours: M-F 9-4:30, Sat-Sun
    inquire. Information: 612-882-2782.
    Donations requested.

This motorcycle museum is administered by the American Motorcycle Heri-

205

The Motorcycle Heritage Museum of Westerville, OH serves to educate and entertain the American public on motorcycling in America.

tage Foundation and serves to educate and entertain the American public on the influence of the motorcycle from the late 19th century to the present. Displays in the museum depict many domestic and international influences on motorcycling in America. Most of the museum's collection of motorcycles are on loan on a 2 year basis so the displays are ever-changing. The museum, though, is acquiring its own collection.

End of Columbus Area △

▼ DAYTON AREA

ALOTTA AUTO PARTS (Salvage)
8426 Upper Miamisburg Rd (SR 725)
MIAMISBURG, OH 45342
(Southern suburb of Dayton off I-75)
Phone: 937-866-1849
Hours: M-F 8:30-5, Sat 8:30-2

There is about 600 vehicles on this six-acre lot, mostly GM products. Fords can also be seen along with some orphans. There is a nice selection of convertibles. Ages of the cars run from the 1940s through the 1970s with the bulk being in the 1960s. Customers may browse the lot and remove some of their own parts with permission. The yard is owned by Joe Pierce and run by his son, Doug. In business since 1967.

CARILLON HISTORICAL PARK (Museum complex)
2001 S Patterson Blvd
DAYTON, OH 45409
Phone: 937-293-2841
Hours: May thru Oct Tues-Sat 9:30-5, Sun noon-5. Admission charged.

Two of the buildings in Carillon Historical Park include an early automobile dealership, left, and a 1924 Sun Oil Co. service station, right.

In this large city park there is a collection of historic buildings and exhibits near the river which trace the early history of Dayton and the progress of transportation from the beginning of the 1900s. Buildings of interest to car buffs include a 1924 Sun Oil Co. service station, an early automobile dealership and a replica of the Deeds Barn, the building in which Charles F. Kettering invented the automobile electric starter. His invention overcame one of the major problems of the early automobile industry, that of hand-cranking internal combustion engines. This limitation dictated that gasoline engines be of relatively small size and low compression so that the average man could turn the crank. Unfortunately not all men, and very few women, could crank a car. Kettering's invention eliminated this problem and eventually made the internal combustion engine the engine of choice for most automobiles. It also spelled the end of steam and electric-powered cars which had sold well because they required no cranking.

Other items of interest on display in the complex is a Concord stagecoach, an early steam locomotive and caboose, a trolley car, a restored 1905 Wright Brothers airplane, a replica of the Wright Brothers bicycle shop and a number of vintage cars, some of which were made in Dayton. Among the autos is a 1908 Stoddard-Dayton, a 1910 Courier, a 1910 Speedwell, a 1912 Cadillac, the first car equipped with Charles Kettering's electric starter, a 1914 Xenia Cyclecar and a 1923 Maxwell. There is a fine museum store with many auto-related items for sale.

THE CITIZENS MOTORCAR CO., AMERICA'S PACKARD MUSEUM
420 S Ludlow St
DAYTON, OH 45402
Phone: 513-226-1917
Hours: M-F noon-5, Sat-Sun 1-5

This museum, near downtown Dayton, is in a building built in 1917 by the Packard Motor Car Co. as a branch office and a sales service center. The interior of the building has been restored to look like a 1930s Packard dealership.

207

Ohio

The Citizen's Motor Car Co., America's Packard Museum is convenient from either I-70 or I-75.

The museum has about 20 PACKARD vehicles on display which represents the largest display in the world of "Packards only". In the museum's collection is a 1903 Packard restoration/recreation, on loan from Packard Electric Corp., known as "Old Pacific II". In 1903, the Packard Motorcar Company, then in its infancy, built three of these cars and one of them was driven to the Pacific coast by a company driver. This brought the young company much publicity and helped to insure its later success.

Also on display is a Roll-Royce Merlin aircraft engine, built by Packard in large numbers during World War II under license from Rolls-Royce. The museum also has displays on the Packard Motorcar Co. including its original paper of incorporation and traces the company's history from its founding in 1899 to its demise in 1956. The museum welcomes tour groups and is available for dinners, meetings and banquets. The Packard Automobile Classics (the national Packard club) is located at the museum. The museum's founder is Bob Sigmon.

STARK WRECKING CO. (Salvage)
7081 Germantown Pike
MIAMISBURG, OH 45342
(A southwestern suburb of Dayton)
Phone: 513-866-5032
Hours: M-Sat 9-5

This is a very old salvage yard with about 3000 vehicles of all makes from the 1920s to the 1980s. Customers may browse the yard and pull their own parts. The company does not accept mail orders. In business at the same location since 1923.

WILHELM'S (Salvage)
1761 Liberty Rd
NEW CARLISLE, OH 45344
(15 miles northeast of downtown Dayton)
Phone: 937-845-8600
Hours: M-F 9-6, Sat 9-5

This yard has about 100 vehicles many of which are from the 1950s and 1960s. There are also a few pre-war vehicles and still others up to the 1980s. Wilhelm's specializes in CHEVROLETs and has a particularly good assortment of that marque from 1953-54. The yard has been in business since 1954. Roger Wilhelm is the owner.

End of Dayton Area △

▼ LIMA AREA (Northwestern Ohio on I-75)

ALLEN COUNTY MUSEUM
620 W Market St
LIMA, OH 45801
Phone: 419-222-9426
Hours: June-Aug Tues-Sat 10-5,
Sun 1-5, rest of year Tues-Sun 1-5,
closed holidays. Free.

This is a nice county museum with local historical exhibits and a library. There is a 15-foot model of Mount Vernon complete with model furniture plus displays on Indians, pioneers, guns, steam and electric railroads, firefighting equipment, bicycles and several vintage cars. One of the cars, a 1910 Locomobile Sports Roadster, is one of the first Locomobiles to have gasoline engines. The museum has a gift and souvenir shop.

The Allen County Museum has an interesting collection of antique vehicles.

ENDLESS ENDEAVORS (Museum)
502 S Dixie Hwy (Exit 118 off I-75)
CRIDERSVILLE, OH 45806
(10 miles south of Lima on I-75)
Phone: 419-645-0650
Hours: M-Sat 9:30-8:30, closed holidays. Admission charged.

Here is a new museum which opened in March 1998. It is the life-long ambition of its founder, Donald E. Miller, Jr., a long-time car collector. It is actually more than a car museum, it is an antique mall covering some 64,000 sq ft with booths and glass-front stores selling all sorts of antiques. In the car museum are about 20 vehicles, most of them owned personally by Mr. Miller. Many of the cars are low-mileage originals. There is a restored 1935 Auburn 851 boattail, a 1934 Buick roadster with rumble seat, a 1964 Thunderbird, a 1973 Plymouth Duster, five Oldsmobiles and seven Chevys. The museum's walls are covered with hundreds of signs and service station-type displays and life-size paintings. In the complex is a gift shop and 50s-style restaurant.

End of Lime area △

Ohio

Twilight Taxi Parts is the only place in the country where one can see some 200 Checkers in one location.

TWILIGHT TAXI PARTS, INC. (Salvage)
14503 Old State Rd 608
MIDDLEFIELD, OH 44062 (25 miles east of Cleveland)
Phone: 440-632-5419
Hours: Irregular, phone for appointment.

This is a small salvage yard specializing in CHECKER motor products. There are about 200 vehicles, mostly from 1960 to 1982. Customers may browse the yard. In business since 1986.

BOB'S AUTO WRECKING (Salvage)
12602 SR 13
MILAN, OH 44846 (10 miles southeast of Sandusky off I-80/90)
Phone: 419-499-2415
Hours: M-F 8-5, Sat 8-noon

This is a large salvage yard offering some 5000 vehicles from 1946 to current. All makes and body types are represented in the yard. Customers may browse the yard. In business since 1961.

PRO TEAM CLASSIC CORVETTE COLLECTION (Dealer)
SR 108 South, PO Box 606
NAPOLEON, OH 43545 (35 miles southwest of Toledo on US 24)
Phone: 888-592-5086 or 419-592-5086
Hours: M-F 9-5

This is a 60,000 sq ft dealership selling CORVETTEs and carrying an inventory of some 150 vehicles at all times. All years of Corvettes are usually available at Pro Team. The company takes trades, arranges financing, insurance and transportation and welcomes inquiries from other dealers. Pro Team has a gift and souvenir shop and visitors are welcome. Terry Michaelis is the president.

MERSHON'S WORLD OF CARS (Dealer)
201 E North St
SPRINGFIELD, OH 45503 (20 miles northeast of Dayton on I-70)
Phone: 937-324-8899
Hours: M-Thurs 9-7, F 9-6, Sat 9-5

Mershon's World of Cars, Springfield, OH, is a specialist in Corvettes and also offers muscle cars, sports cars and collector cars.

This is a large dealer of collector cars specializing in all years of CORVETTEs. Up to 60 vehicles can be seen in their spacious, carpeted and air conditioned indoor showroom with additional cars on their adjacent lot. Other makes of cars are offered with heavy emphasis on muscle cars, sports cars and collector cars. Financing, leasing and shipping can be arranged and the company takes trades. The owner is Dan Mershon.

WELSH JAGUAR CLASSIC CAR MUSEUM
  5th & Washington Sts
  STEUBENVILLE, OH 43952
  (Eastern edge of the state on the Ohio River opposite Weirton, WV)
  Phone: 740-282-8649
  Hours: M-Sat 10-5, Sun noon-5.
  Admission charged.

This privately-owned museum houses several JAGUARs and muscle

cars from vintage to late models. Several car-related murals can also be

The Welsh Jaguar Classic Car Museum, Steubenville, OH.

211

found in the museum. All car clubs and other interested organizations are welcome. The museum has a gift shop offering local arts and crafts, souvenirs and Jaguar memorabilia. Also on the premises is the Jaggin' Around Restaurant & Pub. William E. Welsh is the museum's founder.

▼ TOLEDO AREA

When approaching the Toledo area from the north on I-75 one can see the old Willys manufacturing plant off to the east. In the old brick smoke stack the word "Overland" is still clearly visible. The Plant is operational, making Jeeps. In the area are Jeep Boulevard and Willys Boulevard.

CHERRY AUTO PARTS (Salvage)
5650 N Detroit Av
TOLEDO, OH 43612
Phone: 800-537-8677 or 419-476-7222
Hours: M-F 7-5, Sat 8:30-noon

This 800-vehicle salvage yard specializes in Asian cars and trucks from 1985 to 1991 and European cars from 1980 to 1991. Cherry's has a full machine shop. In business since 1949.

TOLEDO FIREFIGHTERS MUSEUM
918 Sylvania Av
TOLEDO, OH 43612
Phone: 419-478-FIRE (3473) or 245-1140
Hours: June thru Aug Sat noon-4, Sept thru May Sat-Sun noon- 4. Free.

The fire museum is located in Toledo's old fire station #18 and displays antique firefighting equipment, photos, artifacts, books and 6 motorized firefighting vehicles. The oldest is a 1927 American LaFrance fire truck and the newest is a 1948 Buffalo. The museum has a gift shop offering firefighting-related items.

End of Toledo Area △

GENERAL MOTORS LORDSTOWN COMPLEX (Plant tours)
2300 Halleck Young Rd
(SR 45 South)
WARREN, OH 44482
(13 miles northwest of downtown Youngstown)
Phone: 330-824-5000
Hours: M-F tours offered at noon and 6. Please phone for reservations. Free.

This large General Motors facility offers plant tours to the general public. Tours are not offered on holidays or when plant is closed.

AMERICAN PARTS DEPOT (Salvage)
409 N Main St (US 127)
WEST MANCHESTER, OH 45382
(24 miles northwest of Dayton)

Phone: 513-678-7249
Hours: M-F 8-noon and 1-6, plus 7 pm-10 pm Wed evenings.

This is a small but expanding salvage yard specializing in American Motors (AMC) products. The yard has approxi-

mately 60 vehicles and is growing. Most of the vehicles are from the 1960's thru the 1980s. American Parts also carries NOS parts, and all part are inventoried by computer. In business since 1990. Doug Noel is the owner.

▼ ZANESVILLE AREA (50 miles east of Columbus on I-70)

NATIONAL ROAD/ZANE GREY MUSEUM
8850 East Pike
NORWICH, OH 43767 (10 miles east of Zanesville)
Phone: 740-872-3143
Hours: Apr 26 thru Sept 26 M-Sat 9:30-5, Sun noon-5; Mar 3 thru Apr 25 and Sept 29 thru Nov 28 W-Sat 9:30-5, Sun noon-5. Closed Thanksgiving and the rest of the year. Admission charged.

Approximately half of this museum is devoted to the history of the "National Road", the first federally funded road in the US. Funded by Congress in 1806, the road began in Cumberland, MD, passed thru Zanesville and ran to Vandalia, IL. It was built by animal and human power and was instrumental in opening up the Northwest Territory and the areas westward until railroads took over that task. Most of the "National Road" was converted into modern-day US 40 over the years. One of the main displays in the museum is a glass-encased diorama, 136 feet long, showing the evolution of the

"National Road". There are also recreations of early roadside services such as a tavern and a wheelwright shop, covered wagons and restored antique automobiles. The other half of the museum honors Zane Grey, the famous writer of western novels, who was born in Zanesville. One of Grey's favorite themes was the opening of the west beyond the "National Road". His best-known work was "Riders of the Purple Sage". Also, Zane Grey's great-grandfather, Ebenezer Zane, was a well-known road builder. He built the first public road in Ohio known as Zane's Trace, which is in the Zanesville area.

RON'S AUTO PARTS (Salvage)
3590 Center Rd
ZANESVILLE, OH 43701
Phone: 740-453-7234
Hours: M-F 8-5, Sat 8-2

This is a large salvage yard with about 3000 vehicles from the early 1940s to the present. All makes are available. Customers may browse the yard. In business since 1966.

End of Zanesville Area △

OKLAHOMA

 ROUTE 66

Oklahoma is one of several states that has made a concerted effort to preserve portions of the famous Route 66 that runs through their state. Route 66 was the main road from America's heartland to the west coast for many years in the early part of the twentieth century. Oklahoma has over 400 driveable miles of the original route 66, more than any other state. Cities and towns along the route have cooperated in preserving historic and unique landmarks relative to the highway. The State of Oklahoma prints a very informative brochure on the highway entitles "Get Your Kicks on Oklahoma Historic Route 66" that is available from the Oklahoma Tourism and Recreation Department, PO Box 60789, Oklahoma City, OK 73146-0789, phone, 405-521-2406. The route is also well-marked with distinctive brown and white signs.

BUD'S AUTO SALVAGE
Hwy 8 (1 mile east of Aline)
ALINE, OK 73716
(North central part of state
40 miles west-northwest of Enid)
Phone: 580-463-2204
Hours: M-F 8-5:30,
closed weekends.

Look for the 40 ft lumberjack with the ax in his hand. This is Bud's Auto Salvage on the plains of rural Oklahoma. Beneath the ax-man is 20 acres of antique cars dating mostly from the 1950s and 1960s. Actually Bud's has 60 acres of cars and some 5000 total, but only those below the ax-man qualify as antiques. There are several rows of restorable cars that are being sold as a whole. Bud's is a good source for early factory and add-on air conditioning parts. It gets real hot in this part of the country in the summertime. Ask for Rocky. He is the man that knows the antique stuff.

31 AUTO SALVAGE
Rt 5
McALESTER, OK 74501 (East-central part of the state on the Indian Nation Turnpike)
Phone: 918-423-2022
Hours: M-F 8-5, Sat 8-noon

This salvage yard has about 250 vehicles and specializes in GENERAL MOTORS vehicles from 1960 to 1972. Mail order business welcome. Customers may browse the yard. In business since 1978.

McDANIEL SALVAGE
SR 16 (1.5 miles south of Okay, OK)

The Oklahoma Firefighters Museum is one of the larger firefighter museums in the country.

OKAY, OK 74446
(Northern suburb of Muskogee)
Phone: 918-683-5371 or
918-683-6675
Hours: M-F 8-5, Sat 9-2

Here is a good source for MUSTANG and FALCON parts. McDaniel Salvage has a big inventory of both marques from the 1960s. Parts from other domestic cars are also available. Customers may browse the lot escorted, but lot personnel remove all parts. Dean McDaniel is the owner/operator. In business since 1966.

▼ OKLAHOMA CITY AREA

AABAR'S CADILLAC & LINCOLN SALVAGE
9700 NE 23rd St
OKLAHOMA CITY, OK 73141
Phone: 405-769-3318
Hours: M-F 8:30-5

As the name implies, this 7-acre salvage yard specializes in CADILLACs and LINCOLNs. Some of their 600 cars date back to 1939. Aabar's offers a large selection of used, NOS, NORS and reproduction parts which are stocked in their warehouse. Customers may browse the yard. In business since 1960.

OKLAHOMA FIREFIGHTERS MUSEUM

2716 NE 50th St
OKLAHOMA CITY, OK 73111
Phone: 405-424-3440
Hours: Daily 10-4:30. Closed Jan 1, Thanksgiving, and Dec 25. Admission charged.

This is a large firefighting museum displaying horse-drawn, human-drawn and motorized firefighting vehicles and other equipment. Among the motorized vehicles is a 1910 American LaFrance chemical and hose truck which was Oklahoma City's first piece of motorized firefighting equipment. There is also a 1917 REO chemical and hose truck, a 1920 Stutz with a brass engine block and a 1928 Ahrens-Fox front-

215

mounted piston pumper. Other displays include uniforms, photos, awards, paintings and collections of nozzles and alarm boxes.

End of Oklahoma City Area △

BOB TOWNSEND CLASSIC AUTO MUSEUM
SR 18 North (Harrison St) and I-40
SHAWNEE, OK 74801 (35 miles east of downtown Oklahoma City)
Phone: 405-273-0330
Hours: Appointment only. Admission charged.

This is a large privately-owned museum with over 300 antique vehicles. There are many rare and interesting cars in the collection including three celebrity cars; Mae West's 1938 V-12 Cadillac limousine, Elvis Presley's 1956 Lincoln and Sammy Davis Jr's. Stutz. The museum has a large gift and antique shop. Car clubs welcome.

HAUF AUTO SUPPLY (Salvage)
US 177 3 miles south of town
STILLWATER, OK 74076 (35 miles north-northeast of Oklahoma City)
Phone: 405-372-1585
Hours: Tues-F 8-5:30

Hauf's is a 76 acre salvage yard with about 3500 cars and trucks from 1928 to the present with a high concentration of cars and trucks from the 1940s thru 1970s. Customers may browse the yard. In business since 1946 as a 4th generation family business.

▼ TULSA AREA

COURT HOUSE/CITY HALL
Downtown
TULSA, OK.

Buried on the Courthouse/City Hall lawn is a brand new 1957 Plymouth. The car was donated by a local Chrysler Plymouth dealer and was buried there in 1957 in a waterproof chamber along with several drums of gasoline. It is to be exhumed in 2007. Until then a plaque marks the site.

NORTH YALE AUTO PARTS (Salvage)
116th and N Yale (US 75)
SPERRY, OK 74073 (A northern suburb of Tulsa)
Phone: 800-256-NYAP (6927)
and 918-288-7218
Hours: M-F 8-5, Sat 9-noon

There are approximately 1000 vehicles in this lot from 1984 and older. North Yale specializes in CHRYSLER, FORD and GENERAL MOTORS vehicles. Customers may browse the yard. In business since 1960. Contact Walt or Bobby Ward.

End of Tulsa Area △

OREGON

THE UPPERTOWN FIREFIGHTERS MUSEUM

30th St and Marine Dr
ASTORIA, OR 97103 (Northwest corner of the state at the mouth of the Columbia River)
Phone: 503-325-2203
Hours: May-Sept F-Sun 10-5, rest of year F-Sun 11-4. Closed Thanksgiving and Dec 25. Admission charged includes admission to other nearby attractions.

The building that houses this firefighters museum was built in 1896 as a brewery. In 1928 it was modified and converted into Astoria's Uppertown Fire Station #2 and a city equipment maintenance shop. The facility served in those capacities for 33 years. In 1990 it was converted into a museum and houses a collection of firefighting items and equipment from 1877 to 1921. Included in the collection are five motorized pieces of fire equipment, several hand-pulled and horse-drawn pieces of equipment and a wide variety of firefighting items and memorabilia. The living quarters of the firemen on the 2nd floor has been restored and is open to the public.

This was Astoria's Fire Station #2 for 33 years before it became a firefighters' museum.

217

▼ EUGENE AREA (West-central part of the state on I-5)

McCOY'S AUTO AND TRUCK WRECKING (Salvage)

80820 Pacific Highway 99N (South of Creswell, but north of Cottage Grove)
CRESWELL, OR 97426 (A southern suburb of Eugene)
Phone: 503-942-0804
Hours: M-F 8:30-5:30, Sat 8:30-3.

McCoy's has about 700 vehicles crammed onto their 5-acre lot. Most of the cars are GMs, Fords and Chrysler products from the 1950s thru the 1970s with a very good selection of Buicks and Cadillacs from the 1950s and 1960s. McCoy's also has a large inventory of rebuildable engines, wheel covers and miscellaneous parts in their warehouse.

RAINBOW AUTO WRECKERS (Salvage)

25850 Tidball Ln
VENETA, OR 97487
(16 miles west of Eugene)
Phone: 800-303-1828 or 503-935-1828
Hours: M-Sat 8:30-5

This salvage yard specializes in CHEVROLET cars and pickup trucks from 1955 thru 1966. There are, however, other make and models in the yard.

End of Eugene Area △

D & R SALES (Salvage yard — whole vehicles)

Rt 2 Box 2080
HERMISTON, OR 97838 (North-central edge of the state 5 miles south of the Columbia River)
Phone: 800-554-8763 or 503-567-8048
Hours: M-F 9:30-6:30, Sat 10:30-6

This salvage yard sells whole vehicles only. There are some 500 vehicles of mixed makes, mostly of U.S. manufacture. They range in age from 1926 to the late 1960s. An inventory list is available and customers may browse the yard. D & R offers towing, delivery, restoration and searches for specific vehicles.

▼ PORTLAND AREA

AURORA WRECKERS AND RECYCLERS, INC. (Salvage)

2111 Hwy 99 NE
AURORA, OR 97002 (Southern suburb of Portland)
Phone: 503-678-1107
Hours: M-Sat 9-5

They date back to the 1920s in this salvage yard and run up into the 1960s.

CHRYSLER products are a specialty, but other makes of domestic vehicles are available. Some cars are whole and will only be sold as a complete unit. Company personnel remove all parts. Some of the better stuff is stored inside. Ray Hellhake is the owner.

FASPEC BRITISH CARS & PARTS (Salvage)
1036 SE Stark St
PORTLAND, OR 97214
Phone: 800-547-8788 or
503-232-1232
Hours: M-F 9-6, Sat 9-12:30

This is a small salvage yard with about 100 British-made vehicles specializing in MG, Austin-Healy, Triumph, Spridget, Austin-America, Marina and Riley automobiles. Both new and used parts are available, and the company can supply a catalog. Faspec also sells used British-made cars. In business since 1969.

MEMORY LANE MOTORS—THE ORIGINAL (Dealer)
2608 SE Holgate
PORTLAND, OR 97202
Phone: 503-231-1940
Hours: M-Sat 8:30-5

This dealer specializes in quality, affordable, collectible antique automobiles from the 1930s to the 1970s. They inventory about 30 to 35 cars in their inside showroom and adjacent lot. Some cars are sold on consignment. Memory Lane offers an appraisal service, takes trades and welcomes car clubs. Dale Matthews is the owner.

End of Portland Area △

UMAPINE GARAGE & SALVAGE
Rt 2, Box 130
UMAPINE, OR 97862
(Northeastern part of state just across the state line from Walla Walla, WA)
Phone: 503-938-6806
Hours: Seven days a week 8-6

Better phone first for directions to this yard. Umapine is not on all the maps. Once here, though, the trip is worth it. Bring your high boots. This is a pick-your-own-parts operation and the yard is shared with cattle and a pet pony. There are several hundred vehicles from the 1940s through the 1970s on five acres of brush land. Louella Hoskins runs the yard and she has been at it for over 30 years.

PENNSYLVANIA

▼ ALLENTOWN AREA
(40 miles north of Philadelphia)

THE JUNKYARD (Salvage)
201 Cedar St
ALLENTOWN, PA 18102
Phone: 215-435-7278
Hours: M-F 9-6, Sat 9-4

This is a 1000-vehicle salvage yard offering a mix of vehicle makes and models up to 1980. Customers may browse the yard. In business since 1989.

MACK TRUCKS HISTORICAL MUSEUM
997 Postal Rd
(From US 22 exit Airport Rd North. In an industrial park adjacent to the Allentown Airport.)
ALLENTOWN, PA 18103
Phone: 610-226-6767
Hours: M, W and F 10-4, and by appointment. Free.

There are more than two dozen antique trucks on display at the Mack Trucks Historical Museum in Allentown, PA.

This is the MACK Truck Corporation's company museum. On display are about two dozen trucks and vehicles associated with the company. There is a 1900 open-air, 27-passenger Mack touring bus, a 1910 Brockway motor wagon, a nicely restored Model AB Mack tank truck, a 1918 Mack Model AC 5-$\frac{1}{2}$ ton firetruck fully equipped as it was when it was in service in the city of Baltimore, and many other interesting vehicles. The museum has a library of some 80,000 photographs of historic trucks. Don Schumaker and Snowy Doe are the museum's co-curators.

End of Allentown Area △

BOYERTOWN MUSEUM OF HISTORIC VEHICLES

28 Warwick St (Proceed from SR 100 to Jct SRs 73 and 562, then two blocks south to Warwick St.)
BOYERTOWN, PA 19512
(30 miles east of Reading)
Phone: 610-367-2090
Hours: Tues-Sun 9:30-4.
Closed major holidays.
Admission charged.

This museum, in the heart of the Pennsylvania Dutch country, displays many types of vehicles, many of which are associated with the local area. Some of the vehicles were built by local Pennsylvania Dutch craftsmen and sport names such as Duryea, SGV, Daniels, Middleby, Boss, Dile and Fleetwood. Other exhibits include electric vehicles, motorcycles, carriages, sleighs, bicycles, children's vehicles, license plates, tools and other transportation related items. The museum sponsors an annual auto show and flea market called "Duryea Days". The museum was founded in 1965. There is a gift and souvenir shop on the premises offering many auto-related items.

FEEZLE'S AUTO WRECKING (Salvage)

Rt 1 Box 215
ENON VALLEY, PA 16120
(About 25 miles southeast of Youngstown, OH off I-76)
Phone: 412-336-5755 or
412-336-5512
Hours: M-F 8:30-5, Sat 8:30-4

There's almost 6000 cars in this 20-acre salvage yard. The owners estimate that there are 2500 cars, 1200 pickups and 2000 motorcycles. They range in age from the 1930s to the present with a good concentration in the 1950s and 1960s. Many of the best parts are stored inside. Most cars are domestic makes with some orphans such as Studebakers and AMCs. The company also runs a used car lot, but they are not cars from the yard. Brothers Jim and Rick Feezle own and operate the businesses.

EISENHOWER NATIONAL HISTORIC SITE (Historic Home)

Adjacent to Gettysburg National Military Park
GETTYSBURG, PA 17325 (40

miles southwest of Harrisburg near the Maryland state line)
Phone: 717-338-9114
Hours: Vary. Site accessible by shuttle bus from Natl. Park Visitor Center on SR 134. Admission charged.

This was the home and 230-acre farm of President and Mrs. Dwight D. Eisenhower. There is a visitor center, with exhibits on Eisenhower's life, and the home itself in which the Eisenhowers lived during his Presidency and in retirement. Several out-buildings hold and display the personal belongings, awards, gifts, paintings, farm equipment and other memorabilia of the Eisenhower family. In the large garage, which was once a chicken house, is a modified Crosley runabout, jokingly called by Eisenhower the "surry with the fringe on top". The President used the Crosley to take visitors around the farm. Some of the world's most famous people, including Winston Churchill, Nikita Khrushchev and Charles De Gaulle, rode in this little car. Also in the garage is the chauffeur's quarters and a walk-in cooler for meat storage.

ED LUCKE'S AUTO PARTS (Salvage)

Rt 2 Box 2883
GLENVILLE, PA 17329
(15 miles south-southwest of York near the Maryland state line)
Phone: 717-235-2866
Hours: M-F 9-5, Sat 9-noon

This large salvage lot, with some 1800 vehicles, specializes in PACKARDs from 1939 to 1956, CHRYSLER products from 1939 and later and has many CORVAIRs.

There are also some Fords from the 1950s and 1960s. Customers may browse the yard. In business since 1968.

EPERTHENER'S AUTO WRECKING (Salvage)

683 Teiline Rd
GROVE CITY, PA 16127
(25 miles east of Youngstown, OH on PA SRs 58 and 173)
Phone: 814-786-7173
Hours: M-F 9-5, Sat 9-noon

Did you ever see a 1937 Chevrolet full of hub caps? You will see one here at Eperthener's. You will also see hundreds of old cars and trucks dating back to the 1940s. They also have some NOS parts and a nice selection of old manuals dating back to the 1930s. And how about your antique snowmobile? You can get parts for it here too. The Eperthener's used to be dealers for the Polaris snowmobiles. Visitors may browse the yard with permission, but company personnel remove all parts. This is a family-run business. The person that answers the phone will probably be one of the Epertheners. They started in 1957.

STATE MUSEUM OF PENNSYLVANIA

3rd and North Sts
HARRISBURG, PA 17108
(South-central part of the state on I-81, I-76 and I-83)
Phone: 717-787-4978
Hours: Tues-Sat 9-5, Sun noon-5, closed holidays. Free.

This is the official museum of the state of Pennsylvania with displays on a

The Antique Automobile Club of America Library and Research Center, Hershey, PA, was founded in 1981 and is open to visitors and researchers.

wide variety of topics including the history, industry, natural resources, arts and people of the state. There are about 10 antique autos in the museum including a 1902 Gardner Serpollet steam car, a 1903 Pierce Stanhope, a 1904 Franklin with a rear entrance door, a 1905 Autocar roadster and a 1909 Zimmerman high wheel touring car. The museum has an automotive library with 15 volumes of literature plus periodicals and is open to the public by appointment.

ANTIQUE AUTOMOBILE CLUB OF AMERICA LIBRARY AND RESEARCH CENTER

501 W Governor Rd
HERSHEY, PA 17033
(12 miles east of Harrisburg)
Phone: Library 717-534-2082,
National Headquarters 717-534-1910
Hours: M-F 8:30-3:45

This is a large library created and operated by the Antique Automobile Club of America and open to visitors and researchers. The library has a wealth of information on antique cars including books, periodicals, catalogs, sales literature, ads, brochures, owner's manuals, shop manuals, parts books, color charts and chips, photographs, sheet music, postcards, calendars, jokes, cartoons and company annual reports. Materials may not be taken from the library but library personnel will photocopy or otherwise provide working copies for borrowers and researchers. Individuals seeking research information should request a Research Request Form from the Library in order to facilitate the research process. Fees are charged for research work done by library personnel.

The AACA is planning to build a large collector car museum in the near

223

The Swigart Museum of Huntingdon, PA is the oldest antique car museum in the US.

future at a nearby location. In the meantime some of the cars to be displayed in the museum are on display at the Library.

SWIGART MUSEUM
US 22 East (4 miles east of Huntingdon)
HUNTINGDON, PA 16652
(22 miles east of Altoona)
Phone: 814-643-0885
Hours: Memorial Day through Oct 9-5, closed rest of year. Admission charged.

One of the foremost collections of antique cars including DuPont, Carroll, Scripps-Booth, 1930 Model J Dual-Cowl Duesenberg, 1936 Duesenberg Gentlemen's Speedster Prototype and the latest addition—"Herbie the Love Bug". Other exhibits include the world's largest collection of license plates, also name plates, horns, lights, toys and period clothing. William E. Swigart, Jr. is the owner.

▼ PHILADELPHIA AREA

FRANKLIN MINT MUSEUM
Rt 1 (1 mile south of SR 452 on US 1)
FRANKLIN CENTER, PA 19091
(12 miles southwest of Philadelphia on US 1)
Phone: 610-459-6168
Hours: M-Sat 9:30-4:30, Sun 1-4:30. Free.

This is the company museum of the Franklin Mint which displays several thousand of the company's precision molded metal products. Included in the collection are coins, Faberge jewelry, medals, plaques, tableware and plates. Since the Franklin Mint is one of the world's leading manufacturers of precision automobile models the museum has a generous display of these. The company has announced an on-going program with the mission of keeping automotive history alive by continuing to manufacture precision models of automobiles that have historical significance and/or have made a special marque in the automotive world. Therefore, the collection of precision automobile models will be ever-expanding. The museum offers a video presentation showing step-by-step how the models are made. There is also a large gift shop in which many of the models are offered for sale along with items manufactured by the Franklin Mint.

FREE LIBRARY OF PHILADELPHIA AUTOMOBILE

REFERENCE COLLECTION
1901 Vine St
PHILADELPHIA, PA 19103
Phone: 215-686-5404
Hours: Automobile Collection M-F 9-5. Library M-W 9-9, Thurs-F 9-6, Sat 9-5, Sun 1-5, closed on Sundays in the summer and on holidays. Free.

This is a large city library with one of the larger collections of automotive literature in the country. The Automotive Reference Collection is open as noted above. No browsing permitted.

End of Philadelphia Area g

KLINGER'S USED AUTO SALES (Salvage)
RD 3 Box 454
PINE GROVE, PA 17963 (About halfway between Allentown and Harrisburg off I-81)
Phone: 717-345-8778
Hours: M-F 9-5, Sat 8-4

This large salvage lot, with approximately 2500 vehicles, specializes in 1941 to 1956 CHEVROLET cars and trucks and 1963 to 1980 FORD cars and trucks. Customers may browse the yard and an inventory list is available. Klinger's also does radiator repair work. This yard is quite unique in that it is surrounded by a wall of cars stacked up to 4-high. It makes a very effective fence and deterrent to trespassers. Klinger's has been in business since 1982. Dean Klinger is the owner.

▼ PITTSBURGH AREA

THE FRICK ART & HISTORICAL CENTER (Museum)
7227 Reynolds St (In Point Breeze)
PITTSBURGH, PA 15208
Phone: 412-371-0606
Hours: Guided tours Tues-Sat 10-5, Sun noon-6, closed major holidays. Reservations are recommended. Admission charged.

Clayton, the historic home which is the centerpiece of the Frick Art & Historic Center, was the home and estate of the famous industrialist Henry Clay Frick. It is open to the public and is furnished with many of the original belongings of the Frick family. On the grounds is a visitors center, art museum, greenhouse, children's playhouse and a new (1997) 1500 sq ft car and carriage museum. That museum displays many of the Frick's personal vehicles including a 1914 Rolls-Royce Silver Ghost and a 1931 Lincoln as well as rare antique cars from Pittsburgh collectors. Highlights include an 1898 Panhard Tonneau once owned by H. J. Heinz's son Howard, a 1909 Mercedes, a 1931 Pierce-Arrow and other vehicles owned or manufactured in Pittsburgh between 1898-1940. A film in the museum's video theater traces the impact of automobiles on U. S. history and culture.

STATION SQUARE TRANSPORTATION MUSEUM
Bessemer Court at Station Square
PITTSBURGH, PA 15219

Phone: 412-471-5808
Hours: May-Dec 11:30-8, Jan-Apr noon-6. Admission charged.

This museum relates the history of transportation in the Pittsburgh area from its founding to the present. Included in the generous display of transportation vehicles are about a dozen cars. Some of the cars, such as the 1911 Penn 30 and the Artzberger steam wagon, were made in Pittsburgh. Also exhibited is an 1898 Panhard, which was the first car in Pittsburgh, imported from France by the H. J. Heinz family. The museum has an interesting collection of motorcycles, carriages, model cars, toy cars, planes and trains. There is a nice gift and souvenir shop on the premises.

End of Pittsburgh Area △

TYRED WHEELS MUSEUM
Russell Corner Rd (Rt 2, Box 302)
PLEASANTON, PA 16341 (60 miles south of Erie)
Phone: 814-676-0756
Hours: Memorial Day to Sept 1 daily 1-5

This museum is in the heart of Pennsylvania oil country and has some 5000 miniature vehicle models on display. There are Danbury and Franklin Mint miniatures, dealer promotional models, miniature tractors and trains. In addition to the miniatures there are 25 antique automobiles plus airplanes, motorcycles, old radios, bicycles, pedal cars doll houses and tin toys. This is a

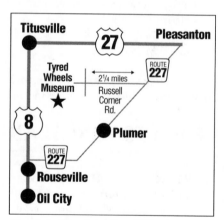

Here is how to get to Tyred Wheels Museum.

family-owned museum run by Gene, Cora and Darrin Burt.

▼ POCONO MOUNTAIN AREA

JEM CLASSIC CAR MUSEUM

SR 443 (10 miles west of
Lehighton)
ANDREAS, PA 18211 (20 miles
northwest of Allentown)
Phone: 717-386-3554
Hours: Memorial Day Weekend
through Oct 31 M-F 10-4. Admission charged

This museum, nestled in the beautiful Pocono Mountains, displays about 45 cars. Cars range in age from 1902 to 1966. Visitors will see a Cord, Gardner, Wills St. Claire, Graham-Page, Auburn, Studebaker, Sears, Maxwell, Cole, Stutz and many others. The museum has a nice collection of motorcycles too. There is a gift shop and a snack bar. Car clubs are always welcome. The museum's executive director is Harry Loder.

POCONO HISTORICAL MUSEUM

Rt 661, Shine Hill Rd
SCOTRUN, PA 18360
Phone: 717-629-0700

Hours: June 15 through Oct 31 daily 10-4. Admission charged.

This historical museum has a diversity of displays which include antique household items, farm equipment, tools, ship models, antique office equipment, toys, fire trucks and antique cars. The oldest car in the car collection dates from 1904 and the newest is a 1966 Lincoln. There is also a 1922 Ford Model T touring car, a 1929 Chevrolet Roadster, a World War II Jeep, several fire trucks and a small 1952 Vespa circus car that could hold 10 clowns. The museum has a nice collection of motorcycles too. Owners are Frank and Norma Young.

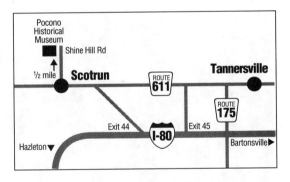

End of Pocono Mountain Area △

WINNICK'S AUTO SALES & PARTS (Salvage)

SR 61 East
SHAMOKIN, PA 17872 (40 miles
northeast of Harrisburg)
Phone: 717-648-6857
Hours: M-F 8-5, Sat 8-noon

This salvage yard has about 500 domestic and imported cars and trucks, and specializes in 1965 to 1975 MUSTANGs and CAMAROs. Other makes of cars can also be found on the lot. Customers may browse the yard. In business since 1963,

Pennsylvania

GAST CLASSIC MOTORCAR EXHIBIT (Museum & dealer)

421 Hartman Bridge Rd
(On SR 896 just north of town)
STRASBURG, PA 17579
(8 miles southeast of Lancaster)
Phone: 717-687-9500
Hours: Daily 9-5, closed Jan 1,
Easter, Thanksgiving, Dec 24 and
25. Admission charged.

This is a beautiful exhibit of approximately 50 restored and fine original vehicles with about 20 of the cars for sale and therefore constantly changing the makeup of the exhibit. Some of the more permanent vehicles include a 1929 MG purchased by Edsel Ford and was the first MG imported into the US, and a 1980 MGB, purchased by Henry Ford, II which was the last MG imported into the US. There is also a 1930 American Austin Deluxe Roadster, a 1938 Lincoln Zephyr, a 1948 Tucker, a 1964-$^1/_2$ Mustang, a 1967 Amphicar and a 1971 Rolls-Royce once owned by entertainer Michael Jackson's family. Gast's has a large gift shop called the "Car Buffs Gift Shop" which offers a generous assortment of automotive-oriented gifts, books, posters, jewelry, etc. Jeffrey A. Gast is the proprietor of the establishment.

TEE-TO-TUM MUSEUM

US 6
WYSOX, PA 18848 (50 miles northwest of Scranton on US 6)
Phone: 717-265-5505 or
717-265-8272

The ever-changing display of vehicles at the Gast Classic Motorcar Exhibit includes autos available for purchase.

Hours: Apr through Nov Tues-F 10-4. Rest of year by appointment. Admission charged.

This is a privately-owned museum displaying over 25 antique cars from 1897 to WW II (but mostly pre-1915) in restored, original or as found condition. There are unique cars such as Grant and Brough and others such as Franklin, Reliable Dayton, REO, Schacht, Waverly, RCH, Buick Cadillac, Bantam, Sears, Autocar, Locomobile, Case, Lafayette and Chase. There are related displays of engines, accessories, advertising, and oil company advertising. In addition there are displays of antique dolls, toys, firearms, tools and many other American antiques.

The museum is managed by Howard and Dietland Crain and there is a small antique shop on the premises.

▼ YORK AREA (25 miles south of Harrisburg on I-83)

AGRICULTURAL AND INDUSTRIAL MUSEUM OF YORK COUNTY
480 E Market St
YORK, PA 17403
Phone: 717-852-7007
Hours: Tues, Thurs and Sat 10-4. Closed major holidays. Admission charged.

This is a large county-owned museum with two locations that trace the history of York County from just before the Civil War thru World War I. Exhibits highlight industrial equipment, agricultural items and products used and made in York County. Many of the exhibits are hands-on for additional educational appeal. In the E. Market St. location is a collection of antique vehicles including several made in York County such as the Pullman automobile, the Bell Car and a Mayflower Huck-

Visitors will see Pullman automobiles like these, which were made in York County, at the Agricultural and Industrial Museum of York County. Left is a 1909 Pullman touring car; right, a 1910 Pullman touring car.

ster Wagon. In the second location, at 217 W. Princess St., is a REO bus with a body made in York County. The museum also has a collection of horse-drawn vehicles, antique farm equipment, engines (some made in York County), an old machine shop, weaving equipment, boats, a locomotive and railroad cars, a grist mill and displays on various automobile components made in York County over the years.

THE FIRE MUSEUM OF YORK COUNTY

757 W Market St
YORK, PA 17404
Phone: 717-843-0464
Hours: Apr 1 thru Oct 31, Sat noon-4, Second Sun of each month noon-4. For rest of the year please phone for special hours.

This fine fire museum is housed in York's old Royal Fire Station and traces the history of firefighting in York County from pre-Revolutionary days to the present. On display are hand-drawn and horse-drawn vehicles, leather buckets, uniforms, fire alarms, Currier & Ives prints, photos and many other items related to firefighting. On the wall of the old fire house are engraved the names of the horses who served the station prior to their being replaced by motorized equipment. The living quarters of

the firemen has been restored complete with a brass slide pole. The museum has several pieces of motorized firefighting equipment including a 1919 Model T firetruck, a 1933 Ahern-Fox and a 1955 American-LaFrance.

RODNEY C. GOTT MUSEUM AND HARLEY-DAVIDSON ASSEMBLY PLANT

1425 Eden Rd
(one mile east of exit 9E of I-83)
YORK, PA 17402 (25 miles east-southeast of Harrisburg)
Phone: 717-848-1177
Hours: Combined plant & museum tours M-F at 10, 12:30 and 1:30. Museum tours only Sat at 10, 11, 1 and 2. Museum closed holidays. Plant closed during model changeover which is from the last week of June through the last week of July. Free.

This is a large motorcycle assembly plant with a company-related motorcycle museum. On the plant tours visitors will see a motorcycle assembled every 90 seconds. In the museum are HARLEY-DAVIDSON motorcycles dating from 1903, their first year of production, to the present. There are exhibits of old motorcycle ads, racing trophies, photographs and other motorcycle memorabilia.

End of York Area △

RHODE ISLAND

BILL'S AUTO PARTS (Salvage)
1 Macondry St
CUMBERLAND HILL, RI 02864
(10 miles north of Providence)
Phone: 401-725-1225
Hours: M-F 8-4:30, Sat 8-4,
Sun 9-3.

This salvage yard has approximately 1000 vehicles of US and imported makes. Most are from the 1970s and 1980s, but there is a good selection of 1950s and 1960s vehicles. An inventory list is available and customers may browse the yard. Bill's also offers new parts. In business since 1963.

ARNOLD'S AUTO PARTS (Salvage)
1484 Crandall Rd
TIVERTON, RI 02878 (5 miles southwest of Fall River, MA)
Phone: 401-624-6936
Hours: M-F 8-5, Sat 8-3

This salvage yard, with about 1000 vehicles, specializes in cars and trucks of mixed makes from the 1930s to the 1970s. Most are domestic. Arnold's also offers a towing service. Customers may browse the yard. In business since 1952.

SOUTH CAROLINA

NMPA STOCK CAR HALL OF FAME AND THE JOE WEATHERLY MUSEUM
SR 34 West (adjoining the Darlington Raceway)
DARLINGTON, SC 29532
(10 miles northwest of Florence)
Phone: 803-395-8821
Hours: Daily 8:30-5. Admission charged.

This hall of fame and museum honors famous individuals in the sport of stock car racing. There are pictures and plaques of those who have been honored in the Hall of Fame and the museum displays a collection of history-making stock cars. Included in the collection is the 1950 Oldsmobile driven by "Buck" Baker which was the first car to qualify in the first Southern 500 here at Darlington, and Johnny Mantz' 1950 Plymouth which won the first race. Other cars include Jim Reed's 1957 Chevrolet, David Pearson's #21 Mercury, Cale Yarborough's #11 Chevrolet, Richard Petty's 1967 Plymouth, Joe Weatherly's #8 Mercury and Bill Elliott's Thunderbird that won NASCAR's $1 millon bonus in 1988. Also on display is the Chevrolet that Darrel Waltrip flipped at Daytona in 1991 with a video of the crash. The museum has a gift and souvenir shop offering stock car-related merchandise.

COOK'S GARAGE (Salvage)
Callison Highway
GREENWOOD, SC 29646 (50 miles south of Greenville on US 25)
Phone: 803-227-2731 and
803 227-9415 after 6 pm.
Hours: M-F 8-6, Sat by appointment.

This salvage yard of about 300 vehicles has Ford Model T's from the 1920s to cars and pickups of the 1970s. All makes are represented. There are some whole cars for sale and Cook's can

Some of the restorable whole cars are displayed in front of Cook's Garage.

232

supply NOS and NORS parts. Services available include engine rebuilding, sandblasting, towing and partial or complete restoration. Customers may browse the yard. In business since 1968. J.P. Cook is the owner.

SCHOOLHOUSE ANTIQUES MUSEUM
517 Flat Rock Rd
LIBERTY, SC 29657 (15 miles west of Greenville on Hwy 135 and Flat Rock Rd)
Phone: 864-843-6827
Hours: W-Sat 11-5, Sun 1-5.
Admission charged.

Entrance to BMW Zentrum Museum and Visitors Center, Spartenburg, SC.

This museum has the largest varied antique collection in the southeast. Browse through an early barber shop, traveling dentist office (fillings are 25 cents), general store, tavern, 7-room house and an early "Auto Supply Store". Twenty some vehicles are on display including a 1904 three-wheel Riley (driven from the rear seat), the only existing 1905 Armac, a 1905 REO, a 1912 Renault, a 1912 belt-driven Yale and a 1920 Indian Power-Plus motorcycle. Guided tours can be provided for one or a dozen visitors with a guarantee you will see things you have never seen before.

BMW ZENTRUM MUSEUM AND VISITORS CENTER AND FACTORY TOUR
PO Box 11000
SPARTENBURG, SC 29304-4100 (Northwest part of state)
Phone: 888-TOUR-BMW
Hours: Tues-Sat 9:30-5:30, Thurs

until 9. Admission charged.

This is the BMW company's museum and visitor center attached to their large manufacturing plant in Spartanburg. The museum traces the history of the company and highlights many of its contributions to the automotive industry. Several historic and antique BMW automobiles are on display in the museum including a 1930 Dixi, Formula I and II championship race cars, and the Z3 roadster used in some of the James Bond movies. Other displays include motorcycles, innovative engines and aircraft engines. In the engine display are engines designed to use alternative fuels. The museum has an extensive art gallery with paintings of auto-related subjects by world-famous artists. There is also a gift shop and a cafe.

To reach the BMW facility take exit 60 from I-85 South, proceed north and then west at the first stop light. Watch for signs leading to the facility.

SOUTH DAKOTA

▼ MITCHELL AREA (65 miles west of Sioux Falls)

The Middle Border Museum of American Indian and Pioneer Life in Mitchell, SD.

THE MIDDLE BORDER MUSEUM OF AMERICAN INDIAN AND PIONEER LIFE
1311 S Duff St
MITCHELL, SD 57301
Phone: 605-996-2122
Hours: June thru Aug M-Sat 8-6, Sun 10-6; May and Sept M-F 9-5, Sat and Sun 1-5; rest of year by appointment. Admission charged.

This is a museum complex of several buildings consisting of the Beckwith House (1886), the Territorial School (1885), a railroad depot (1900), a country church (1909), an art gallery and the main museum. In the museum are many displays of South Dakota history, American Indian artifacts, antique farm equipment, carriages and an exhibit of about 20 antique autos. Most of the au-

234

Telstar Mustang-Shelby-Cobra Museum's 1968 Shelby.

tos are on loan from local car buffs so the exhibit is ever-changing. There is also an old time general store and a gift shop.

TELSTAR MUSTANG-SHELBY-COBRA MUSEUM

1300-1400 S Kimball St
MITCHELL, SD 57301
Phone: 605-996-6550
Open: Mid-May thru mid-Sept, or any time upon request. Admission charged. Guided tours given.

This is the most complete privately-owned collection of MUSTANGs and SHELBYs in existence. Every year of Shelby, GT 350, GT 500, Shelby fastback and Shelby convertible are represented. In addition, there are several Cobras in the collection plus two extremely rare GT 500 428SCJ Drag-Pack convertibles, a 1969 Boss 429 NASCAR KK1318, a Boss 429 "Hemi" Tunnel Ram and a high-performance engine display. All the cars have been restored in Telstar's own restoration shop and are on display in their temperature and humidity-controlled showroom. The owners of the collection are Jerry and Mavis Regynski and Mr. Regynski has personally worked on the restoration of every vehicle in the museum.

End of Mitchell Area △

PIONEER AUTO MUSEUM AND ANTIQUE TOWN

Junction of I-90 and US 16/83
MURDO, SD 57559 (South-central part of the state on I-90)
Phone: 605-669-2691
Hours: June thru Aug daily 7 am-10 pm, Apr-May and Sept-Oct daily 8-6. Admission charged.

This is a large museum complex of more than 30 buildings, most of which comprise the "Antique Town". And, there is an unusually large collection of antique cars... nearly 250. Some of the cars of interest include a 1903 Oldsmobile, a 1904 Fuller touring car, a 1913 Argo electric, a 1921 Stutz, a 1925 Stanley Steamer, a 1921 White motor

Watch for the unique Pioneer Auto signs on your way to Pioneer Auto Museum and Antique Town.

home, a 1921 Cole, a 1930 Pierce-Arrow roadster, a 1931 De Vaux, a 1931 Packard once owned by cowboy movie star Tom Mix, a 1935 Auburn boattail, a 1937 Cord, a 1948 Tucker and a 1954 Kaiser Darrin. As a part of their Ford collection is a replica of Henry Ford's garage in which he built his first car. There is also a display of motorcycles one of which belonged to Elvis Presley. The museum has a cafe and a large and interesting gift shop. The contact person is Vivian Sonder.

MOTION UNLIMITED MUSEUM AND ANTIQUE CAR LOT (Museum and dealer)
6180 S Hwy 79
RAPID CITY, SD 57701
(Southwest corner of the state just east of The Black Hills)
Phone: 605-348-7373

Hours: M-F 9-6, Sat 9-4. Indoor museum open May-Oct, antique car lot open year around.

Here is a place that shows 'em and sells 'em. The best vehicles are, understandably, in the show room where some are for sale and some are not. Currently in the museum is a restored 1933 Dodge Delivery van, a 1926 Ford Model T Marshall's wagon, a 1925 Studebaker Motor Home and many other interesting vehicles. Owners Bill and Peggy Napoli do complete vehicle restorations so many of the vehicles on display are the products of their labor. Altogether, there are some 100 vehicles on display and for sale. Motorcycles are plentiful here too along with over 100 children's pedal cars, tractors and other memorabilia. Vehicles constantly change so this is a place you can visit often.

▼ SIOUX FALLS AREA (Southeastern corner of the state near the MN and IA state lines on I-29 and I-90)

HOWARD'S CORVETTES (Salvage)
Rt 3 Box 162
SIOUX FALLS, SD 57106
Phone: 605-368-5233
Hours: M-F 9-5:30, Sat 9-4

This is a small but very specialized salvage yard specializing in CORVETTEs from 1968-88. There are about 40 vehicles in the yard and an inventory list is available. In business since 1974.

LACEY'S VWs (Salvage)
Rt 1 Box 40
TRENT, SD 57065

(25 miles north of Sioux Falls)
Phone: 605-428-3145
Hours: M-F 9-5, Sat 9-1

Need a part for your Thing - or your Karmann Ghia or VW camper? No Problem! Just contact Lacey's. They have over 250 VWs of all models dating back to the 1950s. They also have a number of restorable cars that will be sold as a whole. Lacey's has some new parts such as rubber, glass, rust repair panels and upholstery. There are a few large trucks on the lot and a few Izusus too. If you have a "Bug" you should know about Lacey's.

End of Sioux Falls Area △

▼ STURGIS AREA (West-central part of the state on I-90)

JIM'S AUTO SALVAGE
Junction of SR 79 and SR 34
STURGIS, SD 57785
Phone: 605-347-2303 or 605-347-5636
Hours: M-F 8-5:30, Sat 8-2

Jim's Auto Salvage has about 1200 vehicles on their 14-acre lot. They specialize in CHEVROLETs, but have many cars and trucks of other makes. About 400 of the cars are pre-1970s with a good selection of 1955-57 models. There are a few cars from the 1920s,

1930s and 1940s. Jim Dempsey is the man to contact.

NATIONAL MOTORCYCLE MUSEUM & HALL OF FAME
1650 Lazelle
STURGIS, SD 57785
Phone: 605-347-4875
Hours: Open daily. Closed major holidays. Admission charged.

This museum pays tribute to those people who have contributed to the role of motorcycling in terms of industry,

237

transportation, recreation and competition. Some 100 motorcycles and motorscooters are on display along with dozens of photographs and other motorcycles memorabilia. Displays highlight the Black Hills Motor Classic, which is one of the biggest events in motorcycling, and J.C. "Pappy" Hoel who started the Classic. In the Hall of Fame are photos and information plaques on motorcyclists who have been honored. The museum has a gift shop offering many rally souvenirs and official logo products. Ed Netterberg is the executive director.

End of Sturgis Area △

MUSEUM OF WILDLIFE, SCIENCE & INDUSTRY
US 12 (1 mile west of its junction with SR 25)
WEBSTER, SD 57274 (10 miles west of Waubay on US 12)
Phone: 605-345-4751
Hours: May thru Sept M-F 9-5, Sat-Sun 1-5; rest of year as weather permits. Donations requested.

This is a fine local museum consisting of several buildings and displaying the attributes and historical assets of this part of South Dakota. Within the museum are a dozen antique vehicles including a 1919 Ford truck, a 1924 International truck, a 1930 Hupmobile, a 1937 Packard Model 120 4dr sedan and a 1966 Oldsmobile Toronado. Also in the museum are pieces of antique farm equipment, including about 70 tractors, horse-drawn equipment, tools and mounted animals. There is a fully furnished South Dakota farm house inside the museum and a small building built in the shape of a shoe.

WAYNE'S AUTO SALVAGE
WINNER, SD 57580 (South-central part of state on US 18\183)
Phone: 605-842-2054
Hours: M-F 9-6, Sat 10-4

American-made cars from 1937 to 1970 are a specialty of this salvage yard with over 1500 vehicles on 20 acres. There is a very good selection of Ford coupes from 1946 to 1948 and there are many "orphans" such as Hudsons, Kaisers, Frazers, Nashes, Studebakers, etc. Customers may browse the yard. Wayne's also does mechanical repair work and has a muffler shop. In business since 1968.

TENNESSEE

SONNY'S AUTO PARTS (Salvage)
US Hwy 11 W
BLAINE, TN 37709
(15 miles east of Knoxville)
Phone: 423-932-2610 or 423-933-9137
Hours: M-Sat 9-5

Three brothers, Sonny, Mike and Gary Reeser run this 3000-vehicle salvage lot in the beautiful hills of eastern Tennessee. Visitors can browse the lot, but dress properly. This is no place for sandals. Sonny's cars and light trucks range in age from the 1940s and up. Most are a mix of domestic makes and models. Parts removal by customers is negotiable. Sonny is an avid antique car collector. Some of his 20+ personal vehicles may be seen at the yard.

INTERNATIONAL TOWING AND RECOVERY MUSEUM

The International Towing and Recovery Museum is located just northwest of downtown Chattanooga.

401 Broad St
CHATTANOOGA, TN 37402
Phone: 423-267-3132
Hours: M-F 10-4:30, Sat-Sun 11-5, closed major holidays. Admission charged.

This is the world's only tow truck museum. For years one of the country's

239

major towing equipment manufacturers was located in Chattanooga and this museum honors that memory as well as the unique nature of the vehicle towing and recovery business. Many restored tow trucks are on display dating back to the pre-World War I era. Displays also tell the history of vehicle towing and recovery. The walls of the museum are generously covered with photos, painting, prints and other towing memorabilia. There is a nice gift shop offering collectibles, toy tow trucks, souvenirs and other interesting items. Remember that good feeling you get when that long-awaited tow truck arrives and pulls your car out of the ditch or snow bank?

CARS AND PARTS (Salvage)
157 Ed. MacDonald Rd
DYER, TN 38330 (Northwestern corner of state on US 45W and 22 miles east of Dyersburg)
Phone: 901-643-6448
Hours: M-Sat 6-8

This is a small salvage yard with only 30 cars, but there are four barns full of parts for FORD Model T's, Model A's and early Ford V-8's. There are also some motorcycle parts, tractor parts, peddle cars and thousands of $^1/_{16}$ and $^1/_{64}$-scale toy farm tractors for sale. Customers may browse the yard. In business since 1963.

▼ KNOXVILLE-SMOKEY MOUNTAIN AREA

**STAR CARS COLLECTION
(Museum)**
914 Parkway
(Next to the Convention Center)
GATLINBURG, TN 37738 (Eastern Tennessee at the entrance to the Smoky Mountain National Park)
Phone: 423-430-7900
Hours: Daily 10-10, admission charged.

Here is a very unique car display - cars used in, and sometimes made for, Hollywood movies and TV shows. Most of the 30 cars on display were created by the famous car designer, George Barris of Hollywood. Here can be seen the world's only stone-age automobile, the Flintstone-mobile, the Dukes of Hazard's "General Lee", the Monster's "Drag-u-la" and cars from the Beverly Hillbillies, Jurassic Park and Knight Rider. There are some celebrity cars here too, cars which belonged to Burt Reynolds, Frank Sinatra, Charlie Sheen and Elvis.

Another unique attraction inside the museum is Celebrity Golf, an 18-hole miniature golf course where golfers play through recreated Hollywood sets and related movie and TV memorabilia. Stop in, you will have fun. Charles Moore is the general manager.

FLOYD GARRETT'S MUSCLE CAR MUSEUM
320 Winfield Dunn Parkway
(Hwy 66)
SEVIERVILLE, TN 37876

This 1941 Buick convertible is one of the interesting cars on display at the Smoky Mountain Car Museum.

(23 miles east of Knoxville near the western entrance to the Smokey Mountain National Park)
Phone: 423-908-0882
Hours: Daily year around except Thanksgiving and Dec 25.

MUSCLE CAR lovers usually smile from ear-to-ear when they walk into this museum. There are 90+ muscle cars—over five million dollars worth—for them to savor. Not surprisingly, this is the largest collection of muscle cars ever permanently assembled in one location. Some of the cars once belonged to famous people such as Richard Petty's Monte Carlo, two of "Smokey" Yunick's Chevrolets and Dale Earnhardt's Goodwrench Monte Carlo. All of the cars are American-made. Also on display are rare engines and other memorabilia as well as NASCAR souvenirs.

SMOKY MOUNTAIN CAR MUSEUM
2970 Parkway (US 441),
PO Box 385
PIGEON FORGE, TN 37868-0385
(Near the western entrance to Smoky Mountain National Park)
Phone: 423-453-3433
Hours: Early spring-late fall daily 10-6, rest of year please inquire. Admission charged.

There are about 30 cars in this museum and some of them are associated with famous, and infamous, people. For example, there is Hank Williams, Jr's. "Silver Dollar" car, James Bond's "007" car used in the movies "Goldfinger" and "Thunderball", Elvis Presley's Mercedes Benz, country comedian Stringbean's Cadillac, Billy Carter's pickup truck, gangster Al Capone's 1928 bullet-proof

Elvis Presley's "Solid Gold" Cadillac is on display in the Country Music Hall of Fame & Museum.

Cadillac, a 1930 Model J Duesenberg, and a 1999 Plymouth Prowler. There is also a 1968 Oldsmobile Toronado used as an unmarked car by the legendary Buford Pusser who was portrayed in the movie "Walking Tall". Other displays include gas pump globes, radiator emblems and other automotive memorabilia. For sale in the museum are automotive books, posters and post cards. B. H. Atchley is the museum's owner.

End Knoxville-Smokey Mountain Area △

▼ MEMPHIS AREA
(Southwestern corner of the state on the Mississippi River)

MEMPHIS AUTO STORAGE
(Salvage & dealer)
2610 Fite Rd
MEMPHIS, TN 38127
Phone: 901-353-9078
Hours: M-F 8-5, Sat 8-noon

There are some 500 vehicles on this 5 acre salvage yard and many of them are offered complete as restorable vehicles. The company specializes in convertibles, muscle cars and special interest cars. There is also a nice selection of 1955-57 Chevrolet and 1964-67 Mustang parts cars. Highest concentration of cars is from late 1950s through the early 1970s. The company has a unique "lay away" plan by which a customer can purchase a car on time. No storage fee or interest is charged. Richard Massey is the owner.

ELVIS PRESLEY AUTOMOBILE MUSEUM

3764 Elvis Presley Blvd
MEMPHIS, TN 38116
Phone: Graceland 800-238-2000,
Corporate Office 901-332-3322, the
museum has no direct phone.
Hours: Memorial Day weekend
thru Labor Day daily 8-7, rest of
year 9-6, closed Jan 1, Thanksgiving
and Dec 25. Admission charged.

This museum is across the street
from Graceland, Elvis Presley's home,
and contains many of his cars and "toys".
There are 8 cars, 2 planes, motorcycles,
jet skis, golf carts and other possessions
he collected during his fascinating, but
short life.

Nearby is the Sincerely Elvis
Museum displaying many of Presley's
personal belongings, stage costumes
and home movies. Graceland is open to
the public and is one of the most popular tourist sites in Tennessee.

End of the Memphis Area △

▼ NASHVILLE AREA

THE COUNTRY MUSIC HALL OF FAME & MUSEUM

4 Music Square East
NASHVILLE, TN 37203
Phone: 615-256-1639 or
615-255-5333
Hours: Memorial Day to Labor Day
daily 8-6, rest of year daily 9-5.
Admission charged.

The Country Music Hall of Fame &
Museum features over 3000 treasures
from country music's legends and su-
perstars. Browse through the numerous
displays of photos, instruments, awards,
original song manuscripts, personal
items, glittering costumes and two cars
. . Elvis Presley's "Solid Gold" Cadillac
and the 1962 "Silver Dollar" Bonneville
owned and customized by the "King of
the Honky Tonk", Webb Pierce. There is
a large museum store offering a wide variety of country music-related items and
souvenirs.

MUSIC VALLEY CAR MUSEUM

2611 W McGavock Pike (Northern
edge of Opryland USA)
NASHVILLE, TN 37214
Phone: 615-885-7400
Hours: Memorial Day to Labor Day
daily 8 am - 10 pm, rest of year
daily 9-5 (hours may vary, please
phone ahead). Closed Thanksgiving
and Dec 25. Admission charged.

This museum is next door to the
Music Valley Wax Museum of the Stars
and displays about 50 vehicles. Many of
the cars belonged to famous country and
western music performers such as Dolly
Parton, Hank Snow, Chet Atkins, Randy
Travis, Tom T. Hall, Ronnie Stoneman,
George Jones, Hank Williams, Jr., Joe
Don Baker and Elvis Presley. Most of the
other cars are antiques and special interest vehicles and some are for sale. The
displays at the museum change weekly.
There is a gift shop offering a wide vari-

243

Marty Robbins' 1934 Packard straight 8 limousine at the World Famous Car Collector Hall of Fame.

ety of items related to the country music scene and the Grand Ole Opry.

JIM REEVES MUSEUM

1023 Joyce Lane (Off Briley Pkwy)
NASHVILLE, TN 37203
Phone: 615-226-2065 or
615-226-2062
Hours: Daily 9-5, closed Jan 1,
Thanksgiving and Dec 25.
Admission charged.

This museum, housed in a magnificent old mansion, honors the memory of the late country singer, Jim Reeves. On display are his guitars and other musical instruments, music awards, stage costumes, his turquoise collection and other personal items. One exhibit details his brief stint as a minor league baseball player. Of special interest to antique car buffs is Reeves' tour bus which he and the members of his entourage used extensively. Also in the museum are two of his personal cars, a 1960 Cadillac and a 1946 Plymouth. The

museum has a gift shop offering many items pertaining to Reeves.

HANK WILLIAMS, JR. MUSEUM

1524 Demonbreun St. (In the heart of Music Row)
NASHVILLE, TN 37203
Phone: 615-242-8313
Hours: Memorial Day thru Labor Day Sun-Thurs 9 am-8 pm, F-Sat 8 am-5 pm. Rest of year daily 8-6. Closed Dec 25. Admission charged.

This museum honors the career of Hank Williams, Jr. and has displays on his hit songs, awards, musical instruments, stage costumes and personal belongings. There are two of Williams' autos in the museum, a 1958 Cadillac and the 1952 Cadillac in which his father, Hank Williams, Sr., was fatally injured. The museum has a gift shop offering many souvenirs and items of interest related to the careers of Hank, Jr. and Hank, Sr.

WALDON AUTO SALVAGE

5356 Murfreesboro Rd
LaVERGNE, TN 37086 (A southeastern suburb of Nashville)
Phone: 615-793-2791
Hours: M-F 8-5, Sat 8-noon

This salvage yard has approximately

1200 American-made cars and trucks and specializes in the years 1960 to 1975. Customers may browse the yard. In business since 1955.

WORLD FAMOUS CAR COLLECTORS HALL OF FAME
1534 Demonbreun St.
(In the heart of Music Row)
NASHVILLE, TN 37203
Phone: 615-255-6804
Hours: May thru Oct 1 daily
9 am-8 pm, rest of year daily 9-5.
Admission charged.

This museum displays about 45 antique cars, all in mint condition. Many of them once belonged to famous coun-

try and western stars. Included in the collection is a 1975 Chrysler Imperial which was Roy Acuff's last car, Louise Mandrell's 1953 MG-TD, Marty Robbins' 1934 Packard, Tammy Wynette's custom-built 1982 Buick Riviera and Elvis Presley's 1976 Cadillac Eldorado. There is also a Delorean, many restored Chevrolets and Ford and the "Batmobile" used in the Batman TV series. Other displays include musical instruments, period fashions and a doctor's parlor. In the museum is the Gift Shop with many souvenirs, gifts and items of memorabilia for sale from Music City. Lori Sweeny is the museum's director.

End of Nashville Area △

DIXIE GUN WORKS OLD CAR MUSEUM
US Hwy 51 SOUTH
UNION CITY, TN 38261 (North-western corner of the state)
Phone: 901-885-0700

Hours: M-F 8-5, Sat 8-noon. Closed holidays. Admission charged to the car museum.

Visitors to this museum will see 34 antique and classic cars, dating from

The Dixie Gun Works has a display of antique automobiles and antique firearms.

Tennessee

1908 thru the 1940s. Included in the collection are 21 Fords, a 1912 Cadillac, the first production car equipped with a Kettering self-starter, a 1926 Pierce-Arrow roadster, a 1930 Packard 7-passenger limousine and a 1936 Packard 7-passenger sedan. Other displays include steam engines, steam whistles, headlights, bulb horns and farm equipment. The Dixie Gun Works is a firm that specializes in supplying parts for antique guns and rifles. Dixie has a display of over 1000 antique guns and a replica of an early American gunsmith's shop. Hunter Kirkland, Vice President, runs the car museum.

GALE SMYTH ANTIQUE AUTO (Salvage)
8316 East A J Hwy
WHITESBURG, TN 37891
(45 miles northeast of Knoxville)
Phone: 615-235-5221
Hours: M-Sat 8-6

This large salvage yard has about 1300 vehicles and specializes primarily in American-made cars and trucks from 1935 to 1972. An inventory list is available and customers may browse the yard. Bumper rechroming service is also offered. In business since 1973.

TEXAS

▼ AMARILLO AREA
(In the center of the Texas panhandle)

PANHANDLE-PLAINS HISTORICAL MUSEUM
2401 4th Av
CANYON, TX 79016 (15 miles south of downtown Amarillo)
Phone: 806-656-2244
Hours: June thru Aug M-Sat 9-6, Sun 1-6, rest of year M-Sat 9-5, Sun 1-6. Closed Jan 1, Thanksgiving and Dec 25. Donations requested.

This is the oldest and largest state-owned museum in Texas. It has major displays on the history, economy, geology, Indians and pioneer settlers of northwestern Texas. Also, there is a reconstructed turn-of-the-century pioneer town with shops, homes and other buildings filled with artifacts of the period. There is a large transportation display with horse-drawn vehicles and about a dozen antique cars. Motorized vehicles of interest include a 1903 Ford Model A, serial number 28, which is believed to be the oldest surviving assembly-line-manufactured car in the world, a 1915 Ford Model T touring car, a 1915 Detroit Electric, a 1933 Pierce-Arrow limousine and a 1954 Nash Metropolitan. The museum has a large transportation library with an extensive automotive section, a snack area and a gift and souvenir shop.

UP-ENDED CADILLACS (Curiosity)
I-40 West of town
AMARILLO, TX

Driving along I-40 west of Amarillo one will note on the south side of the highway 10 Cadillacs from the 1950s up-ended and partially buried in the ground. This is a pop-art sculpture, in a working grain field. It is the brain child of local millionaire Stanley Marsh III and is designed to pay homage to the extravagant automobile tail fins of that era. Locally the site is known as the "Cadillac Ranch".

End of Amarillo Area △

FIRE MUSEUM OF TEXAS
Walnut and Mulberry Sts
BEAUMONT, TX 77701
(East of Houston near the
Louisiana border)
Phone: 409-880-3917
Hours: M-F 8:00-4:30, closed on
major holidays, guided tours
available. Free.

This interesting fire museum, in the
Headquarters of the Beaumont Fire Department building, has 7 antique fire
trucks along with displays of firefighting
equipment such as uniforms, fire extinguishers, alarm systems and other
firefighting memorabilia. A fire safety
area has hands-on exhibits for children.
The museum has an annual car show
and swap meet in the first week of August.

SAM RAYBURN HOUSE MUSEUM
US 82 West
(2 1/4 miles west of town)
BONHAM, TX 75418
(60 miles northeast of Dallas
near the Oklahoma state line)
Phone: 903-583-5558
Hours: M-F 8-5, Sat-Sun noon-5.
Closed Jan 1, Thanksgiving, and
Dec 25. Free.

This was the 12-room farm home of
the famous Democrat politician Sam
Rayburn, Speaker of the US House of
Representatives at various times during
the 1930s, 1940s and 1950s. Rayburn
served in that capacity longer than any
other man in history and was one of the
major political figures of his day. The
home contains many of the Rayburn
family's furnishings and belongings. In
the garage are three cars, a 1945 Dodge
pickup truck used around the farm, a
1947 Plymouth Savoy 4dr sedan which
belonged to Sam's sister and a 1947
Cadillac Fleetwood which was acquired
by Rayburn in the following manner.
After one of the national elections the
Republicans won control of the House
of Representatives and Rayburn, being
a Democrat, had to step down as
Speaker. His Democrat colleagues offered to give him a new Cadillac as a
show of their appreciation for his lead-
ership thru the years. Rayburn declined
the offer, but let it be known that he
would accept personal checks from his
colleagues no larger than $25 each
which would be used toward the purchase of a new Cadillac. His colleagues
obliged and Rayburn was able to buy the
car. Some of the canceled $25 checks are
displayed in the museum.

▼ DALLAS/FORT WORTH AREA

BOLIN WILDLIFE EXHIBIT
(Museum)
1028 N McDonald St (SR 5)
McKINNEY, TX 75069
(20 miles north of Dallas)
Phone: 972-542-2639

Hours: M-F 9-noon and 1-4.
Closed holidays. Free.

This is a privately-owned museum
with a large display of mounted wildlife from around the world. There are

paintings, carvings and photographs of animals as well as a number of displays of the early history of the area. Included among the exhibits are five antique vehicles, all Fords; a 1913 Ford touring car, a 1915 Model T, a 1925 Model T, a 1930 Ford Model A roadster with rumble seat and a 1928 Ford truck that was converted to carry petroleum. Other vehicles include horse-drawn buggies and wagons including a John Deere wagon manufactured by the famous tractor maker before they went into motorized farm equipment.

Part of the antique vehicle display at Bolin Wildlife Exhibit.

CTC AUTO RANCH (Salvage)

I-35 Exit 474
(Between Denton and Sanger)
KRUM, TX 76249 (33 miles north of downtown Ft. Worth)
Phone: 940-482-3007
Hours: M-F 9-5, Sat 9-1.

There are some 1300 vehicles on this 28 acre salvage yard. Most of them are American-made vehicles and there is a respectable number of orphans. Most of the cars range in age from the 1940s through the 1970s. This is a very clean yard with the vehicles in neat rows and grass and weeds are kept mowed. Visitors may browse the yard with permission but yard personnel remove all parts. The yard is run by Dave Williamson and his sons, Dale and Allen. In business since 1985.

GREAT RACE HALL OF FAME (museum and race headquarters)

114 N Crockett St
GRANBURY, TX 76048 (30 miles southwest of Ft. Worth on US 377)
Phone: 817-573-5200 or
817-573-7223
Hours: F 10-5, Sat 10-6, Sun noon-5, M-Thurs go to office in rear for entry to the museum. Free.

This is the national headquarters, Hall of Fame and museum for the national "Great Race", a coast-to-coast race for antique cars that takes place annually. Displayed in the 14,000 sq ft museum are more than a dozen of the cars that have taken part in the race. The cars are still owned by the original owners so the display slowly changes. The Hall of Fame, of course, honors those associated with the race. Also on display are some 300 motorcycles, 100 pedal cars, some 2000 auto-related toys and other items associated with vintage vehicles. There are several events at the museum each year, a Texas regional race and a series of swap meets and sales called the "Great American Car Corral" every third Saturday in the month, March through October. There is lots going on in Granbury because it is a very big tourist town. The museum has a nice gift shop and the museum's manager is Keith Fleshman. Tom McRae is the founder of the Great Race and his wife, Sandi, is president of the association.

HENDERSON AUTO PARTS (Salvage)

307 Ball St
SEAGOVILLE, TX 75159 (10 miles southeast of Dallas on US 175)
Phone: 214-287-4787
Hours: M-Sat 8-6

There are about 750 vehicles of mixed makes on this salvage lot. All are older than 1976. An inventory list is available and customers may browse the lot. In business since 1978.

HONEST JOHN'S CADDY CORNER (Salvage)

2604 Roselawn
DENTON, TX 76201 (25 miles north of Dallas/Fort Worth)
Phone: 888-592-2339 or
817-566-5066
Hours: M-F 9-6

This salvage yard specializes in the parting out of CADILLACs from 1939

to 1980. Over 300 Cadillacs are in inventory and entire cars are offered for sale. NOS and reproduction parts are also available and Honest John's does mechanical work and restorations. In business since 1985. If you phone you can ask for Honest John.

PATE MUSEUM OF TRANSPORTATION

US 377
(3 miles north of Cresson, TX)
FT. WORTH, TX 76101
Phone: 817-332-1161
Hours: Tues-Sun 9-5. Free.

This is a large museum with airplanes, helicopters, railroad cars, a minesweeper and other forms of transportation including about 30 antique cars. Antique vehicles of note include a 1904 Schacht Runabout, a 1926 Franklin coupe, a 1934 Brewster Town Car, a 1934 Pierce-Arrow Silver Arrow, a 1935 Aston Martin Mark II Roadster, a 1938 Hupmobile, a 1950 ZIM sedan (Russian-made) and a 1957 Chrysler Ghia Limousine. There is also an automotive library, with 1500 pieces, which is open to the public. The Pate Museum is the home of the annual Pate Swap Meet, the third largest automotive swap meet in the country.

SOUTHWEST GALLERY OF CARS (Dealer)

6333 Denton Dr (Near southwest corner of Love Field Airport)
DALLAS, TX 75235
Hours: M-Sat 7:30-5:50
Phone: 214-350-9636 or
214-443-1212 (Voice Mail)

The Pate Museum of Ft. Worth, TX and its V-12-powerd 1937 Packard Club Sedan.

Gary Walker, the owner of this dealership, offers the public a very nice selection of muscle cars, sports cars and special interest cars. Most are from the 1940s through the 1970s. On average, about 60 cars are on display in their showroom. The company takes trades, sells on consignment, provides appraisals and offers long-term storage. Car clubs are welcome.

End of Dallas/Ft. Worth Area △

DAVID TAYLOR CLASSIC CAR MUSEUM
1918 Mechanic St
GALVESTON, TX 77550
(Southeastern coast of Texas on the Gulf of Mexico)
Phone: 409-765-6590
Hours: M-F 10-5.
Admission charged.

This museum is housed in three historic buildings on Galveston Island and displays over 50 vehicles. Of interest is a 1934 Chevrolet Master Deluxe Sedan with only 4300 miles on the odometer, a 1931 Packard Cabriolet, a 1940 Lincoln Continental convertible, a 1937 Cord Phaeton convertible and a 1949 Oldsmobile Rocket 88. There are two celebrity cars, a 1940 Mercury given to actress Carole Lombard by her husband, Clark Gable, and a 1941 Cadillac 62 Sedan owned by the Kellogg breakfast cereal family with only 42,000 miles on the odometer. The museum has a gift shop offering automobile-related items. JoBeth Litwin is the museum's director. (See photo, following page.)

David Taylor Classic Car Museum in Galveston.

TEXAS ACRES, MOPAR PARTS (Salvage)
1130 FM 2410
HARKER HEIGHTS, TX 76543
(An eastern suburb of Killeen which is 60 miles north of Austin)
Phone: 817-698-4555
Hours: M-F 8:30-5:30. Sat by appointment.

This is a small salvage yard of 50 vehicles, but all are Chrysler products. Texas Acres specializes in CHRYSLERs, DODGEs, PLYMOUTHs and DESOTOs from 1940 thru 1980. Customers may browse the yard. The company also does collision repairs and partial restorations. In business since 1984.

▼ HOUSTON AREA

NATIONAL MUSEUM OF FUNERAL HISTORY
415 Barren Springs Dr
HOUSTON, TX 77090
Phone: 281-876-3063
Hours: M-F 10-4, Sat-Sun noon-4

Here in this 20,000 sq. ft. Houston museum is the country's largest display of funeral service memorabilia. The museum is of interest to antique car buffs because of its sizeable collection of hearses and other funeral vehicles. There are also horse-drawn funeral vehicles on display. The museum offers group tours and there is a gift shop which can provide a catalog of the items it sells. Gary Sanders is the museum's curator.

THE TOY STORE (Dealer)
321 North Loop West
HOUSTON, TX 77008
Phone: 713-864-2277
Hours: M-F 9-7, Sat 9-3

This company carries more than 50 cars in inventory at any one time on an outdoor lot. Most of the cars are pre-1972 STREET RODS and MUSCLE CARS but vintage vehicles are also to be found. Some cars are sold on consignment and the company will take trades, arrange financing and transportation, do appraisals and search for specific vehicles. Customers will find from the company's inventory list that most of The Toy Store's cars are in the affordable range. Their company motto is "Poor Boys Paradise". Car clubs are welcome. Nobert Kurtz is the owner.

End of Houston area △

GAF AUTO MUSEUM
307 E Woodlawn
KILGORE, TX 75662 (On I-20 70 miles west of Shreveport, LA)
Phone: 800-234-0124 or
214-758-0002
Hours: M-F 8-5, free.

There are about 55 cars in this privately-owned museum ranging in age from 1916 to 1976. Highlights of the collection include a 1916 Ford touring car, a 1918 Chandler, a 1924 Franklin, a 1949 Cadillac convertible, a 1957 Ford Retractable and a 1941 Lincoln Mark I. The owner of the museum is Gordon A. Fenner.

This 1941 Cadillac Fleetwood 60 Special is one of the fine cars to be seen in the GAF collection.

Texas

KING RANCH MUSEUM

405 N 6th St
KINGSVILLE,
TX 78363
(30 miles
southwest
of Corpus
Christi)
Phone:
512-595-1881
Hours: M-Sat
10-4, Sun 1-5,
closed holidays. Admission charged.

A customized hunting car on display at the King Ranch Museum.

The King Ranch Museum is housed in the Henrietta Memorial Center, a renovated ice factory near downtown Kingsville, and displays many antique items from the local area and its famous namesake ranch. Included in the collection are several vintage cars including a customized Buick Eight used as a hunting car. There are also award-winning photographs by Toni Frissell who describe life on the King Ranch in the early 1940s.

ALAMO CLASSIC CAR MUSEUM

I-35 and Ingel Rd
NEW BRAUNFELS, TX 78130
(25 miles northeast of
San Antonio on I-35)
Phone: 830-606-4311

Alamo Classic Car Museum in New Braunfels.

Hours: Daily 9-5, admission charged.

This is a privately-owned museum with about 150 vehicles. Cars of interest include a custom-built 1967 Ford Mustang and a 1927 Dual Cowl Cadillac. The museum has what is claimed to be the world's largest collection of monkey wrenches. There are also displays of engines, automotive tools and hubcaps. Alamo Classic Car Museum is owned by Carl Van Roekel.

This Rolls-Royce Phantom II is one of many fine automobiles on display at the Central Texas Museum of Transportation.

CENTRAL TEXAS MUSEUM OF AUTOMOTIVE HISTORY

SR 304 North (12 miles south of Bastrop)
ROSANKY, TX 78953 (30 miles southeast of Austin on SR 304)
Phone: 512-237-2635
Hours: Apr 1 thru Sept 30 W-Sat 9-5, Sun 1:30-5. Rest of year F-Sat 10-5, Sun 1:30-5. Admission charged.

This is a large museum with over 100 vintage cars, many of them classic and historic vehicles. There is a 1902 Holsman 10 hp air-cooled four-seater, a 1903 Stanley Steamer, a 1911 Napier, a 1917 Pierce-Arrow 66 used by President Woodrow Wilson, a 1920 Empire 20 hp race car, a 1921 and 1924 Mercedes, a 1929 Stutz, a 1930 V-16 Cadillac, a 1933 Duesenberg, a 1948 Tucker and a Rolls-Royce once owned by singer Johnny Cash. Other displays include old gas pumps, license plates, automotive signs, photos, antique furniture and a reconstructed Texaco gas station. The museum has an interesting gift shop.

TEXAS TRANSPORTATION MUSEUM

11731 Wetmore Rd
SAN ANTONIO, TX 78247 (South-central part of the state)
Phone: 210-490-3554
Hours: Thurs, Sat & Sun 9-4. Admission charged.

This is part of the antique car collection on display at the Smokehose Auto Museum.

This is the home of the Longhorn & Wester Railroad and primarily a railroad museum. There are several buildings in the complex displaying locomotives, a large variety of railroad cars, electric rail vehicles, model trains, about a dozen antique cars, several antique trucks, firetrucks, antique farm equipment and horse-drawn vehicles. There is also a restored railroad station and train rides are offered on Sundays. Antique cars of interest include a 1928 Star 2-dr coupe, a 1929 REO Flying Cloud, a 1937 Cord, a 1938 Chevrolet, a 1965 Studebaker Daytona 2-dr sedan and a 1985 Pulse motorcycle/canopy car.

SMOKEHOUSE AUTO MUSEUM
905 West Business Loop 10
VAN HORN, TX 79855 (105 miles southeast of El Paso on I-10)
Hours: Daily 6 am-10:00 pm

This interesting museum is next to the Smokehouse Restaurant on I-10 Business Loop West. On display are more than a dozen vintage cars which are only a small part of a much larger collection. Cars are rotated every two weeks so that the whole collection is eventually displayed. Outstanding in the collection is the world's only 1902 Wheeler (made in Massachusetts) of which only three were made and one—this one—put into production. Also in the collection are many coupes from 1935 to 1942 along with a generous assortment of 1950s cars, some muscle cars and some imports. The museum's walls are covered with a wide assortment of automobilia and there is a nice gift shop selling books, models and many other auto-related items. Mitch Van Horn is the owner of this magnificent collection.

SOUTH SIDE SALVAGE
US 83 South
WELLINGTON, TX 79095
(Eastern edge of the Texas pan-
handle 40 miles south of I-40
near Oklahoma state line)
Phone: 806-447-2391
Hours: M-F 8-6

There are approximately 1200 vehicles
in this 9-acre yard. Most are American-
made. This is a dry area and many vehicles and parts are rust-free. Some vehicles are whole and restorable. In business since 1950. The owners are Marshall
and David Peters.

UTAH

NEPHI AUTO WRECKING (Salvage)
730 N 200 E Moab Rd (North of
Nephi just west of I-15)
NEPHI, UT 84648 (85 miles south
of Salt Lake City on I-15)
Phone: 435-623-2200
Hours: M-Sat 9-5

Over half of the vehicles in this 15
acre 1000-car lot are 20 years old or
older. Most are domestic makes with
some orphans, such as Studebakers and
Hudsons. Some NOS parts are also
available. There are several large trucks,
a collection of farm equipment and
some industrial items. Customers can
remove their own parts if they wish.
Clarence Phillipson is the owner.

UNION STATION MUSEUM
2501 Wall St
OGDEN, UT 84401
(30 miles north of Salt Lake City)
Phone: 801-629-8535
Hours: M-Sat 10-6, Sun (in the
summer) 11-3. Admission charged.

The Union Station Museum car collection has 7 Pierce-Arrows. This is one of them.

This is a small but elegant museum displaying about a dozen cars at a time from a larger collection. All are classics, each with its own unique history. A guide is usually in attendance to walk visitors thru the museum and narrate the history and details about each car. There are other cars in the collection stored elsewhere so those in the museum are rotated every six months. There are three other museums in the Union Station building; the Golden Spike Railroad Museum, the Natural History Museum and the Browning Firearms Museum. Union Station has a gift and souvenir shop which sells items related to all four museums.

▼ SALT LAKE CITY AREA

CLASSIC CAR MUSEUM
INTERNATIONAL
355 West 700 South St
SALT LAKE CITY, UT 84101
Phone: 801-322-5186 or
801-582-6883
Hours: M-F 9-3. Donations requested.

This is a privately owned collection of some 200 vehicles. Only a part of the collection is on display at this location. The cars are regularly rotated. Some are for sale. There are classics, special interest cars, show cars, cars of movie stars and other famous people. Cars of note include a 1904 Stevens-Duryea, a 1906 Cadillac Tulip, a 1929 Pierce-Arrow dual cowl phaeton, a 1929 Duesenberg Model J and a dual windshield 1938 V-12 Lincoln once owned by former Secretary of the Treasury Henry

Morgenthal. The museum is owned by Richard Williams.

REMEMBER WHEN (Dealer)
1450 S 4th West
SALT LAKE CITY, UT 84115
Phone: 801-463-1000
HOURS: M-F 10-6, Sat 10-5

This dealer likes to be known as "The Rocky Mountain Headquarters for Classic and Performance Cars". That accurately depicts the types of cars you will see in their spacious showroom.

An interior view of Classic Cars International Auto Museum.

Utah

Many of Remember When's cars are in the affordable range and there are some high-ticket items, too. The company arranges financing and transportation, takes trades and shuttles customers back and forth to the airport or their hotel. Bring your skis. This is great ski country.

End of Salt Lake city Area △

BONNEVILLE SPEEDWAY MUSEUM
1000 E Wendover Blvd
(I-80 Business)
WENDOVER, UT 84083
(West of Salt Lake City at the Nevada state line)
Phone: 801-665-7721
Hours: May thru Nov daily 10-6.
Admission charged.

Some of the race cars that have raced on the Bonneville salt flats are on dis-play in this museum. There are also antique cars and special interest cars; a total of about 30 altogether. Some of the cars in the collection include a 1909 Rausch & Lang Electric, a 1929 Essex boattail, a 1930 Rolls-Royce 20/25 Sedanca DeVille, a 1953 Studebaker Bonneville race car, a 1957 Thunderbird and a 1963 Rolls-Royce Silver Cloud III. Some of the museum's cars are for sale. Souvenirs, coins and antiques are also offered for sale in the gift shop. Richard Dixon in the museum's owner.

VERMONT

▼ BENNINGTON AREA (Southeastern corner of the state)

BENNINGTON MUSEUM
W Main St
BENNINGTON, VT 05201
Phone: 802-447-1571
Hours: Jun 1-end Oct daily 9-6 and
Easter 1-5. Closed Thanksgiving,
Dec 25 thru Jan 1. Admission
charged.

This museum displays items of early Americana, a large collection of locally made pottery, paintings by Grandma Moses and one antique automobile...a very special automobile. It's a 1924 Wasp Rickshaw-Victoria. This is the last of only 18 large and luxurious, hand-made Wasps made in Bennington from 1919 to 1924. It was made primarily of aluminum and had mahogany trim and red leather. In its day it sold for $10,000 making it one of the most expensive cars in America. The museum has a gift and souvenir shop. This museum is within walking distance of Hemmings Publishing Co., publisher of Hemmings Motor News.

HEMMINGS PUBLISHING COMPANY'S OLD FASHION FILLING STATION
216 Main St
BENNINGTON, VT 05201
Phone: 800-CAR-HERE, Ext 507
Hours: Daily 7 am - 10 pm

Hemmings Motor News, "the bible" of the collector-car hobby, now operates a "Finest Old Fashion Full-Service" filling station at this location, which is next door to Hemmings' publishing headquarters. Filling station personnel give prompt and courteous old fashion service. They pump your gas, check your oil, wash your windshield, headlights, rear windows and taillights. Parked on the station's premises, weather permitting, is an ever-changing display of about half a dozen vintage vehicles. Inside the station is a "car-lovers convenience store" full of books, models and other automobilia. It is a perfect place to shop for gifts for your car crazy friends and relatives.

Tours of Hemmings' publishing facilities are available to car clubs and other groups but only with advanced notice.

End of Bennington Area △

Vermont

THE WESTMINSTER MG CAR MUSEUM

Kimber Close
WESTMINSTER, VT 05158
(Southeastern corner of state on I-91)
Phone: 802-722-3708 or 603-756-4121
Hours: June-Labor Day daily 10-5. Closed rest of year. Admission charged.

Twenty nine MGs, many of them very rare models, are on display at this museum devoted solely to the MG marque. Included in the collection is a rare 1927 14/28 Tourer Flatnose 4-seater, one of only 6 known to exist and thought to be the oldest MG in the US. There is a 1930 Sportsman's Coupe; a 1933 J-4 supercharged racer, number 5 of 9 produced; a 1938 SA 4-door Tourer, one of only 5 known to exist; a 1953 TD Inskip 4-seater, one of 10 known to exist; a 1955 EX 182, the only one known to exist of 4 made and a 1964 MK IV Magnette ex-factory car. The museum has a gift shop with many MG-related items for sale.

VIRGINIA

GLADE MOUNTAIN MUSEUM
(Museum & salvage)
US 11
ATKINS, VA 24311 (Southwestern tip of the state off I-81 and 5 miles east of Marion)
Phone: 540-783-5678
Hours: May thru Aug Sun only 1-8. Donations accepted.

This museum displays local Americana including an 1803 blacksmith shop, household items from the mid-1800s, toys, antiques, farm machinery and about a dozen vintage automobiles in various conditions. Most, but not all of the cars, are Fords from the years 1926 thru 1946. Included in the collection is a 1945 Ford Jeep and a 1946 Ford fire truck. The museum has a gift and souvenir shop. Adjacent to the museum is Jack's Garage, a salvage yard with some 200 vehicles from 1935 to 1970. Customers may browse the yard.

ROARING TWENTIES ANTIQUE CAR MUSEUM
On SR 230 between US 29 and US 33
HOOD, VA 22723 (About 25 miles north-northeast of Charlottesville)
Phone: 540-948-6290
Hours: By appointment only. Admission charged.

This hard-to-find museum has about 32 vehicles, mostly from the 1920s, including a 1920 Dodge touring car, a 1922 Buick roadster, a 1923 Stevens, a 1924 Cleveland 4dr, a 1925 Studebaker Deluxe Roadster, a 1925 Cadillac 4dr, a 1925 Paige 4dr, a 1928 Chrysler Model 72 with rumble seat, a 1929 Hudson coupe, a 1945 Surelsmobile 2dr and a 1948 Playboy. Other displays include horse-drawn vehicles, stationary engines, hood ornaments, radiator caps, advertising signs, glassware, etc. The museum has a gift shop at a separate location.

RALPH'S AUTO SERVICE AND REPAIR (Salvage)
SR 613 (at its junction with SR 783)
LINVILLE, VA 22834
(In western Virginia 5 miles north of Harrisonburg)
Phone: 703-833-6111
Hours: M-F 8-6

This is a 10-acre salvage yard with about 200 vehicles, most of which are domestic cars and light trucks from the 1930s thru the 1970s. The best selections are from the 1940s thru the 1960s. Fords and Chevrolets predominate in the yard, but there is a good selection of other makes too. Many parts have been removed and are stored inside. Some ve-

263

Virginia

hicles are whole and restorable. Visitors may browse the yard. In business since 1941.

CAR AND CARRIAGE CARAVAN (Museum)
Entrance to Luray Caverns
LURAY, VA 22835
(In the Shenandoah Valley
25 miles northwest of
Harrisonburg on US 211)
Phone: 703-743-6551
Hours: Mar 15 thru June 14 daily
10-7:30, June 15 thru Labor Day
10-8:30, after Labor Day thru Oct
31 daily 10-7:30, rest of year M-F
10-5:50, Sat-Sun 10-6:30.
Admission includes guided tour
of Luray Caverns.

This large antique vehicle museum is part of the famous Luray Caverns complex, one of the most famous cave systems in the US. In the museum are about 75 restored vintage cars along with carriages, coaches, buggies and other modes of transportation. One carriage of special note is a 1625 Berline Coupa de Gala built for the Portuguese Royal Family. Included in the car collection is an 1892 Benz, one of the oldest cars in America and in running condition. Other vehicles of interest include a 1908 Baker Electric, a 1910 Maxwell, a 1914 Locomobile, a 1925 Rolls-Royce once owned by movie idol Rudolph Valentino, a 1927 Mercedes-Benz and a 1935 Hispano-Suiza. There is a large gift shop offering a wide variety of items and the complex has its own restaurant.

HAROLD LUDHOLTZ'S SALVAGE YARD
Rt 2, Box 63
MOUNT CRAWFORD, VA 22841
(Southern suburb of Harrisonburg
in the Shenandoah Valley)
Phone: 540-828-3348
Hours: M-Sat 9-5

Harold has so many cars he lost count years ago! But there is a bunch of them tightly packed onto his 15-acre salvage yard. Most range from the 1940s to the 1970s and most are domestic makes. There are many 2-door and 4-door models, some light trucks, some station wagons and a nice old 1962 Pontiac ambulance last used by a travelling Rock & Roll band. It is best to phone Harold before coming out. He might be out with the wrecker bringing in another one. In business since 1957.

PHILBATES AUTO WRECKING, INC. (Salvage)
SR 249 ($^1/_2$ mile west of junction
with SR 33)
NEW KENT, VA 23124 (25 miles
east of downtown Richmond)
Phone: 804-843-9787
Hours: M-F 8-5, Sat 8-3

This is a very large salvage yard with some 6000 vehicles on more than 100 acres of land. All makes are represented and most are between 1940 and 1982 with the majority between the late 1940s and 1960s. MUSCLE CARS are well represented here at Philbates. A parts locating service is offered, as is a towing service. Customers may browse the yard. In business since 1955.

▼ NORFOLK/NEWPORT NEWS/ HAMPTON AREA

CHRYSLER MUSEUM
(Art museum)
Olney Rd and Virginia Beach Blvd
NORFOLK, VA 23510
Phone: 757-622-1211
Hours: Tues-Sat 10-4, Sun 1-5.
Closed Jan 1, July 4, Thanksgiving
and Dec 25. Donations requested.

This is the city art museum of Norfolk renamed after the late Walter P. Chrysler, Jr., son of the founder of the Chrysler Corporation. In 1970 Walter P. Chrysler, Jr. agreed to move his large and valuable art collection from Provincetown, MA to this museum in Norfolk, his wife's home town In gratitude, the city named the museum after him. The Chrysler Museum is considered to be one of the top 20 art museums in the country and contains works from ancient Greece and Rome, pre-

Columbian works from America, works of European and American masters and an 8000-piece glass collection considered to be one of the finest in the world. Walter P. Chrysler, Jr. had a long and successful career at Chrysler Corporation as founder and head of the Air-Temp Division which developed the first air conditioning systems for automobiles.

GENERAL DOUGLAS MacARTHUR MEMORIAL
MacArthur Square
NORFOLK, VA 23510
Phone: 757-441-2965
Hours: M-Sat 10-5, Sun 11-5. Free.

This is the former city hall of Norfolk which has been turned into a museum honoring one of America's most famous World War II commanders, General Douglas MacArthur. Among

The Chrysler Museum, Norfolk, VA.

Virginia

General MacArthur's staff car, a 1950 Chrysler Imperial limousine is displayed at the MacAuthur Memorial. He used it both in Japan and the US from 1950 until his death in 1964.

the many displays of personal belongings, maps, murals, photographs, models, etc., is the General's staff car, a 1950 Chrysler Imperial. It is on display in the gift shop.

US ARMY TRANSPORTATION MUSEUM
Building 300, Besson Hall
FORT EUSTIS, VA 23604
(West of, and adjacent to, Newport News)
Phone: 757-878-1182 or 804-878-1183
Hours: Tues-Sun 9-4:30, closed all Federal holidays. Free.

Fort Eustis is the home of the US Army's Transportation Corps and this museum, which is on the base, displays many of the vehicles used by the Corps over the past 200 years. This includes many trucks and Jeeps, including several prototype Jeeps produced by various manufactures in the early 1940s when the Army was developing that vehicle. There are three Russian-made trucks captured in Grenada

Displayed at the U.S. Army Transportation Museum is the Bantam Motor Car Company's version of the Jeep which was presented to the Army for evaluation.

266

and several DUKWs and other amphibious vehicles. Other displays include aircraft, trains, marine craft, experimental vehicles, models of various vehicles, dioramas, photos, uniforms, medals, weapons and many other items used by the Corps. There is a gift and souvenir shop in the museum.

End of Norfolk/Newport News/Hampton Area △

VIRGINIA MUSEUM OF TRANSPORTATION
303 Norfolk Av
ROANOKE, VA 24016
(In western Virginia on I-80)
Phone: 540-342-5670
Hours: M-Sat 10-5, Sun noon-5. Admission charged.

This city-owned museum displays steam, electric and diesel locomotives, railroad cars, horse-drawn vehicles, a Canadian dog sled, miniature circus vehicles, a railroad station building, a telegraph office and has about 10 antique cars and trucks. Included is a 1927 White truck, a 1930 Chevrolet stake truck, a 1938 Cadillac fire truck

and a 1926 Studebaker taxi. The museum has a picnic area and a gift shop offering many items related to the field of transportation. Eric Alexie is the curator.

The Virginia Museum of Transportation is near the junction of I-81 and I-581.

Virginia

WOODROW WILSON BIRTHPLACE AND MUSEUM

Coalter and Frederick Sts
STAUNTON, VA 24401 (30 miles north-northwest of Charlottesville on I-81 and I-64)
Phone: 703-885-0897
Hours: Mar thru Nov daily 9-5, rest of year daily 9-5. Closed Jan 1, Thanksgiving and Dec 25. Admission charged.

This is the birthplace and boyhood home of President Woodrow Wilson. He was born here in 1856. The home was the manse of the First Presbyterian Church where his father, the Rev. Joseph Ruggles Wilson, was pastor. It has been restored to appear as it did at the time of Woodrow's birth. Among the many family belongings and displays is a Pierce-Arrow limousine used by Wilson when be became President.

LOWREY'S SEAFOOD RESTAURANT

528 Church Ln
TAPPAHANNOCK, VA 22560 (40 miles northeast of Richmond on the Rappahannock River)
Phone: 804-443-2800
Hours: Daily 11 am-9 pm. Closed Christmas Day.

This fine restaurant has a couple of antique cars on display inside their dining room. They are a 1910 Cadillac and a 1926 Chrysler touring car. Upon occasion, additional antique cars are parked outside. There is also automobile memorabilia inside the restaurant and a gift shop. Car clubs are welcome. Contact William Lowrey, co-owner.

WHITE POST RESTORATIONS (Restorer)

1 Old Car Drive (County Rd 658 $^1/_4$ mile southeast of US 340)
WHITE POST, VA 22663 (10 miles southeast of Winchester on SR 277)
Phone: 540-837-1140
Hours: M-F 7-5. Closed holidays.

This is one of the world's largest complete restoration shops, established in 1940. Visitors are welcome. Please phone and join one of our group tours.

WASHINGTON

WHOOP-N-HOLLER RANCH & MUSEUM
1 Whitmore Rd
BICKLETON, WA 99322
(43 miles south of Yakima)
Phone: 509-896-2344
Hours: Apr 1 thru Sept 30
Tues-Sun 9-5. Admission charged.

This is a privately-owned museum consisting of several buildings containing a wide variety of pioneer artifacts from the earliest days of settlement in the area. Most of the items have been collected by Lawrence and Ada Ruth who own the museum and are descendants of homesteaders who first settled the area. There are displays of hand-carved doll furniture, home remedies, pioneer clothing, musical instruments including a pipe organ, Coke cans from around the world and a collection of some 30 antique vehicles. In the auto collection are several Studebakers, a 1916 Maxwell, a Republic truck, an old firetruck, a Ford Model T and two Edsels. There is also a picnic area and playground for the kids. To find the Whoop-N-Holler Ranch & Museum proceed 12 miles south of Bickleton on East Rd. or 11 miles north of Roosevelt on East Rd. and watch for Whitmore Rd. and signs to the museum.

This is only part of the auto collection at the Whoop-N-Holler Museum of Bickleton, WA.

Washington

I-5 AUTO WRECKING

190 Estep Rd (Visible from I-5. Exit
Onalaska off-ramp Exit 71)
CHEHALIS, WA 98552 (25 miles
south of Olympia on I-5)
Phone: 206-262-3550 or 800-551-
4489
Hours: M-Sat 9-5:30

This salvage yard has between 800
and 900 vehicles, mostly US-makes, and
mostly from the 1950s and 1960s. There
are some cars, however, dating back to
the 1930s. Customers may browse the
yard and remove their own parts. In
business since the late 1960s.

PART TIME AUTO WRECKING
(Salvage)

ILWACO, WA 98624
(Southwestern corner of the state at
the mouth of the Columbia River.)
Phone: 206-642-4852
Hours: M-F 9-5, Sat 9-noon

This salvage yard specializes in cars
from 1970s and 1980s but has parts for
cars back to the 1950s. There are about
300 vehicles in the yard and an additional flow of about 250 cars per year.
Customers may browse the yard. In
business since 1980.

LYNDEN PIONEER MUSEUM

217 W Front St
LYNDEN, WA 98264
(8 miles northeast of Bellingham
near the Canadian border)
Phone: 360-354-3675
Hours: M-Sat 10-4, admission
charged.

This museum has displays on early
pioneer life, Indians, agricultural
machinery, military items from the Span-
ish-American War to Viet Nam and other
displays pertaining to the history of the
local area. There are horse-drawn
vehicles including a large collection of

The Lynden Pioneer Museum of Lynden, WA has a sizeable collection of antique cars.

buggies. The museum also has a sizeable antique auto collection. Most of the cars are CHEVROLETs and include a 1914 Baby Grand, a 1918 #490 touring car, a rare 1920 center door, a 1922 roadster, a 1928 touring car, a 1927 roadster, a 1931 coupe and a 1931 Cabriolet. The museum has a gift and souvenir shop.

▼ SEATTLE AREA

FERRILL'S AUTO PARTS, INC. (Salvage)

18306 US 99
LYNNWOOD, WA 98037 (a northern suburb of Seattle on I-5)
Phone: 800-421-3147 or 206-778-3147
Hours: M-F 8-5:30, Sat 8-5

This salvage yard has about 1600 cars in three locations. The vehicles are of mixed makes, both domestic and imported from 1976 to current. Ferrill's has a computerized inventory and walk-in customers may browse the yards. In business since 1955.

FITZ AUTO PARTS (Salvage)

24000 SR 9
WOODINVILLE, WA 98072 (A northeastern suburb of Seattle on SR 9 and SR 202)
Phone: 206-483-1212
Hours: M-F 8:30-5

This yard has approximately 2500 vehicles and specializes in FORDs, GENERAL MOTORS, CHRYSLERs and JEEPs. They also have European and Japanese imports. In business since 1931.

VINTAGE AUTO PARTS (Salvage)

24300 SR 9
WOODINVILLE, WA 98072 (A northeastern suburb of Seattle on SR 9 and SR 202)
Phone: 800-426-5911 or 425-486-0777
Hours: M-F 8-5

This 20-acre salvage yard has about 500 vehicles from the late 1940s to the late 1960s. Most are US makes. They also have thousands of parts stored inside their large warehouse/showroom. Some of the parts are from pre-war vehicles. Vintage does not have many 1955-57 Chevrolets, or 1955-57 Thunderbirds, Mustangs, Cougars, Camaros or Firebirds. Rather, Vintage tries to satisfy the broader market and the orphan market. Orphan brands in the yard include Hudson, REO, Nash, DeSoto, LaSalle, Packard and Studebaker. Customers may browse the yard. Vintage is owned by Terry Jarvis.

End of Seattle Area △

Washington

ANTIQUE AUTO RANCH (Salvage)
N 2225 Dollar Rd
SPOKANE, WA 99212
Phone: 509-535-7789
Hours: M-F 8-5, Sat 8-2

This salvage yard specializes in American-made cars prior to 1961. Over 200 cars are on the lot, and there is a large inventory of NOS parts. Antique Auto Ranch can offer restoration services and has a large antique vehicle library. Customers may browse the yard. In business since 1960.

USA OF YESTERDAY (Dealer)
445 St Helens Av
TACOMA, WA 98402
Phone: 253-627-1052
Hours: M-Sat 10-5:30

This dealer of antique cars is located in a spacious old building built in the 1940s for a Buick dealership. They carry between 40 and 50 vehicles in stock at all times and specialize in American-made cars from the 1930s through the 1970s. The company takes trades, sells on consignment, offers appraisals, rents storage space and welcomes car clubs. They have an annual open house in July or August each summer. There is a large gift and souvenir shop associated with the company called Wheel World that carries models, kits, apparel and other automobilia. USA of Yesterday has a big 1950s-style banquet facility which is available for parties and special occasion. The company is owned by Walt Sharp and Tom Breske is the chief sales associate.

▼ VANCOUVER AREA
(Southeastern WA across from Portland, OR)

ALL AMERICAN CLASSICS, INC (Salvage)
15209 NE Fourth Plain Rd
VANCOUVER, WA 98682
Phone: 360-254-8850
Hours: Tues-F 8:30-5, Sat 8:30-3:30

This a neat and well-kept salvage yard of 18 acres with some 2500 vehicles. And, as the company name implies, they are all American-made. Some cars date back to the 1930s, but most are post-war to the early 1970s. All American has a computerized inventory system and offers a nation-wide locator service. They will ship any part, large or small. Customers may browse the yard, but company personnel will remove all parts. All American also carries NOS and reproduction parts and there are a few whole vehicles suitable for restoring. In business since 1989. The lot is owned and operated by a father and son team, Connie and Todd Toedtli.

DAYBREAK AUTO PARTS (Salvage)
29007 NE 88th St
BATTLE GROUND, WA 98604
(10 miles north of Vancouver on SR 503)
Phone: 509-687-3472
Hours: Tues-Sat 9-5

This neatly groomed salvage yard is full of postwar cars from the late 1940s thru the 1960s. Most all are American-made. Daybreak specializes in MERCURYs but has other makes to offer such as their two dozen 1955-57 Chevrolets and numerous Ford and Chrysler products. Some cars are whole and restorable. In business since 1987. Merlin Wright is the owner.

End of Vancouver Area △

JACKSON'S HUDSONS (Salvage)
Hunzeker Rd
YAKIMA, WA 98908 (South-central part of state on I-82)
Phone: 509-966-2341
Hours: Please phone

If you are a Hudson lover you should know about this place. Brothers Mel and Ken Jackson have about 40 Hudsons, mostly from the 1950s, in their yard that they offer for sale as whole cars only. There also are some Nashes and Cadillacs. Hudson parts are available too from a large inventory of previously stripped cars. Parts are kept indoors. The oldest Hudson on the lot is a 1935 five-window coupe.

WEST VIRGINIA

VINTAGE CLASSIC CARS
401 3rd Av
HUNTINGTON, WV 25701
(Westernmost tip of the state
on the Ohio River and I-64)
Phone: 304-523-6068
Hours: Daily 10-7.
Admission charged.

This is the only antique car museum in West Virginia and it's good one. There are about 65 cars on display and some of them are for sale. The collection rotates, so the next time you visit you will see different cars. Vehicles are a mix of classics, antiques, muscle cars, hot rods, etc. The museum occasionally has some celebrity cars. Every March or April, weather permitting, the museum has a car show. Chuck Runyon is the general manager.

WISCONSIN

RAY'S AUTO REPAIR/SALVAGE

Sanborn Av
ASHLAND, WI 54806 (Northern part of the state on Lake Superior)
Phone: 715-682-6505
Hours: M-F 9-5, Sat 9-2

There are approximately 250 vehicles in this yard ranging in age from 1964 to the present. Services offered are brake shoe rebuilding and exhaust system repairs. Customers may browse the yard. In business since 1961.

STAUFFER CLASSICS, LTD. (Dealer)

10311 Highway ID
BLUE MOUNDS, WI 53517
(20 miles west of Madison on US 18/151)
Phone: 608-437-3000
Hours: M-F 8-5, Sat by appointment.

This dealer specializes in COBRAs and SHELBYs, but also handles other high performance and investment cars such as Ferraris, Jaguars, DeTomasos, Panteras, etc. The company takes trades, offers appraisals, arranges financing and shipping and rents storage space. There is a gift shop and the company can do service and maintenance work. George Stauffer is the owner.

C.L. CHASE USED AUTO AND TRUCK PARTS (Salvage)

Rt Box 291
CAMP DOUGLAS, WI 54618 (48 miles east of LaCrosse on I-90/94)
Phone: 608-427-6734
Hours: M-Sat 8-6

There are some 5000 cars and trucks in this salvage yard dating from the teens to the present. Trucks range from pick-ups to semis. Chase offers a towing service with both light and heavy-duty wreckers and has a 100-ton crane. Customers may browse the yard. In business since 1968.

FOUR WHEEL DRIVE MUSEUM

105 E 12th St
CLINTONVILLE, WI 54929 (35 miles west of Green Bay on US 45)
Phone: 715-823-2141
Hours: Memorial Day thru Labor Day Sat & Sun only 1-4. Weekdays by appointment. Free but donations appreciated.

This museum displays four wheel drive vehicles and traces the history of the FWD Corp. of Clintonville, a leading manufacturer of four wheel drives for trucks and other vehicles. Included in the collection is a 1909 four wheel drive automobile known as the "Battle-

275

Wisconsin

ship", the first gasoline-powered car produced by the Four Wheel Drive Auto Company, the forerunner of the FWD Corp. Also in the collection is a 1911 Nancy Hank, the last car built by the Four Wheel Drive Auto company, a 1932 Indy four wheel drive 500 race car, a 1908 four wheel drive steam car, several trucks, a 1926 Seagrave firetruck and several military vehicles. There is a video offered on the birth of four wheel drive vehicles.

FRASCONA CHRYSLER, PLYMOUTH, DODGE AND CLASSIC CARS (Dealer)
2606 Main St
EAST TROY, WI 53120 (30 miles SE of Milwaukee on I-43)
Phone: 414-642-3921 (Nationwide) or 414-933-0668 (from Milwaukee)
Hours: M-F 7 am-8 pm, Sat 7-5

This is a new car dealer that also sells antique vehicles. They will normally have more than 20 vintage cars on hand from which to choose. When dealing in old cars Frascona takes trades, offers appraisals, sells on consignment, arranges financing and shipping and searches for specific vehicles. They also do repairs on old cars and offer storage. Car clubs are welcome.

HARTFORD HERITAGE AUTO MUSEUM
147 N Rural St
(Downtown Hartford)
HARTFORD, WI 53027
(35 miles northwest of Milwaukee)
Phone: 414-673-7999
Hours: May thru Sept M-Sat 10-5, Sun noon-5; rest of year W-Sat 10-5, Sun noon-5. Closed Jan 1, Easter, Thanksgiving and Dec 25. Admission charged.

The Hartford Heritage Auto Museum has the world's largest collection of Kissel Cars.

This museum has the world's largest collection of KISSEL automobiles and trucks. Kissels were made in Hartford from 1906 to 1931 and only about 200 still exist today out of some 36,000 manufactured. Other makes of vintage cars are also displayed making a total of about 90 cars altogether. Included in the display are many cars from the 1960s and a good variety of trucks and fire trucks. The museum has a NASH Room displaying about a dozen Nashes which were made in nearby Kenosha, WI. There are also Nash-related art and memorabilia on display. Other exhibits include gas & steam engines, gasoline pumps and related automobilia. The museum has a gift shop, a banquet hall and an automotive library.

JIM CARLSON'S AUTO CENTER (Dealer and restorer)

N6411 Holmen Dr
PO Box 98
HOLMEN, WI 54636-0098
(4 miles north of LaCross on I-90 and the Mississippi River)
Phone: 608-526-3358
Hours: M-Sat 8-5

This is a complete service center for the antique car buff. They specialize in CHEVROLETs. Customers can buy an antique car here and drive it away, or leave it and have it restored by the company customers may bring in their own car for complete or partial restoration. Carlson's carries about 25 cars in inventory at all times and can provide an inventory list. They take trades, arrange financing and transportation, offer appraisals, lease cars, rent storage and search for specific vehicles. Furthermore,

the company sells restoration supplies for all makes and models and has an inventory of rust-free used parts. Jim Carlson, a former race car driver, is the owner.

NORTHERN TIRE & AUTO SALES (Salvage)

North 8219 US 51
IRMA, WI 54442
(28 miles north of Wausau)
Phone: 715-453-5050
Hours: M-F 8-5, Sat 8-3

This salvage yard has about 1500 vehicles of mixed makes from the 1920s to the 1970s. Towing service is offered. Customers may browse the yard. In business since 1973.

GENERAL MOTORS ASSEMBLY DIVISION (Plant tours)

1000 Industrial Av
(On the southeastern side of town)
JANESVILLE, WI 53545
(South-central part of state near the IL state line)
Phone: 608-765-7681
Hours: M-Thurs tours at 9:30 and 1 except holidays and model changeover. Free.

This is a large General Motors assembly plant that offers conducted factory tours to the public. Tours last about 1 1/2 hours. No cameras permitted. Children must be accompanied by an adult.

AMC AND NASH MUSEUM (Museum-to-be)

KENOSHA, WI
Phone: 414-653-4030
(Information)

Wisconsin

The city of Kenosha is working on a project called the Harbor Park Plan. A part of the project will be the construction of a museum honoring the Nash Motor Car Company and its successor, the American Motors Corporation, which manufactured cars here in Kenosha for many years. At the time of this printing (October 1998) the project was still in its beginning stages. But, keep an eye on this one. It would certainly be of interest to antique car buffs.

LARRY McGRAY'S ANTIQUE AUTOMOTIVE (Dealer and restorer)

Jct US 141 and SR 22
(Stiles Junction)
LENA, WI 54139
(20 miles north of Green Bay)
Phone: 920-834-4447 or
920-834-4246
Hours: M-F 8-5
(Best to phone first)

This company is both a dealer in vintage vehicles and a restorer of same. They carry 6 to 8 cars in inventory most of the time that are for sale as is or candidates for a partial or complete restoration. They do a lot of 1950s cars and trucks. McGray's will take trades, sell on consignment, search for specific vehicles and rent storage space. Their office is quite unique in that it is a replica of an old Mobile Oil gas station decorated generously with automobilia. Some auto-related items are for sale in a small gift shop. The company is owned and operated by Larry McGray.

ZONOTTI (Dealer)

5153 Anton Dr
MADISON, WI 53719
Phone: 608-288-1688
Hours: M-F 10-6, Sat 10-4

CORVETTES are the name of the game here, but Zonotti will also have other sports cars and exotics to offer from their spacious showroom. They carry between 18-22 cars in inventory and will provide an inventory list upon request. They sell cars on consignment, offer appraisals, arrange financing and transportation and will search for that one-and-only car of your choice. Zonotti has a lot of storage space for lease - room for up to 120 cars. This is a good place to park your precious beauty through the winter months. Rick Anderson, the owner, welcomes all car clubs.

ZUNKER'S ANTIQUE CAR MUSEUM

3722 MacArthur Dr
MANITOWOC, WI 54220
(35 miles southeast of Green Bay on Lake Michigan)
Phone: 414-684-4005
Hours: May thru Sept daily 10-5, rest of year by appointment.
Admission charged.

This museum has some 45 antique cars including a 1928 Overland Whippet roadster with rumble seat, a 1929 Auburn 850 brougham, a 1930 Marquette roadster with rumble seat, a 1947 Hudson pickup truck, a 1948 Crosley station wagon and a 1961 Nash Metropolitan. Other displays include

278

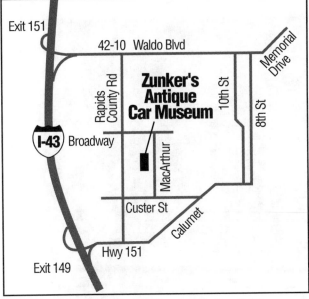

Zunker's Antique Car Museum is accessible from I-43.

SEWARD AUTO SALVAGE
2506 Vincent Rd
MILTON, WI
53563 (25 miles southeast of Madison off I-90)
Phone:
608-752-5166
Hours: M-Sat 8-5

There are approximately 2000 cars and light trucks in the yard. The oldest vehicle is 1937 and the newer ones are current models. An inventory list is available and customers may browse the yard. There are also some whole cars available for restoration. In business since 1978.

motorcycles, bicycles, dolls, children's lunch boxes, automobilia and an antique gas station.

▼ MILWAUKEE AREA

MILWAUKEE PUBLIC MUSEUM
800 Wells St
MILWAUKEE, WI 53233
Phone: 414-278-2700
Hours: Daily 9-5, closed July 4, Thanksgiving and Dec 25. Admission charged.

This is a large city museum that depicts the natural history and geologic processes of the local area and the cultural development of different civilizations. There is a display entitled The Streets of Old Milwaukee and simulated sites in Africa, Asia, Central America and Oceania. In addition, the museum has one very special automobile, a Schloemer Motor Wagon, which is claimed to be the oldest motor vehicle in America. This claim is made for other vehicles around the country, but the claim for the Schloemer is credible and based on an affidavit signed by its builder, Gottfried Schloemer, in 1920, that he built the car in 1890 and ran it for the first time on the streets of Mil-

The Schloemer Motor Wagon, believed by some to be the oldest car in America. Its builder, Gottfried Schloemer is at the tiller.

waukee in 1892. He further claimed that the car was built at his home, 439 3rd Ave. in Milwaukee. The motor in the museum's Schloemer Motor Wagon is, however, not the original motor, but a later motor c. 1897. There is, however, physical and documentary evidence that another motor was previously mounted in the vehicle. There the controversy stands for present-day historians to ponder.

DAVID V. UIHLEIN ANTIQUE RACE CAR MUSEUM
236 Hamilton Dr

CEDARBURG, WI 53012 (A northern suburb of Milwaukee)
Phone: 414-253-2661
Hours: Normally open Memorial Day thru Labor Day Wed-Sat 10-5, Sun 1-5, but best to phone first. Admission charged.

This is a private collection of more than a dozen race cars. Some are very early models. Uihlein's collection of race cars and antique cars is too large to fit into the museum so those at the museum frequently rotate. Some of the cars are used in various activities from time to time and Uihlein buys and sells cars.

This is Valenti Classic, Inc. just south of Milwaukee, off I-94.

VALENTI CLASSICS, INC. (Dealer)
355 S US 41 (Parallels I-94. Valenti can be seen from I-94.)
CALEDONIA, WI 53108 (A southern suburb of Milwaukee)
Phone: 414-835-2070
Hours: M-F 9-6, Sat 9-5

This dealer, on the south side of Milwaukee, specializes in CORVETTES as well as classic and collectible automobiles. Also available are affordable antique cars and muscle cars. They carry from 50 to 75 vehicles in inventory in their indoor showroom and adjacent lot. An inventory list is available. Valenti does some restorations, repair work, service work, sells cars on consignment, searches for vehicles upon request, takes trades and provides appraisals. There is a large selection of gas station memorabilia available for sale, too. Car clubs are welcome. Valenti has a gift shop in the dealership and next door is an antique store run by members of the Valenti family.

End of Milwaukee Area △

KEN'S KLASSICS (Restorer)
20803 SR 60
MUSCODA, WI 53573 (50 miles west of Madison)
Phone: 608-739-4242
Hours: M-F 8-5. After hours or weekend by appointment.

This is a full service restorer of antique, classic and special interest vehicles. Ken's does meticulous frame-up, body-off complete restorations or partial restorations. They also offer appraisals and can provide enclosed trailering of vehicles. A brochure and references are available. Car clubs and visitors welcome. Ken Stadele is the owner.

ALL AUTO ACRES (Salvage)
W 3862 SR 16
RIO, WI 53960 (20 miles north of Madison on SR 16)

Collector Showcase of Sturgeon Bay, WI.

Phone: 800-637-4661 (WI) or
414-992-5362
Hours: M-F 8-5, Sat 8-noon

This salvage yard specializes in American-made cars and trucks from 1955 to 1985, but some older vehicles are also available. Vehicles from the 1960s and 1970s are plentiful among the approximately 2000 vehicles in the yard. New replacement fenders and doors in metal or fiberglass are available. Customers may browse the yard. In business since 1984.

SOMERSET AUTO SALVAGE & REPAIR
Rt 1 Box 39A
SOMERSET, WI 54025 (
Northwestern edge of the state
20 miles northeast of Minneapolis/
St Paul, MN)
Phone: 715-247-5136
Hours: M-Sat 8-5

This salvage lot has 300 vehicles, old and new, cars and pickups and some semis. Services offered are complete engine and drive train repairs, body work and painting. Customers may browse the yard. In business since 1976.

COLLECTOR SHOWCASE (Museum)
3910 SR 42/57 (3 miles north)
STURGEON BAY, WI 54235 (35 miles northeast of Green Bay)
Phone: 414-743-6788
Hours: Mid-May thru mid-Oct daily 9-5, closed rest of year.
Admission charged.

This museum has exhibits of toys, dolls, animated window displays, streets of yesteryear featuring "Old Town" with old store fronts, a gas station, board walk, merry-go-round and an old hotel. There is also a collection of about 35 antique autos including a 1916 Maxwell, a King Midget, 1928, 1929 and

1930 Ford Model A's, a 1958 Edsel and a Delorean. The museum has a gift and souvenir shop.

WIESE AUTO RECYCLING (Salvage)
Hwy TW
THERESA, WI 53091 (30 miles northwest of Milwaukee)
Phone: 414-488-3030
Hours: M-F 8-5, Sat 8-noon

This yard specializes in domestic vehicles from the late 1960s to the present. There are approximately 500 vehicles in the yard. Some imports are included. A partial inventory list is available and customers may browse the yard. Services offered are mechanical repairs, body work, frame work, towing and storage. In business since 1970.

ZEB'S SALVAGE
2426 Bernitt Rd
TIGERTON, WI 54486 (30 miles southeast of Wausau on US 45)
Phone: 715-754-5885
Hours: M-Sat 8-5

There are approximately 900 vehicles in this yard from the 1930s to the 1970s. Trucks and farm machinery will also be found. Services offered are engine work, valve jobs, welding and snow plowing. Customers may browse the yard and a one-hour video of the vehicles in the yard is available. The yard has been here since 1961 and under current ownership since 1984.

CLASSIC MOTORS, INC. (Dealer)
103 200th Av
UNION GROVE, WI 53182
(25 miles south of Milwaukee)
Phone: 414-878-2525 or
414-878-5304
Hours: M-F 9-6, Sat 9-1

This dealer carries about a hundred or so antique cars in inventory at all times in their indoor showroom and adjacent lot. Late model used cars are also available. Most of the antique cars are in the affordable range and some are being sold on consignment. The company provides appraisals, takes trades, rents storage and searches for specific vehicles for customers. There is a gift shop and car clubs are always welcome at Classic Motors/Classic Cars. Partners Rich Adams and Al Goll manage the company.

RAY'S AUTOMOTIVE ENTERPRISES, INC. (Salvage)
605 W Bayfield St
WASHBURN, WI 54891 (Northern edge of state on Chequamegon Bay of Lake Superior)
Phone: 715-373-2669
Hours: M-Sat 8-5

This yard specializes in domestic and imported cars and trucks from the 1960s to the present. There are about 1500 vehicles on the lot. They offer services in towing, body work and frame work. Customers may browse the yard. In business since 1971.

Wisconsin

JACK'S AUTO RANCH (Salvage)
6848 N Island View Rd
WATERTOWN, WI 53094 (Midway between Milwaukee and Madison on SR 26)
Phone: 920-699-2521
Hours: M-F 8-5, Sat 8-noon

To get to Jack's take the Sullivan exit off I-94, go south one mile to Hwy B and follow the signs. When you arrive you'll find some 3500 vehicles on Jack's 40-acre lot dating back to the 1930s. Most of the cars are GM, Ford and Chrysler, but there are a respectable number of orphans. The yard is neat and orderly and the various makes are grouped together. Jack's specializes in engines and transmissions and keeps an inventory of between 250-300 on hand at all times. This is a family operation run by Jack Bender and his two sons, John and Chris. The company was founded in 1964.

VAN'S AUTO SALVAGE
Rt Box 164
WAPUN, WI 53963 (15 miles southwest of Fond Du Lac on US 151)
Phone: 414-324-2481
Hours: Tues-F 9-5, Sat 8-noon

This is a large lot with some 4000 cars and trucks. They range in age from the 1930s to the 1980s, but with the best selections being from 1947 to 1976. Customers may browse the yard. In business since 1964.

▼ WISCONSIN DELLS AREA
(40 miles northwest of Madison on I-90/94)

DELLS AUTO MUSEUM
591 Wisconsin Dells Parkway (US 12 and SR 23 on the "Strip")
WISCONSIN DELLS, WI 53965
Phone: 608-254-2008 (Summer) and 608-221-1964 (Winter)
Hours: May 15 thru Labor Day daily 9-9, after Labor Day to Oct 1 Sat & Sun 9-5, rest of year by

This 1969 Camaro Indy 500 Pace Car is on display at the Dells Auto Museum.

appointment. Admission charged.

This museum exhibits about 25 of its 200 vehicles on a rotating basis on the museum floor. Many of the cars are convertibles and there is a goodly number of Indy 500 pace cars. Some of the cars displayed in the museum are for sale. Some of the permanent cars include a 1907 International touring car, a 1933 Rolls-Royce Phantom II, a 1940 Studebaker Indy 500 pace car, a 1940 Packard convertible, a 1953 Ford pace car, a 1954 Dodge pace car, a 1957 Mercury pace car and a 1969 Camero pace car. Other displays include license plates, antique dolls, toys and period clothing. There is an automotive library and a souvenir shop with many antique car-oriented items.

DUCK RIDES
Amphibious vehicle tours)

In the Wisconsin Dells area there are two companies that offer rides in World War II-era amphibious vehicles known a DUKWs (pronounced "ducks"). These vehicles were used extensively during the war to ferry men and supplies from ship to shore. Today they are used to take people on joy rides thru the magnificent scenery of the Wisconsin River, Dell Creek and Lake Delton. The companies offering these rides pick up passengers at their offices or at various locations in the area, proceed along the local streets and roads and into the river. The "captain" narrates the history of the Ducks as well as local history as the tour progresses. The Ducks are inspected by the U.S. Coast Guard and are well equipped for both safety and comfort.

The companies offering the Duck rides are:

DELLS DUCK TOURS, INC.
1.5 miles south on US 12 and SR 23
WISCONSIN DELLS, WI 43965
Phone: 608-254-6080
Hours: May-Oct, daily 9-6

An amphibious "Duck" pulls out of the water and onto the land during an amphibious Duck ride.

Wisconsin

ORIGINAL WISCONSIN DUCKS, INC.

1 mile south on US 12 and SR 23
(Watch for the green and white
sign)
WISCONSIN DELLS, WI 43965
Phone: 608-254-8751
Hours: June 1-Labor Day daily 8-7,
Apr-May daily 9-5, day after Labor
Day-late Oct daily 9-4.

End of Wisconsin Dells Area △

CANADA

ALBERTA

SOUTH PEACE CENTENNIAL MUSEUM
Hwy 34 North 2 Km
BEAVERLODGE, Alberta T0H 0C0
(West-central part of the province
28 miles west of
Grande Prairie)
Phone: 403-354-8869
Hours: May 15 thru Sept 6 daily
10-6. Admission charged.

This museum displays pioneer artifacts, equipment and furnishings from the early 1900s. There is a pioneer home, circa 1928; a fully stocked general store; a flour mill; a schoolhouse; an Anglican church; a railway caboose; farm machinery and a collection of about 20 antique cars and trucks. Some of the vehicles on display include a 1927 Chevrolet truck, a 1929 Graham-Paige, a 1955 Oldsmobile and several Ford Model A's. The museum has a well-supplied gift and souvenir shop. They also have an old-time clay baking oven in working order and from time to time sell freshly baked bread. Jim and Beth Albrecht are the curators.

HOMESTEAD ANTIQUE MUSEUM
Dinosaur Trail
(Hwy 838 $1/2$ mile west of Hwy 9)
DRUMHELLER, Alberta T0J 0Y0
(60 miles northeast of Calgary on Hwy 9)
Phone: 403-823-2600

This is the entrance to the Homestead Museum of Drumheller, Alberta.

Alberta

Hours: May 15 thru Oct 15 daily 9-8. Admission charged.

Pioneer and Indian artifacts are highlighted in this museum including clothing, home furnishings, clocks, musical instruments, gramophones, radios, horse-drawn vehicles, farm equipment, steam-powered tractors, a 1919 catalog-ordered house and several antique cars and trucks. Cars and trucks displayed include a 1919 Ford Model T, a 1914 Ford 4 door touring car, a 1919 Chevrolet roadster, a 1920 Canadian-built Gray-Dort pickup truck, a 1919 International Homestead truck and a 1928 Plymouth 4 dr sedan. All of the cars and trucks are in running order. There is an interesting gift and souvenir shop in the museum.

REG'S STORAGE (Salvage)
10820 Winterburn Rd NW
EDMONTON, Alberta T5S 2C3
Phone: 403-447-3610
Hours: M-F 8-6, Sat 8-4

This salvage yard has approximately 500 cars and light trucks, all of North American makes. The vehicles range in age from 1940 to 1986. Customers may browse the yard and an inventory list is available. In business since 1963.

C. R. AUTO (Salvage)
Box 237
HAY LAKES, Alberta TOB 1WO
(38 miles southeast of Edmonton on Hwy 21)
Phone: 403-878-3263
Hours: M-F 8-7, Sat 9-6

This salvage yard specializes in CADILLACs from 1947 thru 1979. There are 240 cars in the yard. Bumpers are available for most models. C.R. also does restoration work on Cadillacs only. In business since 1988.

ALDON AUTO SALVAGE, LTD.
Hwy 831
LAMONT, Alberta T0B 2R0
(30 miles northeast of Edmonton)
Phone: 403-895-2524
Hours: M-F 8-5:30, Sat 8:30-3

This is a large salvage yard of some 4000 cars and light trucks. Aldon specializes in North American-made vehicles and has vehicles ranging in age from 1940 to current. Customers may browse the yard. Additional services offered include towing, engine rebuilding and parts locating. In business since 1971.

INTERNATIONAL TRUCK MUSEUM
Box 813 (Pas-Ka-Poo Historic Park)
RIMBEY, Alberta T0C 2J0
(about halfway between Edmonton and Calgary on Hwy 20)
Phone: 403-843-2004 or 403-843-2084
Hours: Daily 10-6.
Admission charged.

This museum displays a collection of 19 restored INTERNATIONAL half-ton trucks. There is one example for each model change during the life of the truck from 1935 to 1974. The trucks were restored by Ken Smithson, a local IHC enthusiast, and purchased by the

A 1935 C-1 International Truck is one of the many International half-ton trucks on display at this museum.

town of Rimbey. There are several other vehicles in the museum including an old Canadian police car and a car covered with 365 license plates that has been submitted to the Guinness Book of World Records. The museum also has antique farm equipment, a collection of IHC signs and other automobilia. The museum has a gift shop offering souvenirs and other collectibles. Ken and Rosie Smithson are often available for conducted tours.

▼ WETASKIWIN AREA
(45 miles southwest of Edmonton)

REYNOLDS MUSEUM
4110 57th St
WETASKIWIN, Alberta T9A 2B6
Phone: 403-352-5201 or
403-352-5201
Hours: May 15 thru Sept 13 daily 9-5 and by appointment the rest of the year. Admission charged.

This is a large museum with air-planes, military vehicles, farm equipment, steam engines, horse-drawn vehicles, musical instruments, household appliances, weapons and antique cars and trucks. Altogether there are about 400 vehicles on display. Of note among the cars is an 1899 Innes, built in Scotland; a 1904 Oldsmobile; a 1907 Tudhope McIntyre, built in Sarnia, Ontario; a 1907 Mitchell; a 1908

Alberta

McLaughlin-Buick, built in Canada; a 1911 Hupp Yeats electric; a 1911 Franklin; a 1912 Brockville-Atlas; a 1915 Ford race car; a 1917 National; a 1918 Gray-Dort, built in Canada; a 1922 Franklin; a 1925 Lincoln; a 1927 REO Flying Cloud coupe and 1929, 1930 and 1936 Cords. There is also a large automotive library open to the public by appointment. The museum has a small gift shop.

REYNOLDS-ALBERTA MUSEUM
Hwy 13 West (2 miles west of town)
WETASKIWIN, Alberta T9A 2G1

Phone: 403-361-1351 or
800-661-4726
Hours: Admission charged.

This is a publicly-owned museum and the largest museum in western Canada. It has a collection of some 50 vehicles including antique cars, farming equipment, aircraft and many other items. Cars of interest include a 1911 Cadillac and a 1937 Cord 812 sedan. One display is a reproduction of a small drive-in theater complete with old films, metal speakers and seats shaped like the back end of 1950s-era automobiles.

End of Wetaskiwin Area △

BRITISH COLUMBIA

A & H USED AUTO PARTS (Salvage)
Sawmill Rd
OLIVER, British Columbia
V0H 1T0 (South-central edge of
the province on Hwy 3A/97 near
the US border)
Phone: 604-498-3188
Hours: M-F 8-5

There are about 400 vehicles of all
makes in this salvage yard, most from
the 1940s to the 1960s. There are some
1930s vehicles and an inventory list is
available. Full repair services are offered
and customers may browse the yard. In
business since 1968.

MANITOBA

MANITOBA AGRICULTURAL MUSEUM

Hwy 34 South
(1.6 miles south of Jct, Hwy 34 and TransCanada Hwy 1)
AUSTIN, Manitoba R0H 0C0
(78 miles west of Winnipeg)
Phone: 204-637-2354
Hours: Mid-May thru mid-Oct daily 9-5. Admission charged.

This is a large agricultural museum consisting of several buildings displaying antique tractors, various types of old farming equipment, a large collection of steam engines, a Pioneer village, an old railway station and several railroad cars. There is also a collection of about 20 antique cars and trucks including a 1907 Cadillac, a Stanley Steamer, a 1929 Pontiac Landau, a 1929 International 1-ton flat bed truck and two old firetrucks. The annual Manitoba Threshermen's Reunion and Stampede is held here in late July. The museum has a gift and souvenir shop, a campground and an airstrip. Terry Farley is the museum's manager.

MANITOBA AUTOMOBILE MUSEUM FOUNDATION

TransCanada Hwy #1 East
ELKHORN, Manitoba R0M 0N0
(Southwestern corner of the province 10 miles from the Saskatchewan border)
Phone: 204-845-2604
Hours: May 1 thru late Sept. daily 9-9. Admission charged.

This museum has about 75 vintage

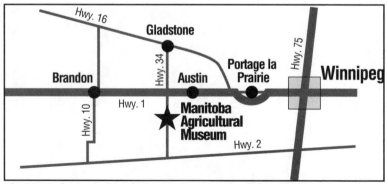

The Manitoba Agricultural Museum is easy to reach from the TransCanada Highway by going 1.6 miles south on Hwy. 34.

autos and trucks, most of them in running condition. Included in the collection is a 1904 Holzman rope drive, a 1908 REO, a 1909 Metz, a 1918 Canadian-made Gray-Dort, a 1913 Russell-Knight, a 1914 Briscoe, a 1914 Hupmobile, a 1918 Chevrolet V-8 and many other interesting cars including McLaughlins and Fords. Other displays include agricultural equipment, Indian and pioneer artifacts, china, license plates and other memorabilia. The museum has a small gift and souvenir shop.

WATSON CROSSLEY COMMUNITY MUSEUM

Railway Av (west side of town at the sports ground)
GRANDVIEW, Manitoba R0L 0Y0
(West-central part of province
on Hwy 5)
Phone: 204-546-2040 (summer)
and 204-546-2467 (rest of year)
Hours: Mid-June thru early Sept
daily 10-6, rest of year by appointment. Admission charged.

This museum displays artifacts of local history, a miniature lumber mill, a restored homesteader's cabin, farm equipment including a large number of antique tractors and about 15 vintage cars and trucks. In the car collection is a 1915 Ford half-ton Model T truck, a 1916 Overland, a 1926 Essex and a rare 1952 Dodge style-side truck. There is also a restoration shop and visitors may watch restoration work in progress. Gerald Morran is the museum's manager.

ARCHIBALD HISTORICAL MUSEUM

Hwy 3 East
(4 miles west of Manitou)
LA RIVIERE, Manitoba R0G 1A0
(South-central part of the
province near the US border.)
Phone: 204-242-2825 or
204-242-2554
Hours: Mid-May to Labour Day
F-Tues noon-8. Admission charged.

Antique furniture, household items, farm machinery, tools, buggies and several vintage cars can be seen in this nice local museum. One of the main exhibits is a log house built in 1878 which was the residence of Canadian authoress Nellie McClung from 1890 to 1891, and a second frame home, fully furnished, where Nellie and her husband, Wes McClung, lived in Manitou from 1904 to 1911. LaRiviere's Canadian Pacific Railroad station has been relocated to the museum and is a Provincial Historic Site.

NEW BRUNSWICK

AUTOMOBILE MUSEUM
TransCanada Hwy #2 (6 miles
northwest in Les Jardins de la
Republique Provincial Park)
ST. JACQUES, New Brunswick
E0L 1K0 (Northwestern corner
of the province on the northern
border of Maine)
Phone: 506-735-2525
Hours: Late June thru Labour Day
daily 10 am to 8 pm. Admission
charged.

This museum, in a beautiful park
setting, exhibits about 20 vintage cars
and related automobilia. Of interest in
the collection is a 1910 Detroit Electric,
a 1929 Stutz Black Hawk, a 1928 Willys
Knight, a 1933 Rolls-Royce limousine,
a 1937 Diamond T firetruck, a 1956
Corvette and a 1942 Plymouth 45-ton
locomotive. There are also displays of
early steam engines and bicycles. The
museum was founded in 1976.

NOVA SCOTIA

**FIREFIGHTERS MUSEUM OF
NOVA SCOTIA**
451 Main St
YARMOUTH, Nova Scotia
B5A 1G9 (Southwestern tip of the
province on the Atlantic Ocean)
Phone: 902-742-5525
Hours: July thru Aug M-Sat 9-9,
Sun 10-5, June and Sept M-Sat 9-5,
Oct thru May 31st M-F 9-4.
Admission charged.

This museum has many displays on
the history of firefighting in Nova Scotia
and exhibits of antique firefighting
equipment such as horse-drawn, hand-
drawn, steam powered and gasoline engine powered vehicles, uniforms, hoses,
fittings, badges, photos, awards, etc. Included among the display of engine
powered vehicles is an 1880 Silsby
steamer, a 1906 Orient car, a 1922 Ford
Model T hose truck, a 1925 American
LaFrance foamite pumper and a 1931
Dodge hose truck. The museum also has
a fire-related library open to the public.

ONTARIO

SILVESTER COLLECTOR CAR STORE (Dealer and restorer)
3027 Brigden Rd
BRIGDEN, Ont N0N 1B0 (12 miles southeast of Sarnia/Pt Huron, MI)
Phone: 519-864-1646
Hours: M-F 8-5, Sat by appointment.

This is a restorer that also offers cars for sale in an indoor showroom. Silvester's is a full-service restoration shop that offers service work and repairs on old cars. In their showroom they carry about a dozen North-American affordable antique vehicles for sale, some restored, some as-is. They will sell cars on consignment, do appraisals and take trades. Car clubs are welcome. The owners are Ernie and Sharon Silvester.

R.M. RESTORATION, LTD. (Restorer and dealer)
825 Park Av West
CHATHAM, Ontario N7M 5J6 (45 miles east of the Detroit/Windsor area)
Phone: 519-352-4575
Hours: M-F 8-5, Sat by appointment

This is a large, full service, antique automobile restorer and dealer. R.M. car-

This is the Silvester Collector Car Store in Brigden, Ontario.

ries up to 75 vehicles in stock for sale. They also offer some parts and will make body panels for Cadillac, Mercedes-Benz, Rolls-Royce, Stutz, Packard, Ferrari, Jaguar and Duesenberg.

SOUTHWESTERN ONTARIO HERITAGE VILLAGE (Museum)
County Rd 23/Arner Town Line (10 minutes south of Essex)
KINGSVILLE, Ontario NOR IGO (25 miles southeast of the Detroit/ Windsor on Lake Erie)
Phone: 519-776-6909
Hours: July and Aug daily 10-5, Apr thru June and Sept thru Nov W-Sun 11-5. Admission charged.

This is a large museum complex with 12 buildings which date from 1826 to 1930. There is an old time general store, a church, a one-room schoolhouse, a barber/shoe shop, a train station, several homes, a gift shop and a transportation building housing a number of vintage automobiles. In the auto collection is a rare 1893 Shamrock horseless carriage built in Wardsville, Ontario, a 1904 Mitchell hearse, a 1906 Buick, a 1913 International Highwheeler truck, a 1913 Studebaker, a 1918 3-passenger Dodge with a sliding steering wheel and other custom features built for Mrs. Dodge, a 1919 Essex, a 1923 Ford truck, a 1924 Oakland, a 1927 Ford Model T roadster, a 1939 Plymouth, a 1959 Hudson and several firetrucks. Some of the cars are on loan from local collectors. The museum hosts several antique car events during the year. The Village has a gift shop and picnic facilities. Dawn Thompson is the curator.

MINAKER'S AUTO PARTS (Salvage)
King St
MILFORD, Ontario KOK 2PO (20 miles southeast of Belleville)
Phone: 613-476-4547
Hours: M-F 9-5, Sat 9-4. Closed Thurs at noon.

This salvage yard of approximately 3000 vehicles specializes in North American-made cars from 1930 to 1980 with about half the cars and trucks being pre-1970. There is a good selection of sedans from the 1940s and light trucks from the 1950s. They also offer NOS and NORS parts including suspension parts and thousands of brake shoes, master wheel cylinders and wheel cylinders. Some whole cars are offered for sale. Customers may browse the yard. Founded in 1925.

▼ OSHAWA AREA (15 miles east of Toronto on Lake Erie)

Oshawa is the center of Canada's automobile industry and there are several historic sites in the area related to that industry. The city's largest employer is General Motors of Canada which was formed in Oshawa in 1918 with the merger of the McLaughlin Carriage Co. and the Canadian branch of Chevrolet. One-third of the population of Oshawa is employed in the automotive industry and its related services.

Ontario

CANADIAN AUTOMOTIVE MUSEUM

99 Simcoe St South
OSHAWA, Ontario L1H 4G7
Phone: 905-576-1222
Hours: M-F 9-5, Sat, Sun and holidays 10-6. Closed Dec 25.
Admission charged.

This is a large museum with some 70 vehicles and it has the largest collection of Canadian-made vehicles in the world. It is located in an old 1920s automobile dealership building where Chevrolets, Pontiacs and Oaklands were once sold. Integrated into the auto displays are other items of the same period, such as washing machines, printing presses, etc., to give the displays an historic perspective. In the auto collection there is a 1903 Redpath, a 1910 McKay, a 1911 Carter Car Tourer, a 1912 McLaughlin-Buick, a 1912 Brockville Atlas, a 1912 Metz, a 1914 Galt Canada Tourist, a 1921 Gray-Dort Tourer, a 1924 Brooks steamer, a 1927 Rolls-Royce, a 1929 Marquette se-dan, a 1931 Gardner, a 1932 Frontenac coupe, a 1949 Meteor and a 1965 Amphicar with only 84 miles on the odometer. Other exhibits include spark plugs, model cars, automotive lighting components, pinball machines, juke-boxes, pianos and stoves. There is a 10,000 piece automotive library open by appointment only and an impressive gift shop. The museum was founded in 1961.

FAWCETT MOTOR CARRIAGE
(Restorer, dealer, salvage)

106 Palmerston Av
WHITBY, Ontario L1N 3G5 (A western suburb of Oshawa)
Phone: 905-668-4446
Hours: M-Sat 7-5

This versatile company offers full or partial restoration services, sells used, restorable or restored vehicles and has a 5-acre 400-vehicle salvage yard. They also do appraisals and offer a parts lo-

The Canadian Automotive Museum of Oshawa, Ontario has the world's largest collection of Canadian-built vehicles.

cator service. The salvage yard has a good selection of North American-made vehicles from the late 1940s thru the 1960s. Visitors may browse the yard.

PARKWOOD ESTATE & GARDENS (Historic Home)
270 Simcoe St North
OSHAWA, Ontario L1G 4T5
Phone: 905-433-4311
Hours: June thru Labour Day
Tues-Sun 10:30-4, Sept thru May

Tues-Sun 1:30-4. Admission charged.

Parkwood Estate & Gardens was featured in America's Castle and Canadian Gardening Television. This National Historic Site was once home to Col. R. S. McLaughlin (Founder General Motors of Canada). Guided tours of the 55-room mansion highlight lavish original furnishings/garden spaces from serene to spectacular/garden Tea House or greenhouse Tea Room.

End of Oshawa Area △

▼ OTTAWA AREA

CANADIAN WAR MUSEUM
330 Sussex Dr
OTTAWA, Ontario K1A 0M8
Phone: 819-776-8600
Hours: Daily 9-30-5 (also Thurs 5-8), admission charged.

This is Canada's largest war museum and has an excellent collection of military and war-related artifacts and memorabilia from colonial days to the present. Included in the collection are some 50 cars and trucks, mostly from the World War II era. Outstanding in the collection is Hitler's 1940 770 W150 Mercedes-Benz delivered to him in July 1940 just weeks after Germany had defeated France. Another car of interest is General Sir Harold Alexander's customized 1941 Ford. Alexander was commander of all British forces in North Africa after August 1942. Alexander's Ford began life as an ordinary 1941 Ford

4-door sedan. It was shipped to Cairo for his use and there customized for desert warfare. The customizing was done in the British workshops in Cairo in an amazing 36 hours. The car was used extensively by him and others and by the time it was retired to the Canadian War Museum it had logged 180,000 miles. Other vehicles of interest in the collection are an assortment of vehicles known as "CMPs" (Canadian Military Pattern). These were vehicles made in Canada with a universal chassis upon which a variety of bodies were mounted. They were used as staff cars, ambulances, trucks, tankers, etc. Over a million of these vehicles were made during World War II and used in every war theater.

Only the Hitler car is on permanent display in the museum. The others are in a nearby warehouse, but they can be seen by the public from July through

Ontario

The National Museum of Science and Technology is just south of Queensway East on St. Laurent Blvd.

Labour Day (early September) each year. Dr. Cameron Plusifer is the museum's Senior Historian.

NATIONAL MUSEUM OF SCIENCE AND TECHNOLOGY

1867 St Laurent Blvd
OTTAWA, Ontario K1G 5A3
Phone: 613-991-3044
Hours: May 1 to Labour Day M-Thurs 9-6, F 9-9, rest of year Tues thru Sun 9-5. Admission charged.

This is one of Canada's largest and finest museums. It has numerous exhibits on science and technology illustrating the paths from which we have come and the points to where we are going. Located in a 35 acre garden-like park setting the museum contains 140,000 square feet of exhibit space divided into galleries. Displayed in the transportation collection are automobiles, carriages, sleighs, motorcycles and bicycles. The museum's automobile collection consists of about 90 cars and trucks, many of them Canadian-made, but only about a dozen are on display at any one time. In the collection is an 1867 Seth Taylor steam carriage said to be the first self-propelled vehicle in Canada, an 1898 Delahaye, a 1901 Locomobile; a 1902 LeRoy, the first production car made in Canada; a 1906 Peugeot-Lion; a 1907 Comet made in Montreal, Quebec; a 1908 Baker Electric; a 1926 Brooks Steam Motor; a 1931 McLaughlin-Buick made in Canada; a 1932 Nash motor home; 1956 and 1958 Jaguar Mk.II salons, 1970 and 1971 Manic GTPAI coupes; a 1975 Marathon Electric; a 1975 Bricklin made in New Brunswick, Canada and a 1986 Nexus. The museum maintains a large automotive library which is open to the public. The museum has a gift shop, cafe and picnic facilities.

End of Ottawa Area △

THE GUILD OF AUTOMOTIVE RESTORERS, INC. (Restorer and dealer)

18237 Woodbine Av
SHARON, Ont L0G 1V0 (18 miles north of Toronto near Newmarket)
Phone: 905-895-0035
Hours: M-F 9-5, Sat 9-1

This is a full-service restorer that also sells antique cars from an indoor showroom. They specialize in pre-1970 vehicles both in restoration and sales. The Guild carries about 16 cars for sale in the showroom but can offer many more cars stored in other locations. They sell cars on consignment, search for specific vehicles, offer appraisals and provide an inventory list. Visitors are taken through the restoration facility upon request where they can see work in progress on anything from body-off restoration projects to service work and repairs. In the Guild's showroom are many antiques such as gas station memorabilia, antique furniture, bicycles and the like, some of which are for sale. Car clubs are always welcome at The Guild. The owner is David Grainger.

CANADIAN MOTORSPORT MUSEUM AND HALL OF FAME

477 Bay St, PO Box 154 (Downtown Toronto)
TORONTO, Ont M5G 2C8
Phone: 416-597-2643
Hours: M-Sat 10-5, donations accepted.

This is Canada's first and only motorsport museum. It is new and growing and will cover all disciplines of motor car racing including oval track racing, drag racing and Indy type racing. The museum has about a dozen cars and expects to add more. The hall of fame honors racing personalities from North American with emphasis on Canadians honorees, and there is a growing archives collection. Of interest among the race cars on display is a 1978 Walter Wolf Formula 1 car, driven by Jody Scheckter, which won the 1978 South African Grand Prix, and an early 1960s Sadler "Formula Ferocious" rear-engine single-seater. This car started the rear-engine revolution in auto racing. Also to be seen in the museum are photos, trophies and other racing memorabilia. The museum and hall of fame are run by a board of governors from all over Canada.

PRINCE EDWARD ISLAND

CAR LIFE MUSEUM
TransCanada Hwy
BONSHAW, PEI (13 miles south-west of Charlottetown)
Phone: 902-675-3555
Hours: July thru Aug 9-4, June and Sept daily 10-5. Admission charged.

This is a very nice museum in one of the most picturesque areas of North America. On display are many antique agricultural vehicles, tractors and about 20 antique cars. The cars range in age from 1898 to 1959. There is one very unusual automobile powered by a two-cylinder, 5 hp engine that runs on naphtha. Car Life Museum also has one of Elvis Presley's cars, a 1959 pink Cadillac. All vehicles on display are restored. There is a gift shop and a picnic area.

QUEBEC

JEAN-MARIE PARADIS ANTIQUE CAR MUSEUM
411 Route 138
ST. AUGUSTIN PORTNEUF,
Quebec (12 miles west of
Quebec City)
Phone: 418-878-2940
Hours: M-F 9-6. Admission
charged.

This museum displays about 25 vintage automobiles including a 1907 International, a 1915 Ford touring car, a 1926 Franklin touring car, a 1928 Pierce-Arrow limousine, a 1929 Ford roadster, a 1930 Buick roadster, a 1930 Packard roadster, a 1931 Ford pickup truck, a 1932 Cadillac limousine, a 1935 Ford panel truck and a 1967 Amphicar. Other exhibits include motorcycles, airplane motors and juke boxes. The museum was founded in 1968.

SASKATCHEWAN

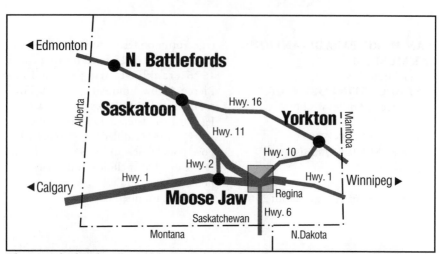

These are the four locations of the Western Development Museum of Saskatchewan.

SPECIAL NOTE: The Western Development Museum of Saskatchewan consists of four separate museums, one each in Moose Jaw, North Battleford, Saskatoon and Yorktown. Each portrays a different theme. All four have antique cars, but the majority of cars are in Moose Jaw and Saskatoon.

BARR COLONY HERITAGE CULTURAL CENTRE
Weaver Park
Hwy 16E at 44th St and 45th Av
LLOYDMINSTER, Saskatchewan
S9V 0T8 (In the west-central part of province on the Saskatchewan/ Alberta line)
Phone: 306-825-5655

Hours: Mid-May to mid-Sept daily 10-8, rest of year W-F noon-5, Sat-Sun 1-5. Closed M and Tues. Admission charged.

In Weaver Park there are a number of new and restored buildings marking the spot where the Barr colonists first settled this part of Saskatchewan in 1903. Some of the buildings that visitors will see are Lloydminster's first church, a schoolhouse circa 1906, a log cabin furnished in the style of 1906-1915, an old time filling station and the Barr Colony Heritage Cultural Centre. In the Centre is a display of about a dozen vintage vehicles which include Lloydminster's first firetruck, a 1924 Model T one-ton truck, a 1925 Hudson brougham, a 1930

Durant and several Edsels. Other attractions in the Park consist of an art gallery, a wildlife display, an oil refinery display, a gift shop, a picnic area and a camp ground. Barbara McKeand is the Historical/Cultural Supervisor.

▼ MOOSE JAW AREA (40 miles west of Regina)

This is the auto museum at the Sukanen Ship Pioneer Village and Museum.

SUKANEN SHIP PIONEER VILLAGE AND MUSEUM
Hwy. #2
(Eight miles south of town)
MOOSE JAW, Saskatchewan
S6H 5V0
Phone: 306-693-7315
Hours: June thru mid-Sept. daily 9-5. Admission charged.

This is a village museum with several historic buildings, and at the entrance, the very unusual Sukanen ship. The ship is a hand-made vessel built locally by an eccentric Finnish immigrant, Tom Sukanen. It was his dream to sail the ship from Saskatchewan back to his native Finland. Sukanen, however, died before the voyage could be attempted. He is buried on the grounds near his ship.

In one of the village buildings are about 40 antique vehicles, most of which belong to local car collectors. There is also a sizeable collection of antique farm equipment. Among the more permanent cars on display is a 1910 Brush, a 1916 Mack 12, a 1927 Chandler, a 1929 Whippet panel truck, a 1938 Ford V8 roadster, a 1938 Willys coupe and a Model A Ford converted into a snowmobile. Other buildings in the complex include a community hall, a fire house, a barber shop, a service station, a blacksmith shop, a post office, a carriage house and a town office. The museum has a gift and souvenir shop with many interesting items.

WESTERN DEVELOPMENT MUSEUM'S HISTORY OF TRANSPORTATION

50 Diefenbaker Dr (Jct of the TransCanada Hwy & Hwy 2)
MOOSE JAW, Saskatchewan
S6H 4N8

Phone: 306-693-5989
Hours: Daily 10-6 except Jan-Mar closed M. Admission charged.

This is a large museum tracing the history of the development of transportation in western Canada. There are displays of horse-drawn vehicles, trains, vintage cars, airplanes, riverboats, streetcars and snowmobiles. More than 40 cars and trucks are on display including a locally-built 1902 Holsman, a 1907 Russell, a 1909 White steamer, a 1912 Rauch & Lang, a 1921 Franklin and a 1931 LaSalle. There is an interesting gift shop here, too.

End of Moose Jaw Area △

WESTERN DEVELOPMENT MUSEUM'S HERITAGE FARM AND VILLAGE

Jct Hwy 16 and Hwy 40
NORTH BATTLEFORD,
Saskatchewan S9A 2Y1 (80 miles northwest of Saskatoon)
Phone: 306-445-8033
Hours: Mid-May thru mid-Sept daily 10-6, rest of year inquire. Admission charged.

This is a reconstructed village showing life as it was in the pioneer days of western Canada during the 1920s. In the village are stores, homes, businesses, a school house, a grain elevator and an 80 acre working farm that is worked as it was in the 1920s. There are also displays of agricultural equipment and several antique automobiles.

WESTERN DEVELOPMENT MUSEUM'S 1910 BOOMTOWN

2610 Lorne Av South
SASKATOON, Saskatchewan
S7J 0S6
Phone: 306-931-1910
Hours: Daily 9-5 except Jan-Mar closed M. Admission charged.

This is a reconstructed village of about 30 buildings showing life as it was in a Saskatchewan prairie boomtown around 1910. Among the numerous displays and exhibits are several vintage cars and trucks. Included is a 1907 Russell, a 1911 Rauch & Lang, a 1912 Peerless 36 and a 1926 Brooks steamer. There is an automotive library of about 2400 pieces open to the public. There are other displays of wagons, buggies and farm machinery. The museum has a gift shop and a restaurant. Each summer, during the last week in June, the museum has a festival called "Pion-Era" in which their cars are displayed along with much of their vintage farming equipment.

WESTERN DEVELOPMENT MUSEUM'S STORY OF PEOPLE
Hwy 16 West
YORKTOWN, Saskatchewan
S3N 2V6
(110 miles northeast of Regina)
Phone: 306-783-8361
Hours: Mid-May thru Sept 30 daily 9-6. Admission charged.

This Western Development Museum focuses on the roots of the people who settled western Canada. Depicted in displays are the customs, homes, clothing, tools, musical instruments, crafts, etc. of the early settlers whose nationalities included Ukrainians, English, Germans, Icelanders, Swedes, Doukhobors, Americans and others. Additional exhibits include a trapper's cabin, a tea room, a music room, a 1930s kitchen, farm machinery and several vintage automobiles. There is a gift shop and each summer during the first weekend in August the museum holds the "Threashermen's Show and Seniors' Festival" at which their antique cars are displayed and some of their farm equipment is put into operation.

MARQUE SPECIALISTS

AMC (NASH)
GENERAL LINE OF PRODUCTS:

American Auto Parts, West Manchester, OH (salvage)

Bob & Art's Auto Parts, Schodack Center, Castleton-On-Hudson, NY (salvage)

Hartford Heritage Auto Museum, Hartford, WI (museum)

Ken's Auto Wrecking, Las Vegas, NV (salvage)

Metropolitan Historical Collection, North Hollywood, CA (museum)

Vintage Auto Part, Mountain Home, ID (salvage)

Vintage Coach, Fontana, CA (salvage)

Webb's Classic Auto Parts, Huntington, IN (salvage)

BENTLEY (see Rolls-Royce)

BMW:

BMW Zentrum Museum and Visitor's Center, Spartenburg, SC (museum)

BRITISH-MADE:

British Auto, Macedon, NY (salvage)

Faspec British Cars & Parts, Portland, OR (salvage)

BUICK:

B & B Used Auto Parts, Big Pine Key, FL (salvage)

Speedway Automotive, Phoenix, AZ (salvage)

CADILLAC:

Aabar's Cadillac & Lincoln Salvage, Oklahoma City, OK (salvage)

All Cadillacs of the Forties, Sylmar, CA (parts and auto display)

B & B Used Auto Parts, Big Pine Key, FL (salvage)

C.R. Auto, Hay Lakes, Alberta (salvage)

Honest John's Caddy Corner, Denton, TX (salvage)

Appendix

CAMARO:

Auto Haven, Bloomington, IN (salvage)

Coast GM Salvage, Long Beach, CA (salvage)

Hillside Auto Salvage, Joplin, MO (salvage)

Winnick's Auto Sales & Parts, Shamokin, PA (salvage)

Z & Z Auto Salvage, Orange, CA (salvage)

CHECKER:

Twilight Taxi Parts, Inc., Middlefield, OH (salvage)

CHEVELLE:

Coast GM Salvage, Long Beach, CA (salvage)

Versailles Auto Salvage, Versailles, MO (salvage)

CHEVROLET:

Adler's Antique Autos, Inc., Stephentown, NY (salvage)

AllChevy Auto Parts, Vacaville, CA (salvage)

B & B Used Auto Parts, Big Pine Key, FL (salvage)

Jim Carlson's Auto Center, Holmen, WI (dealer and restorer)

Classic Chevy International, Orlando, FL (dealer, parts)

Alan Dent Antique Auto Museum, Light Street, PA (museum)

Doug's Auto Parts, Marshall, MN (salvage)

East End Auto Parts, Dickinson, ND (salvage)

Jim's Auto Salvage, Sturgis, SD (salvage)

K & L Auto Wrecking, Las Vegas, NV (salvage)

Klinger's Used Auto Parts, Pine Grove, PA (salvage)

Lynden Pioneer Museum, Lynden, WA (museum)

Memory Lane Collector Car Dismantlers, Sun Valley, CA (salvage)

Nostalgic Cars, Inc., Charlotte, NC (dealer)

Osintowski's Repair, Genoa, NE (salvage)

Rainbow Auto Wreckers, Veneta, OR (salvage)

Wilhelm's, New Carlisle, OH (salvage)

CHRYSLER (MOPAR)
GENERAL LINE OF PRODUCTS:

Aurora Wreckers & Recyclers, Aurora, OR (salvage)

B & B Used Auto Parts, Big Pine Key, FL (salvage)

Big Ben's Used Cars and Salvage, Fordyce, AR (salvage)

Art Coffer Auto Dismantlers, Inc., Phoenix, AZ (salvage)

Fitz Auto Parts, Woodinville, WA (salvage)

Ken's Auto Wrecking, Las Vegas, NV (salvage)

Ed Lucke's Auto Parts, Glenville, PA (salvage)

North Yale Auto Parts, Sperry, OK (salvage)

Osintowski's Repair, Genoa, NE (salvage)

R & R Salvage, Aurora, MO (salvage)

Texas Acres, Mopar Parts, Harker Heights, TX (salvage)

Wheels and Spokes Classic Auto Display, Hays, KS (museum and dealer)

COBRA
(See Mustang-Shelby-Cobra)

CORVAIR:

Ed Lucke's Auto Parts, Glenville, PA (salvage)

CORVETTE:

Antique Cars, Parts and Trains, Millville, NJ (dealer, parts and literature)

Bonanza Corvettes, San Diego, CA (dealer)

Cedar Auto Parts, Jordan, MN (salvage)

CNV, Tempe, AZ (dealer)

Chuck's Used Auto Parts, Marlow Heights, MD (salvage)

Coast GM Salvage, Long Beach, CA (salvage)

Corvette Americana Hall of Fame, Cooperstown, NY (museum)

Corvette Mike, Anaheim, CA (dealer)

Corvette Mike-New England, Plymouth, MA (dealer)

Hillside Auto Salvage, Joplin, MO (salvage)

Howard's Corvettes, Sioux Falls, SD (salvage)

Lussier's Corvette City, Manchester, NH (dealer and parts)

Mershone's World of Cars, Springfield, OH (dealer)

My Garage, Effingham, IL (museum)

National Corvette Museum, Bowling Green, KY (museum)

Pro Team Classic Corvette Collection, Napoleon, OH (dealer)

Unique Corvettes, Inc., Setauket, NY (dealer and restorer)

Valenti Classics, Inc., Caledonia, WI (dealer)

Zonotti, Madison, WI (dealer)

DESOTO:

Texas Acres, Mopar Parts, Harker Heights, TX (salvage)

DODGE:

East End Auto Parts, Dickinson, ND (salvage)

Texas Acres, Mopar Parts, Harker Heights, TX (salvage)

EDSEL:

Show Cars, Ft. Myers, FL (dealer)

Walker's Garage, Beulah, ND (salvage)

FALCON:

McDaniel Salvage, Okay, OK (salvage)

FERRARI:

Motorcar Gallery, Ft. Lauderdale, FL (dealer)

FIAT:

Giant Auto Wreckers, Newhall, CA (salvage)

FIREBIRD:

Auto Haven, Bloomington, IN (salvage)

Hillside Auto Salvage, Joplin, MO (salvage)

Z & Z Auto Salvage, Orange, CA (salvage)

FORD
GENERAL LINE OF PRODUCTS:

B & B Used Auto Parts, Big Pine Key, FL (salvage)

Cars & Parts, Dyer, TN (salvage)

Classic Ford Sales, East Dixfield, ME (salvage)

Coronado Classics, Couer D'Alene, ID (dealer)

Doug's Auto Sales, Marshall, MN (salvage)

East End Auto Parts, Dickinson, ND (salvage)

Fitz Auto Parts, Woodinville, WA (salvage)

Randy Hallman Specialty Cars, Iron Mountain, MI (dealer and restorer)

Hillside Auto Salvage, Joplin, MO (salvage)

Joe's Auto Sales, Hastings, MN (salvage, dealer)

Medicine Bow Motors, Missoula, MT (salvage)

Memory Lane Collector Car Dismantlers, Sun Valley, CA (salvage)

North Yale Auto Parts, Sperry, OK (salvage)

Speedway Automotive, Phoenix, AZ (salvage)

FORD MODEL A:

Cars & Parts, Dyer, TN (salvage)

The Old Car Company, Tampa, FL (dealer)

FRANKLIN:

H. H. Franklin Museum, Tucson, AZ (museum)

Northeast Classic Car Museum, Norwich, NY (museum)

GENERAL MOTORS
GENERAL LINE OF PRODUCTS:

Alotta Auto Parts, Miamisburg, OH (salvage)

Chuck's Used Auto Parts, Marlow Heights, MD (salvage)

Coast GM Salvage, Long Beach, CA (salvage)

Fitz Auto Parts, Woodinville, WA (salvage)

North Yale Auto Parts, Sperry, OK (salvage)

Schultz's Auto Salvage, Millington, MI (salvage)

31 Auto Salvage, McAlester, OK (salvage)

HARLEY-DAVIDSON
(motorcycle):

Rodney C. Gott Museum & Harley-Davidson Assembly Plant, York, PA (museum and plant tour)

HUDSON:

Vintage Coach, Fontana, CA (salvage)

INDIAN (motorcycle):

Indian Motorcycle Museum, Springfield, MA (museum)

INTERNATIONAL:

B & B Used Auto Parts, Big Pine Key, FL (salvage)

International Truck Museum, Rimbey, Alberta (museum)

JAGUAR:

The Stable, Ltd., Gladstone NJ (dealer)

Welsh Jaguar Classic Car Museum, Steubenville, OH (museum)

JEEP:

Fitz Auto Parts, Woodinville, WA (salvage)

Willys Works, Tucson, AZ (salvage)

315

Appendix

LAMBORGHINI:

Motorcar Gallery, Ft. Lauderdale, FL (dealer)

LEMANS:

Auto Haven, Bloomington, IN (salvage)

LINCOLN:

Aabar's Cadillac & Lincoln Salvage, Oklahoma City, OK (salvage)

Classique Cars Unlimited, Lakeshore, MS (storage, dealer, parts and museum)

L & L Classic Auto, Wendell, ID (salvage)

Show Cars, Ft. Myers, FL (dealer)

MACK:

Mack Trucks Historical Museum, Macungie, PA (museum)

MASERATI:

Motorcar Gallery, Ft. Lauderdale, FL (dealer)

MERCEDES-BENZ:

Aase Brothers, Inc., Anaheim, CA (salvage)

Chicago Car Exchange, Inc., Libertyville, IL (dealer and museum)

Embee Parts, Inc., Smyrna, GA (salvage)

Mercedes-Benz Visitors Center, Tuscaloosa, AL (museum & plant tours)

Potomac German Auto, Frederick, MD (salvage)

Showroom Auto Sales, San Jose, CA (dealer and restorer)

Tri-State Pete, Tempe, AZ (salvage)

MERCURY:

L & L Auto, Wendell, ID (salvage)

Joe's Auto Sales, Hastings, MN (salvage and dealer)

MG:

M & G Vintage Auto, Tuxedo Park, NY (restorer and dealer)

O'Connor Classic Autos, Santa Clara, CA (dealer and parts)

The Westminster MG Car Museum, Westminster, VT (museum)

MOPAR (see Chrysler)

MUSCLE CARS:

Randy Blythe's, Fort Smith, AR (dealer)

Floyd Garrett's Muscle Car Museum, Sevierville, TN (museum)

Lussier's Corvette City, Manchester, NH (dealer)

Philbates Auto Wrecking, New Kent, VA (salvage)

Towne & Country Motors, Decatur, MI (dealer)

The Toy Store, Houston, TX (dealer)

Vicksburg Classic Car Sales, Vicksburg, MI (dealer)

MUSTANG-SHELBY-COBRA:

Crossroads Classic Mustang, Mira Loma, CA (salvage)

McDaniel Salvage, Okay, OK (salvage)

Stauffer Classics, Ltd., Blue Mound, WI (dealer)

Telstar Mustang-Shelby-Cobra Museum, Mitchell, SD (museum)

Vail's Classic Cars, Greenfield, IN (restorer)

Versailles Auto Salvage, Versailles, MO (salvage)

Winnick's Auto Sales & Parts, Shamokin, PA (salvage)

NASH (see AMC)

OLDSMOBILE:

Hall's Oldsmobile Salvage, Soldier, KS (salvage)

R.E. Olds Transportation Museum, Lansing, MI (museum)

PACKARD:

The Citizens Motorcar Co.— A Packard Museum, Dayton, OH (museum)

Ed Lucke's Auto Parts, Glenville, PA (salvage)

PANOZ:

Cars Dawydiak, San Francisco, CA (dealer)

PICKUP TRUCKS:

Joe's Auto Sales, Hastings, MN (salvage and dealer)

PLAYBOY:

Bellingham Auto Parts, Bellingham, MA (salvage)

PLYMOUTH:

Texas Acres, Mopar Parts, Harker Heights, TX (salvage)

PONTIAC:

Boneyard Stan, Phoenix, AZ (salvage)

317

Appendix

K & L Auto Wrecking, Las Vegas, NV (salvage)

Osintowski's Repair, Genoa, NE (salvage)

Pontiac Grill, Santa Cruz, CA (theme restaurant)

PORSCHE:

Aase Brothers, Inc., Anaheim, CA (salvage)

Cars Dawydiak, San Francisco, CA (dealer)

REO:

R.E. Olds Transportation Museum, Lansing, MI (museum)

REO Antique Auto Museum, Lindsborg, KS (museum)

ROLLS-ROYCE:

Motorcar Gallery, Ft. Lauderdale, FL (dealer)

SHELBY (See Mustang-Shelby-Cobra)

STANLEY STEAMERS:

Stanley Hotel and Conference Center, Estes Park, CO (hotel)

The Stanley Museum, Kingfield, ME (museum)

STUDEBAKER:

Jim's Auto Sales, Inman, KS (salvage)

Studebaker National Museum, South Bend, IN (museum)

Tucker's Auto Salvage, Burke, NY (salvage)

TEMPEST:

Auto Haven, Bloomington, IN (salvage)

THUNDERBIRD:

Classique Cars Unlimited, Lakeshore, MS (storage, dealer, parts and museum)

Ken's Auto Wrecking, Las Vegas, NV (salvage)

Prestige Thunderbird, Santa Fe Springs, CA (restorer and dealer)

T-Bird Specialists, Tucson, AZ (salvage)

Thunderbird Barn, North Wilkesboro, NC (salvage)

VOLKSWAGEN:

Discount Auto Parts, Albuquerque, NM (salvage)

Lacey's VW, Trent, SD (salvage)

VOLVO:

Revolvstore, Tucson, AZ (salvage)

INDEX

319

Index

Index

Index

Index